APPLICATIONS IN PERSONNEL/
HUMAN RESOURCE MANAGEMENT

Kent Series in Management

Barnett/Wilsted, *Strategic Management: Concepts and Cases*

Berkman/Neider, *The Human Relations of Organizations*

Crane, *Personnel: The Management of Human Resources,* Fourth Edition

Davis/Cosenza, *Business Research for Decision Making,* Second Edition

Kirkpatrick, *Supervision: A Situational Approach*

Klein/Ritti, *Understanding Organizational Behavior,* Second Edition

Kolde, *Environment of International Business,* Second Edition

Plunkett/Attner, *Introduction to Management,* Second Edition

Scarpello/Ledvinka: *Personnel/Human Resource Management: Environments and Functions*

Starling: *The Changing Environment of Business: A Managerial Approach,* Third Edition

Starling/Baskin, *Issues in Business and Society: Capitalism and Public Purpose*

Steers/Ungson/Mowday, *Managing Effective Organizations: An Introduction*

Kent Series in Human Resource Management

Bernardin/Beatty, *Performance Appraisal: Assessing Human Behavior at Work*

Cascio, *Costing Human Resources: The Financial Impact of Behavior in Organizations,* Second Edition

Ledvinka, *Federal Regulation of Personnel and Human Resource Management*

McCaffery, *Employee Benefit Programs: A Total Compensation Perspective*

Wallace/Fay, *Compensation Theory and Practice,* Second Edition

APPLICATIONS IN PERSONNEL/ HUMAN RESOURCE MANAGEMENT

Cases, Exercises, and Skill Builders

Stella M. Nkomo
University of North Carolina at Charlotte

Myron D. Fottler
University of Alabama at Birmingham

R. Bruce McAfee
Old Dominion University

 PWS-KENT PUBLISHING COMPANY, BOSTON

PWS–KENT
Publishing Company

Editor: *Rolf Janke*
Production Editor: *Eve Mendelsohn*
Interior Design: *Ex Libris*
Cover Designer: *Julie Gecha*
Manufacturing Manager: *Linda Siegrist*

PWS-KENT Publishing Company is a division of Wadsworth, Inc.

Printed in the United States of America

2 3 4 5 6 7 8 9 — 91 90 89 88

Library of Congress Cataloging-in-Publication Data

Nkomo, Stella M., 1947-
    Applications in personnel/human resource management: cases, exercises, and skill builders / Stella M. Nkomo, Myron D. Fottler, R. Bruce McAfee.
        p. cm.
    ISBN 0-534-87210-7
    1. Personnel management--Case studies. 2. Personnel management--Problems, exercises, etc. I. Fottler, Myron D. II. McAfee, R. Bruce. III. Title
HF5549.N56 1988
658.3—dc19   88-1893
                                                                          CIP

To my parents, Fred and Eva Brown, who started me on the right path.

Stella M. Nkomo

To my wife, Carol, and my doctoral students.

Myron D. Fottler

To my wife, Chris, and my son, Ethan.

R. Bruce McAfee

PREFACE

The purpose of this book is to provide a single source of cases, exercises, incidents, and skill builders to supplement the basic text in personnel/human resource management. These materials offer a fresh approach to the personnel management student based on dynamic, "real life" organizational events confronting both personnel/human resource managers and line managers who often implement personnel programs and policies. The book's content is uniquely designed to increase analytical problem-solving skills and may be used in basic courses at the undergraduate and graduate level. Topics range from traditional applications of personnel theory to the more controversial issues of AIDS, alcohol and drug abuse on the job, new federal legislation on discrimination issues, employment-at-will, and the human resource aspects of merger activities. The settings cover a wide variety of organizations with an emphasis on the growing service sector.

The book offers the opportunity for learning experiences in its eight major sections: (1) Introduction to Personnel/Human Resource Management; (2) The Legal and Regulatory Environment of Personnel/Human Resource Management; (3) Planning for Human Resources; (4) Recruiting and Staffing; (5) Compensation and Salary Administration; (6) Orientation, Training, and Development; (7) Labor Relations; and (8) Performance Management and Control. Each of these sections contains cases, exercises, incidents, and skill builders. Suggestions for group projects and/or term assignments are offered in the final section of the book.

Most cases are based on actual personnel events occurring in private and public sector organizations. All names have been disguised, except in "The Alcohol/Drug Abuse Program" in Part 8. The two cases in the introductory section are designed to act as a potential pre- and post-measure of the students' knowledge of personnel/human resource management. That is, the cases in Part 1 can be used at the beginning of the course and/or at the end to test how much students have learned. The student becomes the decision maker in these classroom-tested cases. The instructor may use the skill builder in Part 1 to prepare students to complete additional library work for each case or each case may be considered a class-contained learning tool. Questions are provided at the end of each case and incident to guide discussion, and/or the instructor may ask students to use the case analysis model suggested by the authors.

The exercises include opportunities for students to simulate the personnel work environment through role playing, identifying and solving personnel problems, completing in-baskets, and applying personnel theories. The role plays and in-basket exercises require students to act just as they might in a real management siutation. Virtually all of the exercises can be completed within 45 minutes and all contain a set of detailed procedures to follow.

The incidents are mini-cases composed of critical personnel events and are designed to help students develop problem-solving skills. They are intended to raise questions around an issue without definitive answers and may be used to stimulate class discussions or as a means of introducing students to a topic in personnel/human resource management.

Skill builders are short, individual assignments that can be completed by students outside of class to allow them to develop specific technical skills needed by personnel/human resource professionals and line managers to effectively manage human resources.

The final section of the book provides a set of suggestions for group projects and/or term assignments: a potpourri of field exercises, class presentations, group projects, and creative exercises to enhance the learning of personnel/human resource management. These projects are designed to be challenging and comprehensive by requiring students to draw upon material learned throughout the course.

The instructor's manual includes an analysis of the cases and incidents, solutions to the exercises and skill builders, and alternative approaches for using and presenting the materials in the book. The manual also provides reference sources to aid in the analysis and discussion of the cases and exercises. A cross-reference key of the cases/exercises to current major editions of personnel/human resource management texts is also provided.

Acknowledgments

Many people have assisted in making this book possible. We are grateful to our colleagues who contributed cases: Deborah R. Bishop, Gerald Calvasina, Max. B. Jones, Ronald Karren, Diane Kellogg, Arno F. Knapper, and Mua Narakes. Special thanks to Juanita Craig, Ralph Pederson, Jim Bavis, David Abernethy, Diane Marie Eckland, Rusty Rainey, and other friends who shared their professional knowledge and experiences in personnel management with us in developing materials for the book.

The authors wish to acknowledge the contributions of Dorothy Moore of The Citadel and Fraya Andrews of Eastern Michigan University who reviewed the manuscript and offered helpful suggestions and comments. We would like to thank Patricia Washington, Judy Mitchell, and Patricia McClenney who typed drafts of the original materials. We owe special thanks to Margaret Pettus who painstakingly typed the entire manuscript and who did an outstanding job of meeting impossible deadlines, often working with minimal instructions.

Stella Nkomo would like to thank her graduate assistants, Debbie Phillips and Sheila Goldbach, who diligently helped with the research and the seemingly endless day-to-day drudgery of proofreading and verifiying details. They are probably happier than we are to see this project completed. But I am sure that my husband, Mokubung, and my son, Sebenza are even more relieved. I appreciate their steadfast encouragement and support.

Myron Fottler would like to thank his wife, Carol, for her assistance and input into the book. Her contributions and ideas were particularly important in the development of several cases. Thanks are also due to Dean Gene Newport of the School of Business, Dean Keith Blayney of the School of Allied Health Profes-

sions, and Dr. Charles Austin, Chair of the Department of Health Services Administration at the University of Alabama at Birmingham for providing support
for the preparation of this book.

This book would have been impossible without the hard work of the people at
PWS-KENT. We are indebted to Rolf Janke, Associate Editor, for bringing us
together on this project and convincing us that it was doable. Eve Mendelsohn,
Production Editor, offered many wise suggestions for polishing the manuscript.
Her patience and professional competence helped to alleviate our anxieties. Justi
Echeles always made sure that our requests were promptly answered.

Finally, we would like to thank our students for their invaluable suggestions for
revising and clarifying the materials in this book.

Stella Nkomo
Myron D. Fottler
R. Bruce McAfee

CONTENTS

A MODEL FOR ANALYZING CASES IN PERSONNEL/HUMAN RESOURCE MANAGEMENT

PURPOSE OF CASES

A case is a written description of events and activities that have taken place in an organization. Cases allow you to experience a different kind of learning—learning by doing. They are intended to give you an opportunity to actively experience the reality and complexity of the issues facing practicing managers and personnel executives. While other disciplines like physical science allow you to test theories in a laboratory, performing a case analysis allows you to apply personnel theories to specific organizational problems. The cases and other materials in this book will help you develop your analytical and problem-solving skills. Cases enable you to analyze organization problems and to generate solutions based on your understanding of theories and models of effective personnel/human resource management (P/HRM).

Both a "decision-maker" and an "evaluator" approach are used in the cases. In the decision-maker approach, the primary goal is to sort out information given and to propose a viable solution to the problem(s) identified. In the evaluator approach, the personnel/human resource management decisions have already been implemented, and the primary goal is to evaluate outcomes and consequences and to propose alternative solutions.

STUDENT PREPARATION OF WRITTEN CASES

There are any number of possible approaches to analyzing a case. The most important point to remember is that case analysis involves decision making. There is no absolutely right or wrong solution to a case problem. Your major task as a decision maker is to present a coherent and defensible analysis of the situation based on personnel concepts and theories. Just as managers in the "real world" must persuade their colleagues and superiors that their proposals are sound, so must you persuade your fellow students and your instructor that your analysis of the case and proposed solution are best.

There are a few preliminary steps you should follow before preparing your written analysis. First, give the case a general reading to get an overall sense of the situation. Put it aside for a while, then read it a second time and make notes on the critical facts. Case facts provide information and data on attitudes and values, relative power and influence, the nature and quality of relationships, the organization's objectives and personnel policies/functions, and other pertinent aspects about the organization. Keep two key questions in mind as you review the facts of the case? First, are there any discernible patterns in the facts? Second, what can be inferred about personnel/human resource management practices in this organization from the facts presented? You should attempt to classify, sort, and evaluate the information you have identified in this preliminary step. Once you have a clear understanding of the critical facts in the case, you can prepare your written analysis using the five-step model that follows.

Written Case Analysis Model

Step 1. Problem Identification. The first step in your analysis is to explicitly identify the major problem(s) in the case in one or two clear and precise sentences. For example, "The major problem in this case is a 15 percent increase in employee turnover compared to last year's rate." Herbert Simon, who received a Nobel Prize for his work on management decision making, has defined a problem as "a deviation from a standard." In other words, one way to identify a problem is to compare some desired state or objective with the actual situation. A problem or series of problems may prevent the organization from reaching its objectives or goals. A key point here is that in order to define a problem, there must be some type of standard for comparison. Possible standards include the organization's stated objectives or goals, objectives or goals of competing organizations, or standards based on normative prescriptions from personnel/human resource management theory.

Step 2. Identify the Causes of the Problem. Before proposing alternative solutions, the decision maker must have a clear understanding of the underlying causes of the problem. P/HRM problems are usually embedded in a larger context. This means the decision maker must examine internal and external environmental factors over time to isolate causal factors. Causes of problems tend to be historical in nature. To formulate a solid understanding of the specific causes, you should search for root causes and use relevant course concepts and theories to better define them. The "question syndrome" approach may be beneficial here: Why did the problem occur? When did it begin? Where does it occur? Where doesn't it occur? What effective P/HRM practices should the organization be using? What has the organization failed to do? What are the antecedents of the problem? Posing these questions will help you to probe beyond the symptoms to the root causes of the problem.

The process of identifying causes of a problem is very much like hypothesis testing. You should set forth possible causes and then test them against the facts in the case. In writing this section, it is important to present a plausible discussion of the causes so as to convince the reader that your analysis is correct.

Step 3. Alternative Solutions. This step involves developing alternative solutions and evaluating their contributions to resolving the problem(s) identified. Proposed alternatives should be consistent with the problem(s) and cause(s) identified. You should attempt to develop at least three possible alternatives. For many cases, you may be able to propose more than three. List each of your alternatives and the advantages and disadvantages associated with each. Keep the following criteria in mind as you evaluate your alternatives: time constraints, feasibility, cost, contribution to meeting the organization's objectives, and possible negative side effects. Developing a list of good alternatives involves creativity and avoiding preconceived attitudes and assumptions. It may be useful to brainstorm possible solutions before weighing their advantages and disadvantages.

Step 4. Select the Best Alternative. Indicate the alternative you have chosen to solve the problem. It is important here to justify why you chose a particular solution and why it will best resolve the problem(s).

Step 5. Implementation Steps. Now that you have a solution, you must develop appropriate action plans to implement it. In this section of your written analysis, you want to specify, as much as possible, what should be done, by whom, when, where, and in what sequence. For example: Who should implement the decision? To whom should it be communicated? What actions need to be taken now? What actions need to be taken later? If you recommend that the organization revise its performance appraisal process, give as much detail as possible on the content of the revisions. Finally, in this section you should also indicate what follow-up procedures should be used to monitor the implementation of your solution to ensure that the intended actions are taken and that the problem is corrected.

While these steps have been presented in a linear fashion, case analysis does not involve linear thinking. You will probably find yourself thinking about all of the parts of the analysis simultaneously. This is perfectly normal and underscores the complexity of decision making. To present a clear written analysis, however, it is important to write up your report in the analytical form just described. As you gain experience with the case method, you will end the course with a better understanding of both your problem-solving ability and effective personnel/human resource management practices.

Pitfalls in Analysis

Amateurs at case analysis often encounter the pitfall of jumping to a conclusion, which in effect bypasses analysis. For example, a student may readily observe some overt behavior, quickly identify it as objectionable and, therefore, assume it is a basic problem. Later, with some dismay, the student may discover that the prescribed action had no effect on the "problem" and that the objectionable behavior was only a symptom and not the actual problem.

Another common mistake is for students to reject a case because they think there is insufficient information. All desirable or useful information is seldom available for analyzing and resolving actual problems in real organizations. Consequently, managers must do the best they can with the information available to them. Furthermore, the main issue in solving the problems of many organizations is to determine what additional and relevant information is available or can be obtained before adequate analysis can be made and appropriate action taken. If additional information is available, the manager must decide whether it is worth getting, whether it is meaningful and relevant, and whether it can be secured in time to be useful. Thus, an apparent lack of information in cases is actually a reflection of reality that students must learn to accept and overcome.

Students occasionally search for the "right" answer or solutions to cases, and sometimes they ask their instructor what actually happened in a case. Although some answers or solutions are better than others, there really are no "right" answers or solutions to cases. What actually happened in a case is usually irrelevant—the focus of case study should be on the process of analysis, the diagnosis of problems, and the prescription of remedial action rather than on the discovery of answers or end results. Many of the cases and incidents in this book were in the process of being studied and resolved at the time the pieces were written. Consequently, what actually happened was not always available. Although some of the cases do include what happened, no case is intended to illustrate either right or wrong, effective or ineffective solutions to personnel/human resource management problems.

APPLICATIONS IN PERSONNEL/ HUMAN RESOURCE MANAGEMENT

Part 1

Introduction to Personnel/ Human Resource Management

This section introduces the field of personnel/human resource management. Personnel and human resource management has changed substantially over the past few years. Historically, personnel was viewed as a maintenance function not critical to the strategic success of the organization. Complex changes in the external environment of organizations in the 1970s—chief among them government regulation and a sagging economy—led to a revitalized role for personnel management with greater emphasis on its strategic importance to organization effectiveness. This changing role is reflected in the increasing use of the term "human resource management" to refer to the field. There is a growing awareness of the need to better integrate the various functions and activities of personnel and human resource management into a unified whole to achieve harmony with the organization's strategic mission.

The cases in this section, "The New Personnel Director" and "The Personnel Function at Harrison Brothers Corporation," present comprehensive descriptions of two different organizations and allow for an analysis of the internal and external environment of personnel systems. The issues addressed in both cases are crucial to understanding the changing roles and functions of personnel/human resource management in organizations. The exercise, "Scanning the Contemporary Work Environment," allows for an exploration of the impact of trends and changes in the external environment on the design and implementation of personnel/human resource management practices. The skill builder provides an opportunity for you to become familiar with both practitioner and academic research journals available to personnel managers.

CASE:
THE NEW PERSONNEL DIRECTOR

Mount Ridge Engineering Systems designs, builds, and operates standardized, coal-fired utility plants in Kentucky. These small generating plants (35 megawatts and 55 megawatts) are built adjacent to an industrial plant that utilizes steam in its operations. Mount Ridge sells the steam to the industrial plant and electricity to the local utility. Under federal regulations, utilities are required to purchase this independently produced power if it is cost competitive. When Garrett Levinson founded the company, he firmly believed that the future of electric generation in the United States would depend upon coal as the primary fuel and standardization as a method of cost control and efficiency. This new technology, known as "cogeneration," is rapidly coming of age as many companies turn to these systems as a way to cut energy costs.

When the firm was formed four years ago, Joyce Newcombe was hired as Director of Personnel. Newcombe had recently graduated with an M.B.A. degree from a large southeastern university. At the time of its establishment, the company had a total of four employees in addition to Newcombe: the President and founder, a Senior Vice President of Operations, a Vice President for Administration, and a Vice President of Cost & Estimation. From the start, Mount Ridge had both the financing and plans to build seven plants over the next five- to eight-year period. Joyce Newcombe was hired to develop all of the necessary personnel programs, plans, and policies needed to staff the plants once they became operational. She explained, "When I was hired, all we had was a dream and a plan. I had an office with a desk, chair, and telephone. I literally had to develop an entire personnel program." During the first year, Newcombe developed benefit packages for both corporate and plant personnel, an employee handbook, job descriptions, a salary program, a supervisor's manual, and other basic personnel policies. In less than three years the company had built five plants. The size of the work force grew from five to thirty-nine people at corporate headquarters and from 0 to 183 employees in the plants. The company had been remarkably successful in a short period of time (see Exhibit 1.1 for the company's organization structure). In addition to having two plants currently under construction in the state, Mount Ridge plans to build an additional two to three plants in the Northeast. The demand for cogeneration plants is strong in New Jersey, Connecticut, Maine, and Massachusetts, where state energy regulations are concerned about high electricity prices. Forecasts indicate that the company will grow to a total of nine plants and approximately 450 corporate and plant employees over the next two to three years.

A major constraint faced by the company was the need not to compete with its industrial hosts and the local utility for employees. Benefits and salaries had to be competitive but not too high to attract workers from Mount Ridge's "customers." In addition, since profits were to be put back into the business to finance future plant expansion, a profit sharing plan was not feasible. Another important goal of the company was to remain nonunion by offering employees a good quality of work life and attractive benefits. Balancing these two goals was often difficult. The importance of these goals is reflected in the words of Mr. Levinson: "Mount Ridge places great value on its relationship with our industrial and utility clients. Our internal employee relationship has an equally important role in order to maintain an enjoyable and productive work force for the future. Management believes that companies who are good to their employees reap the benefits in terms of increased productivity and loyalty." As part of an effort to build this philosophy into its personnel programs, employee appreciation dinners are held annually at each of the five plants. The president and other corporate officers attend each of the dinners given throughout the state. These dinners have been well received by employees.

Plant Operations

Most of Mount Ridge's plants are scattered throughout the state. Each plant employs approximately forty-five workers. The typical plant structure is shown in Exhibit 1.2. Each plant is run by a plant superintendent who reports directly to the manager of plant operations and maintenance. While personnel operations are generally centralized at corporate headquarters, the plant superintendent and shift supervisor of each plant are largely responsible for the day-to-day administration of personnel policies. Newcombe stated that, "One of our biggest problems has been getting management—especially plant management—to understand the legal and governmental regulations affecting personnel procedures." Although Newcombe had developed a detailed employee handbook and supervisor's manual, over the years there had been situations where supervisors had not followed company policy. Newcombe recounted one such incident that occurred in one of the older plants during her third year with the company.

The Termination

One of the first plants built was the Edison plant. It is located in a medium-sized rural community in the eastern region of Kentucky and employs forty-five workers. Bud Johnson had worked as an auxiliary operator for the plant for two years and had worked his way to that position after starting as a laborer. An auxiliary operator was responsible for assisting the control room operator and the equipment operator in the basic operations and maintenance of the plant's generating system. Over the years, Johnson had learned quickly and knew a good deal about the equipment operator's job. On many occasions, Johnson was asked to fill in when the equipment operator was absent or when there was a problem no one else could handle. One day Johnson approached the plant superintendent, Larry Braxton, about a promotion to equipment operator:

Johnson: Larry, you know I can handle the equipment operator position and I'd like to be considered for a promotion.

Braxton: That's not the point. We all know you are capable, but we just don't have any openings right now. Besides, the job qualifications require that you spend sufficient time as an auxiliary operator before moving up to an equipment operator. Just sit tight.

Johnson: Well, I hope some openings will come up soon. I really would like to make more money, and I know that I am qualified. You know I can learn quickly. Look at how fast I moved up from being a laborer.

After this conversation, Johnson was again called on several times to help out with the equipment operator's job and to explain the readings and gauges to Wilma Barker, one of the equipment room operators. When Johnson did not receive a pay increase or promotion after his annual evaluation, he met with Braxton and told him that he was dissatisfied with his pay and felt that since he often performed the equipment operator's job that he ought to be paid at that rate instead of his present rate as an auxiliary operator. Braxton told him he would have to remain at the pay of an auxiliary operator and that he should be satisfied with that for the time being. Johnson became quite upset and stormed out of Braxton's office. The next day Johnson did not report to work and did not call in to report his absence.

Company policy stated that when an employee is absent and fails to notify his or her supervisor, the employee may be terminated. When Johnson returned to work the following day, he told Braxton that he had decided to quit his job because he was very dissatisfied with his pay. Johnson was asked to sign a termination notice form required by company policy and was told by Braxton that he would receive a copy of the form in the mail.

A week later Joyce Newcombe received a phone call from Johnson. Johnson told her that the reason given on the copy of the termination form he had just received in the mail was incorrect (see Exhibit 1.3). He had not left to take another job but had left because he was dissatisfied with his pay and lack of promotion at the plant and that he had spoken with the plant superintendent about this several times. Johnson also told her that he wanted his personnel records to be corrected and that he had been asked by Braxton to sign a blank form. He alleged that Braxton had added the incorrect reason after he had signed the form. Johnson also stated that he thought the Department of Labor would have something to say about this whole incident.

Questions

1. Discuss the relationship between corporate personnel structure and operations at the plant level. What impact, if any, did it have on the present situation?
2. How should Joyce Newcombe have handled this situation?
3. What, if any, disciplinary action should have been taken against the shift supervisor?

4. If Johnson's allegations were true, what are the legal ramifications of Braxton's behavior?
5. What can be done to prevent a reoccurrence of this type of situation?
6. What personnel issues will Newcombe likely face as the company expands to the Northeast? How might this expansion affect the structure of the organization and its personnel department?

Exhibit 1.1 Organization Structure

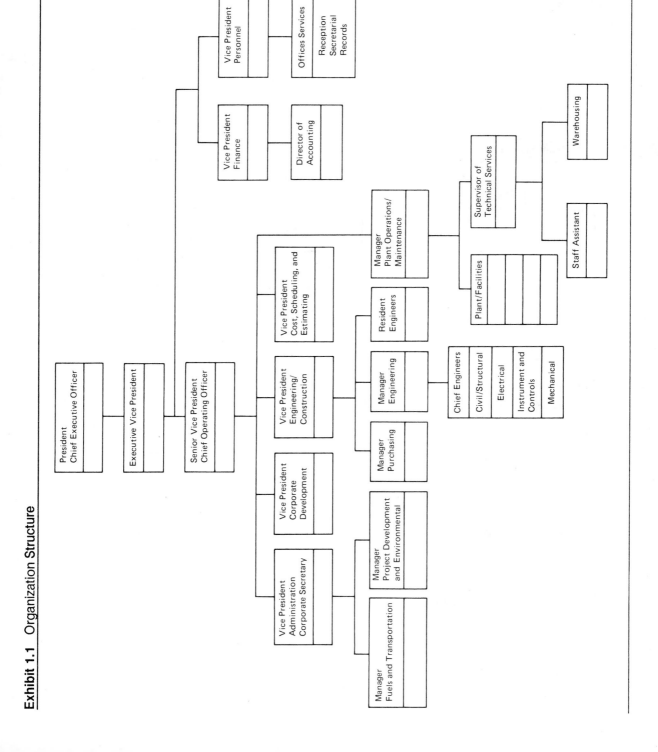

Exhibit 1.2   Typical Plant Structure

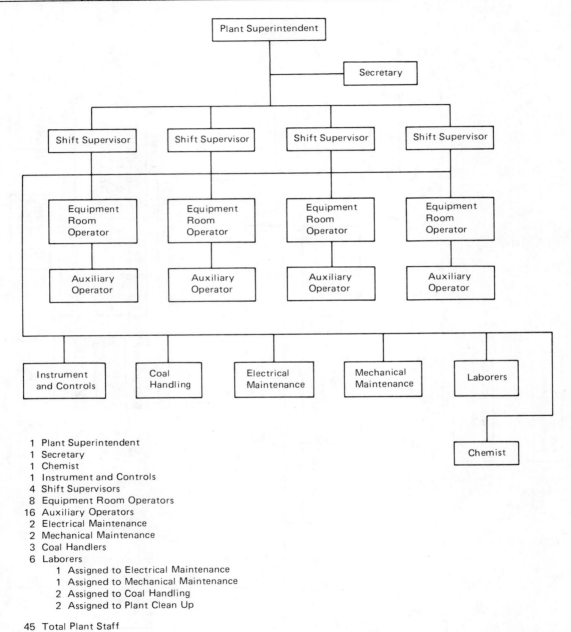

1 Plant Superintendent
1 Secretary
1 Chemist
1 Instrument and Controls
4 Shift Supervisors
8 Equipment Room Operators
16 Auxiliary Operators
2 Electrical Maintenance
2 Mechanical Maintenance
3 Coal Handlers
6 Laborers
    1 Assigned to Electrical Maintenance
    1 Assigned to Mechanical Maintenance
    2 Assigned to Coal Handling
    2 Assigned to Plant Clean Up

45 Total Plant Staff

Exhibit 1.3

NOTICE OF TERMINATION

This form MUST BE completed for EVERY termination

DEPARTMENT USE ONLY

	REASON FOR TERMINATION	PAYROLL DEPARTMENT

1. SOCIAL SECURITY NUMBER

1	2	3	-	0	9	-	7	6	2	5

Johnson Bud O.

2. NAME   Last   First   Middle

348 Bismark Street

3. MAILING ADDRESS   Number   Street

Mount Ridge, Kentucky

City   587-6089   State   Zip

4. HOME PHONE

Auxiliary Operator

5. JOB TITLE

6. Termination date	Last day worked
11/1/86	10/31/86

7. Recommended for other employment Yes ☐ No ☒	Replacement Required Yes ☒ No ☐

9. Immediate Supervisor   Phone

Larry Braxton

10. Plant Location

Edison

11. Sex   M ☒   F ☐

white

12. Ethnic Background

REASON FOR TERMINATION

13. LAY-OFF — No replacement required ☐

14. DISCHARGE
- ☐ Absenteeism (give dates)
- ☐ Not qualified (explain)
- ☐ Other (explain)

15. VOLUNTARY QUIT
- ☐ Leave of absence granted (ending . . . .)
- ☐ Dissatisfied pay (overtime, rate, etc.)
- ☐ Dissatisfied distance to work (miles . . . .)
- ☒ To take another job (employer, rate)
- ☐ Leaving town
- ☐ Dissatisfied working conditions (explain)
- ☐ Other (explain)

16. EXPLANATION (Use additional sheet if necessary)

PAYROLL DEPARTMENT

17. EMPLOYEE No.   _____

18. HIRE DATE   _____

19. RATE   _____

20. HOURLY ☐   SALARIED ☐

                 Days $

Regular pay thru

Vacation

Severance

Pay in lieu of notice

Deductions:
- W/H (Federal & State)   (_____)
- FICA   (_____)
- Other, ie. Insurance   (_____)

         TOTAL $ _____

EMPLOYMENT OFFICE

Larry Braxton   *Bud Johnson*

23. Plant supervisor   24. Employee Signature

_____ , SIGNATURE ACKNOWLEDGES RECEIPT OF THIS NOTICE

Date

SUPERVISOR'S REPORT OF TERMINATION

WERE WRITTEN WARNING NOTICES OR PERFORMANCE EVALUATION GIVEN?

☐ YES (ATTACH COPIES)   ☐ NO

WHAT WAS EMPLOYEE'S REACTION TO COUNSEL, WARNING, NOTICES, OR PERFORMANCE EVALUATIONS?

REASON FOR TERMINATION. (UNEMPLOYMENT INSURANCE CLAIMS ARE A MAJOR COST TO THE COMPANY. WHEN FACTUAL INFORMATION IS LACKING, THE STATE EMPLOYMENT DEVELOPMENT DEPARTMENT GENERALLY FAVORS THE EMPLOYEE'S CLAIM – EVEN THOUGH IT MAY NOT BE MERITED. THEREFORE, THE EXACT REASONS FOR TERMINATION ARE EXTREMELY IMPORTANT. IN ADDITION, THIS INFORMATION CAN BE ESSENTIAL FOR THE RESOLUTION OF UNFAIR LABOR PRACTICE AND EQUAL EMPLOYMENT CASES.)

CASE:
THE PERSONNEL FUNCTION AT HARRISON BROTHERS CORPORATION

Harrison Brothers Corporation was founded in upstate New York on September 15, 1898 by Aubrey and William Harrison. Harrison's is a general merchandise department store dealing mainly with men's, women's, and children's clothing. In recent years the store has expanded to include household furnishings and other items for the home. The long-term goal of the company is to become the leading specialty store in the Northeast selling moderate- to better-priced merchandise to middle-class, fashion-conscious customers. Harrison Brothers is one of the largest privately owned retail stores in the United States. A majority of its ten stores are located in the Northeast. Its largest store is located in a major urban center.

The Westpark Store

Brenda McCain has been Personnel Manager at the Westpark store for the past four years. Prior to her employment at Harrison Brothers, Brenda had several years of experience in retail stores and had come to Harrison's after being a buyer at one of its major competitors. McCain has a degree in fashion merchandising from a college in New Jersey. Currently there are 525 employees at the Westpark store. The staff includes salespeople, sales support employees (dock, marking room, clerical, and accounting), maintenance, security, and management. The Personnel Department consists of five people (see Exhibit 1.4). During the peak holiday season a number of people are hired as floating sales staff. These temporary workers may number close to a hundred during the busy Christmas season.

The Personnel Manager's Job

McCain talked about the areas of responsibility of the Personnel Department: "Our business has really grown in the last two years. We are carrying more specialty and designer clothing lines and have added items we hope will appeal to moderate- to high-income customers. When I came here four years ago, I found too many of the personnel operations being performed by the operations manager, Pat Hartlake, and one of the department heads, Rich Jenkins. Since that time I have attempted to set up procedures and policies to assure proper staffing of the store. I spend most of my time just managing the Personnel Department. I think it is important to keep abreast of the performance of workers, and I like to observe their work habits regularly. I also spend a good deal of time on selecting applicants for the sales and support jobs. There is a good deal of turnover on the sales floor in our business and the average salesperson at Harrison

Brothers is either part-time, an older employee, or one who is 'in-between jobs' — if a better job came along they would snap it up immediately."

McCain went on to explain their selection procedures: "The main sources of our applicants are through newspaper ads and word-of-mouth by present or past employees. We select people based on how well they do in the interview. Right now I conduct about twenty-five to thirty interviews a week and perhaps more during the Christmas rush. I have enough experience in retail to know what it takes to be a good salesperson. We place a lot of weight on their motivation, personality and drive. Little or no useful information is gained from high school or college records or references. I do check their application form for an indication of job stability, though.

"The training of new salespeople occurs every two weeks and every week during the Christmas season. Now and then we get some employees who cannot effectively complete the cash register training. Our trainer, Joanne Flynn, tries to expose them to selling techniques and how to properly interact with customers. Although we have a trainer, I do spend a good deal of time with her and will help out if the training classes are too large.

"When I came here, discipline was a continual bone of contention between the employees and supervisors. Employees felt the present procedures were inconsistently enforced and applied. Each supervisor was administering punishment depending on his or her own interpretation of the problem. Now, I am totally responsible for all disciplinary actions. I discuss the alleged wrongful act with the employee's supervisor to assess the magnitude of the act. I then talk with the employee before deciding upon the appropriate consequences. In this way, we have better consistency in the application of disciplinary rules. Any employee who receives three disciplinary actions is eligible for dismissal.

"While we hire our salespeople at the minimum wage, we do perform an annual evaluation of their performance to determine merit increases. We use sales productivity as the major criterion. Performance is evaluated on average sales per hour. For example, say an employee works in an 8 percent department. The hourly quota would be calculated by dividing the hourly wage by the percent level. This determines how much the sales clerk would have to sell to break even. For any sales above that level, the clerk receives a commission. At evaluation time, if the clerk's sales per hour are above the breakeven point, the new hourly wage is determined by multiplying the sales per hour by the percent level. For example, assume that a salesperson works in an 8 percent department and earns $5 per hour. The employee would have to sell $62.50 per hour to break even. Any sales above that level would receive a commission. If sales at evaluation time were actually $95 per hour, hourly pay would increase to $7.60 per hour (95 times .08). We have had moderate success with this system, although I'm not sure how much it helps us to retain good employees.

"For our sales support staff, we have supervisors basically evaluate the employee's quality and quantity of work. Last year, though, we incorporated a form of 'employee development' into the evaluation process. Supervisors are required to discuss the employees' career opportunities and professional development with them. I initiated this as a form of career planning and hopefully as a way to keep good employees. Unfortunately, supervisors have been slack in doing the assessment. They seem to be more anxious to get the performance evaluation completed. I have had several employees come to me to say they had not received a 'professional assessment' since the program was instituted.

"There is a lot more we need to do here in personnel, but we are somewhat constrained by cost considerations and the realities of the retail industry. The turnover in the sales areas gives me little free time to develop new programs and ideas."

Interview with the Operations Manager

Pat Hartlake, the operations manager, talked about interactions with the Personnel Department: "I have a good working relationship with the Personnel Department, but it took some time to develop that relationship. McCain has a good understanding of the retail business, and I am impressed with her knowledge of store operations. They have been somewhat slow in filling the vacant sales positions, and they don't always respond as quickly as they should. They seem terribly understaffed and overworked most of the time.

"Let me give you an example of what I mean. A few weeks ago I was faced with an employee situation which was evolving to the point where I felt termination was necessary. I went to the Personnel Department to discuss the case to be sure I had covered all bases. With all of the laws today, one needs to be careful in making decisions. They never seem to be able to produce answers to questions without hedging. I had to wait almost two weeks before I got any help from them. In the meantime the situation with the employee continued to deteriorate. I can understand their reluctance to terminate sales staff because of the difficulty in recruiting new people. In a way, however, the old system seemed to be a lot less complicated. Department managers knew how to handle situations that came up in their departments. Don't get me wrong! I know that as we continue to grow we're probably going to need even a larger personnel department."

Questions

1. How does McCain view her role as personnel manager?
2. Evaluate Hartlake's observation that the Personnel Department seems "terribly understaffed and overworked most of the time."
3. Given the organization's size and long-term goals, evaluate the development of the personnel function at Harrison Brothers. How could its major personnel functions be improved?

Exhibit 1.4 Harrison Brothers Organization Chart

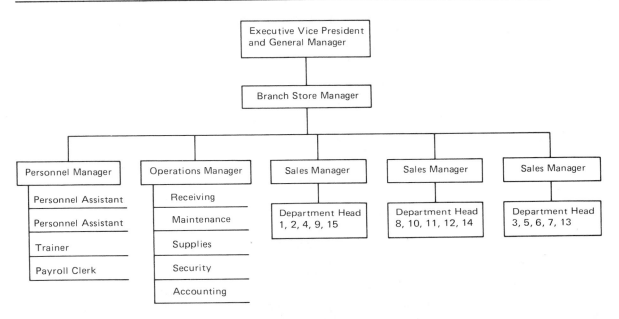

Department Identification

1. Children (boys, girls, infants)
2. Shoes
3. Dresses
4. Men's
5. Women's coats
6. Fashion accessories
7. Intimate apparel
8. Furniture/Carpet/Bedding
9. Cosmetics
10. Domestics
11. China/etc.
12. Housewares
13. Fine Jewelry
14. Sporting Goods
15. Toys
(Each department head supervises several sales clerks)

EXERCISE:
SCANNING THE CONTEMPORARY WORK ENVIRONMENT

I. *Objective:* The purpose of this exercise is to help you understand the potential influence of trends and changes in the external environment on the design and implementation of personnel/human resource management practices.

II. *Out-of-Class Preparation Time:* None

III. *In-Class Time Suggested:* 20 - 30 minutes

IV. *Procedures:*

    1. This exercise should be done in groups of four to five students.

    2. After completion of the exercise, each group will present its ideas to the rest of the class.

    3. Listed below are some of the major predictions about changes or trends in the labor/employment environment that will take place in the 1990s. Read each trend and list some ideas about the impact of these trends on the major personnel/human resource management functions: staffing and placement, training and development, salary administration, performance evaluation, job design, promotions, and career planning. That is, what personnel issues will organizations face because of these changes?

Trend	Impact on P/HRM
1. Shortage of inexperienced and low-skilled workers	
2. Aging of the labor force	
3. Growth of prime-age workers (25 - 54)	
4. Shift from a manufacturing economy to a service economy	
5. More professional/managerial and technical workers than "blue-collar" workers	
6. Increasing number of dual-career families	

7. Increasing number of women with young children

8. Increasing number of minority workers in the labor force

SKILL BUILDER:
REFERENCE MATERIALS
FOR PERSONNEL/HUMAN
RESOURCE MANAGEMENT

I. *Objectives:*
   1. To familiarize you with journals and research publications used by personnel managers.
   2. To allow you to compare and contrast the content of academic and practitioner-oriented journals.
II. *Time Required to Complete:* 4 - 5 hours
III. *Instructions:* Go to the school library and select six articles on one of the functional areas of personnel listed below. Other topics may be selected with your instructor's approval. Select three articles from three different academic journals and three from three different practitioner journals. The journals you may choose from are listed below. Read each article and prepare a short report in which you: (a) Summarize the major findings from each article; (b) Present an analysis of the differences and similarities of the findings in the two types of journals. Are the conclusions drawn from the practitioner journals about your topic similar to the research findings reported in the academic journals? (c) List the strengths and weaknesses of each type of journal. Be sure to include a bibliography that cites the author, article title, journal name, date of publication, and pages.

SUGGESTED FUNCTIONAL TOPICS

Role of the Human Resources
    Manager
Job Analysis
Job Design

Career Development
Performance Evaluation
Job Satisfaction
Labor Relations

Human Resource Planning
Recruitment
Affirmative Action/Equal
    Employment Opportunity
Selection/Staffing
Training and Development

Collective Bargaining
Job Evaluation
Executive Compensation
Compensation/Salary Administration
Safety and Health
Employee Benefits

JOURNALS

Academic

Academy of Management Journal
Academy of Management Review
Human Resource Management
Industrial Relations
Journal of Applied Psychology
Organization Behavior & Human
    Performance
Personnel Psychology

Practitioner

Academy of Management Executive
Human Resource Planning
Management Review
Personnel
Personnel Administrator
Personnel Journal
Training & Development Journal

Part 2

The Legal and Regulatory Environment of Personnel/ Human Resource Management

The passage of Title VII of the 1964 Civil Rights Act signaled the beginning of increased governmental regulation of employment practices in organizations. Since that time numerous other laws, executive orders, and guidelines have been added to ensure fair employment practices in organizations. The legal environment has become increasingly complex, affecting virtually all personnel/human resource management activities. As a consequence, personnel professionals must continually monitor court cases and compliance requirements to avoid charges of discrimination or unfair employment practices.

The two cases in this section, "The Storage Room Massage" and "Unfair Promotions at Food Chain Supermarkets," address the recurring issues of sexual harassment and treatment discrimination. The exercise, "Age Discrimination Role Play," provides the student with an opportunity to experience the influence of age on employment decisions. The exercise, "Is this Unlawful Discrimination?" offers scenarios which cover all the major federal Equal Employment Opportunity (EEO) laws prohibiting discrimination in employment, particularly discrimination because of race, color, sex, age, religion, national origin, and handicap status. The two incidents, "The Employee with AIDS" and "The Employee's Pregnancy," cover important personnel-related issues which are very much part of the contemporary work environment today. Finally, the skill builder requires you to complete the necessary data analyses for preparing an affirmative action plan under Executive Order 11246 Guidelines.

CASE:
THE STORAGE ROOM MASSAGE: A CASE OF SEXUAL HARASSMENT?

Background

Standard Valve & Gauge Company manufactures safety relief valves, pressure gauges, thermometers, testing instruments, and spring disks. The company has three small plants scattered throughout the Southeast. Each plant employs approximately 325 workers. Personnel operations are generally centralized at corporate headquarters located in Atlanta, Georgia. However, the plant superintendent of each plant is largely responsible for the day-to-day administration of personnel policies.

The Incident

Bill Winthrop, a Shift Supervisor at the Marshfield plant, had been employed with the company for five years. On June 11, 1986, Winthrop was terminated by the Plant Superintendent, Jim Hudson, for sexual harassment of a female employee, Mary Harper Jones, on June 9 (see Exhibit 2.1). Jones was employed as a laborer in the Marshfield plant and had accused Winthrop of unwanted sexual advances (see Exhibit 2.2).

A few months after Winthrop had been terminated, the company received a Notice of Charge of Discrimination from the Equal Employment Opportunity Commission (EEOC), filed by Winthrop alleging that he had been sexually harassed by Jones on three occasions and that her actions had unreasonably interfered with his work performance and had created a negative work atmosphere. He further alleged that the company had failed to take action on his complaints about Ms. Jones and that he had been unduly discharged (see Exhibit 2.3).

The Company's Position

In its reply to the EEOC, the company maintained that Winthrop was terminated for sexual harassment and not on the basis of his race, sex, or any other manner of retaliation. The company also pointed out that after his termination on June 11, Winthrop had applied for unemployment compensation and the Employment Security Commission office hearing his appeal agreed that Winthrop was terminated for just cause. Consequently, Winthrop was disqualified for unemployment benefits for a period of nine weeks. The commission's report stated, "Winthrop displayed poor judgment in requesting the 'massage' and the employer's discharge of the claimant was for good business reasons to avoid instances of like nature in the future." The company argued that his sexual harass-

ment charges were unsubstantiated and should be dismissed (see Exhibit 2.4).
Two weeks after forwarding the letter in Exhibit 2.4 to the EEOC, the personnel
director, J. Bevins, received a letter back from the EEOC (Exhibit 2.5) requesting
additional information about the charges.

Questions

1. Evaluate the company's handling of Winthrop's termination. Was he ter-
    minated for just cause?
2. Under the Title VII guidelines on sexual harassment, what are the legal
    ramifications of a supervisor accusing an employee of sexual harassment?
3. What alternative actions could Mary Harper Jones have taken in dealing with
    Winthrop?

Exhibit 2.1 Memo from Plant Superintendent to the Personnel Director
on Winthrop's Termination

MEMORANDUM

To: J. Bevins, Personnel Director
From: Jim Hudson, Plant Superintendent
Date: June 11, 1986
Subject: Termination of Bill Winthrop (Shift Supervisor, Marshfield Plant)

Based on allegations substantiated by others (allegations of Mary Harper
Jones, black female, who is employed as a laborer at the above plant site), a
personal interview was conducted at approximately 11:00 a.m. this date and
as a result of the interview Mr. Winthrop was relieved of his duties and terminated effective this date.

Mr. Bill Winthrop admitted he allowed Miss Jones to physically rub his
back and allowed such action to take place at the workplace on or about
noon on Monday, June 9, and was witnessed by another employee (Jim
Joyner, electrician). Bill disavowed other allegations made by Miss Jones. By
his admission of the above contact, Bill was informed that a possible sex discrimination and/or harassment suit could result. Bill stated it was all in jest. I
informed Bill of the dire consequences of his actions and the fact that Miss
Jones had in fact made it serious as she called his actions to the attention of
the plant superintendent and others. A copy of Miss Jones' statement is attached for your information.

Respectfully submitted,

Jim Hudson

Jim Hudson

Exhibit 2.2 Statement from Mary Harper Jones
Concerning the Events of June 9, 1986

TO WHOM IT MAY CONCERN:

I was cleaning up on the first level of the plant and Bill (Winthrop) came up to me and asked how much I would charge for a massage. I said a professional would charge $35.00 an hour. I said I was not a professional. He asked me if I would meet him in the storage room. I thought he was joking. I smiled and he walked away. He had asked in general if the storage room was locked.

Later, I was on the other end of the plant floor and Bill was in the supervisor's booth motioning for me to come in. I went in and he said, "Sit down and rest; it is hot out there." I sat in J.P.'s chair. Jim Joyner came in at that point. Bill said to me, "Don't sit in that chair; it belongs to J. P. Garnett (Supervisor on shift)." I said it was okay because he is my friend. Bill asked Jim to listen to what I was saying. Jim asked me why I liked J.P., and I told Jim that J.P. has been the same person since the day I met him. Bill then said to me, "I'm going to give you a piece of advice, Mary. Stay away from J.P. because he will get you in trouble." Bill asked Jim what he had done over the weekend. Jim was talking about his weekend, and Bill cut him off saying, "Mary, give me $5.00 worth." Jim looked at me funny, and I had forgotten about the massage. Bill looked at Jim and smiled. Jim left. Bill said, "Mary, come on and stand behind me and massage my shoulders." And then I said, "You told me to come in here and rest and now you are putting me to work." Mr. Hudson (Plant Superintendent) walked in at that point and Bill told me to get over by J.P.'s chair, and I stepped over to it. Mr. Hudson came to where we were, and Bill started talking to him about the shift operations. Mr. Hudson and Bill were talking for a while. Eventually, Mr. Hudson left and went to the plant floor.

Bill told me to go the storage room and to go one way while he went another way. When I got there he was already there. I walked in and asked him, "What's up?" He sat down on a bucket of cleaning fluid and asked if there was any way to lock the door. I told him there was no way to lock the door. I told him that no one ever came up there except the other laborers and he had sent all three to dump the trash. Then he told me to come on and finish massaging his shoulders. Before I started, I asked him if his wife ever did this and he said she was too puny and did not have the grip that I did. I felt funny because he asked me to do it now and had asked me to stop earlier when Mr. Hudson had walked into the supervisor's booth. After I massaged him 3 or 4 times, I patted him on the shoulder and said, "Okay, Bill, time is up. I am finished." I asked him if something was wrong. He said it was all of the pressure here and his son had gotten hurt over the weekend. He said, "Thanks a lot Mary," and then stood there for a few minutes. I started to leave

continued

Exhibit 2.2 *continued*

and he grabbed my arm and pulled me to him and hugged me. I left. When I got downstairs I saw Donald (an engineer) and told him I needed to talk to him. I told him the story and he suggested I go to J. P. Garnett (Supervisor on the shift) and talk to him. Garnett suggested I talk to Joan (secretary). I then went to the office and told the story to Joan.

Mary Harper Jones

Mary Harper Jones

Exhibit 2.3 Charge of Discrimination Filed by Bill Winthrop with the EEOC

```
                 CHARGE OF DISCRIMINATION          ENTER CHARGE NUMBER
This form is affected by the Privacy Act          ___ FEPA
of 1974;  See Privacy Act Statement on            _X_ EEOC      1910897654
reverse before completing this form.
```

```
                                                  and EEOC
_____
  (State or local Agency, if any)
```

Name (Indicate Mr., Miss, or Mrs.)	Home Telephone No. & Area Code
Mr. Bill Winthrop	(404) 459-3145

Street Address	City, State and Zip Code	County
229 Hitchkock Street	Marshfield, GA 29768	Macon

NAMED IS THE EMPLOYER, LABOR ORGANIZATION, EMPLOYMENT AGENCY, APPRENTICESHIP COMMITTEE, STATE OR LOCAL GOVERNMENT AGENCY WHO DISCRIMINATED AGAINST ME (IF MORE THAN ONE LIST BELOW)

Name	No. of Employees	Telephone No. & Area Code
Standard Valve & Gauge Co.	325	(404) 299-4590

Street Address	City, State and Zip Code	
P. O. Box 34517	Atlanta, GA 25843	

Cause of Discrimination Based on (Check Appropriate one). | Date most recent or continuing discrimination took place

X Race   ___ Color X Sex   ___ Religion   ___ Age
___ National Origin X Retaliation   ___ Other (specify)

June 11, 1986

The particulars are (If additional space is needed, attach extra sheet(s)):

I. On or around April 8, 1986, on or around April 18, 1986, and on June 9, 1986, I was sexually harassed. I was initially hired in November 1985 and have been employed as a Shift Supervisor since my hire. Respondent employs approximately 325 persons, of whom 300 are males.

Exhibit 2.3 *continued*

II. On or around April 8, 1986, I reported to Jim Hudson (male),
Plant Superintendent, that I had been sexually harassed by
Mary Harper Jones (female), laborer.

I am not aware of Respondent's policy regarding sexual
harassment.

III. I believe that I have been discriminated against on the basis
of my sex (male) because:

A. On or around April 8, 1986, Mary Harper Jones (female),
laborer, propositioned me. On or around April 18, 1986, Ms.
Jones made a sexually derogatory statement. On or around
June 9, 1986, Ms. Jones propositioned me again. Jones'
sexual advances unreasonably interfered with my work performance and created a negative work atmosphere.

B. When I informed Jim Hudson (male), Plant Superintendent,
about Ms. Jones' sexual advances, he stated that Ms. Jones
had propositioned him, too. However, no action was taken
regarding my complaint.

___I also want this charge filed with the EEOC. I will advise the agencies if I change my address or telephone number and I will cooperate fully with them in processing my charge in accordance with their procedures.	NOTARY - (When necessary to meet State and Local Requirements) .
	I swear or affirm that I have read the above charge and that it is true to the best of my knowledge, information and belief.
I declare under penalty of perjury that the foregoing is true and correct.	SIGNATURE OF COMPLAINANT
10-1-86 *Bill Winthrop* Date Charging Party (Signature)	SUBSCRIBED AND SWORN TO BEFORE ME THIS DATE (Day, month, and year)

continued

Exhibit 2.3 *continued*

PAGE __2__ of __2__ CHARGE OF DISCRIMINATION   ENTER CHARGE NUMBER
This form is affected by the Privacy Act of   ____ FEPA
1974; see Privacy Act Statement on reverse   __X__ EEOC   1910897654
before completing this form.

REF: BILL WINTHROP ^{VS.} STANDARD VALVE & GAUGE COMPANY

I.   On June 11, 1986, I was discharged from my position as Shift Supervisor. Respondent employs approximately 325 persons, of whom 295 are Caucasians. Similarly, of these 325 persons, 300 are males.

II. Jim Hudson (Caucasian, male), Plant Superintendent, stated I was being discharged because I received a complaint of sexual harassment.

     According to the Respondent's employee handbook, I can be discharged due to the following reasons: (1) decrease in Respondent's business; (2) accepting employment with another company; (3) leaving work without properly being relieved; (4) reporting to work in a condition not suitable for normal performance; (5) gross insubordination; (6) bringing on-site drugs or alcohol; (7) fighting; (8) bringing on-site any type of weapon; (9) failure for any reason to perform assigned duties; (10) excessive tardiness or absenteeism; and (11) conduct not in the best interest of the company.

III. I believe I have been discriminated against on the bases of race (Caucasian), sex (male) and in retaliation for complaining about acts made unlawful by Title VII inasmuch as:

     A. On or around April 8, 1986, I informed Jim Hudson (Caucasian, male), Plant Superintendent, that I had been sexually harassed by Mary Harper Jones (black, female). No action was taken regarding my complaint.

     B. Ms. Jones alleged that I sexually harassed her on June 9, 1986. Actually, Ms. Jones sexually harassed me on that date.

     C. I am not aware of any management employee who received a complaint of sexual harassment.

____ I also want this charge filed with the EEOC. I will advise the agencies if I change my address or telephone number and I will cooperate fully with them in processing my charge in accordance with their procedures.	NOTARY - (When necessary to meet State and Local Requirements).
	I swear or affirm that I have read the above charge and that it is true to the best of my knowledge, information and belief.
I declare under penalty of perjury that the foregoing is true and correct.	SIGNATURE OF COMPLAINANT

10-1-86   *Bill Winthrop*   SUBSCRIBED AND SWORN TO BEFORE
                                          ME THIS DATE (Day, Month, Year)
Date   Charging Party (Signature)

Exhibit 2.4 Letter from Company Vice President of Personnel to EEOC

October 5, 1986

Atlanta District Office--EEOC
5500 Peachtree Street
Atlanta, Georgia

Attention: Ms. Harriet Burton

RE: EEOC #1910897654
      Bill Winthrop

Dear Ms. Burton:

This letter is to advise your office of our company's position with regard to the above referenced claim. Mr. Winthrop was terminated from our employ June 11, 1986 for sexual harassment. He was not terminated on the basis of his race, his sex or for any manner of retaliation.

We emphatically deny the sexual harassment charge against our employee. Several unusual circumstances surround this incident. For your information Mr. Winthrop has applied for unemployment compensation and the office hearing his appeal agreed that Mr. Winthrop was terminated for just cause, and he was penalized his unemployment compensation for the appropriate number of weeks. We have interrogated Mr. Jim Hudson, Plant Superintendent, over the phone and he has emphatically denied that Mr. Winthrop had at any time told him he was sexually harassed; and had he done so, Mr. Hudson would have conducted an investigation immediately. It is interesting that the reason for Mr. Winthrop's termination is the same as his charge against his employer.

With reference to Item III, Section B: The superintendent, Mr. Hudson, in our telephone conversation of October 3, 1986, stated that during the last part of April, Mary Harper Jones did come to him and inquire if the company extended employee loans since she needed a down payment for a car. Mr. Hudson told Ms. Jones that the company did not have a Credit Union nor did they give employees loans. She made the comment, "Golly, I would do most anything for a down payment for a car." Mr. Hudson remarked he was sorry he could not help her out. Mr. Hudson did not interpret this as a proposition and neither does our company.

In regard to Item III, Section A: We have reviewed our company records and the dates mentioned in the charge are not documented so we cannot establish the exact date of Mr. Winthrop's allegations and we, therefore, assume he is not being factual.

continued

Exhibit 2.4 *continued*

Because of Mr. Winthrop's position as a Shift Supervisor, we in no way can see how Ms. Jones, a subordinate, could influence Mr. Winthrop's receiving advances, promotions, pay increases, etc.   Due to the fact that Mr. Hudson's allegations were not known by anyone at the plant, we find these charges to be made without fact and that they should be dismissed.

Very truly yours,

J. Bevins

J. Bevins, Vice President of Personnel

JB:tf

cc: Jim Hudson, Marshfield
     Bill Winthrop File

Exhibit 2.5   Request for Additional Information from EEOC
to Standard Valve & Gauge

REQUEST FOR ADDITIONAL INFORMATION
CHARGE #1910897654

1.   Please provide a signed statement from Jim Hudson concerning what Charging Party told him about being sexually harassed. Also include whether or not Hudson told Winthrop that Mary Harper Jones had propositioned him.

2.   If Charging Party reported being sexually harassed to management, to whom did he report this and what were the specifics?

3.   Provide your company's policy on sexual harassment.

4.   Please provide the personnel files of Charging Party and Mary Harper Jones.

5.   Please provide your company's policy on discipline and discharge.

6.   Please explain in detail the reasons for Charging Party's discharge.

continued

Exhibit 2.5 *continued*

7. Please provide a list of employees that were discharged during the last year, indicating their name, race, sex, date of hire, position held, reason for discharge, date of discharge, and prior disciplinary history. Provide the personnel file of an employee that was discharged who was a black female.

8. Please provide a signed statement from Mary Harper Jones concerning whether or not Charging Party sexually harassed her on June 9, 1986.

9. Please provide signed statements from witnesses concerning whether or not Charging Party was sexually harassed or Mary Harper Jones was sexually harassed.

10. Please provide a position statement on every point raised on the face of the charge.

CASE:
UNFAIR PROMOTIONS AT FOOD CHAIN SUPERMARKETS

Thomas L. Rutherford, Personnel Director of Food Chain Supermarkets, Inc., was jolted by the conversation he just had with Walter Jackson, an employee in the company's distribution warehouse. Jackson had complained that black employees were being passed over for promotions in favor of white employees who had less experience and seniority. Jackson had gone on to explain that he had resigned his position in the meat department of the warehouse because, despite his experience and job performance, he felt he would not get promoted. He explained that he had been passed over for promotion three times since he started work with Food Chain.

After Jackson left his office, Rutherford began to immediately investigate his claims. He called in Mark Walters, his personnel assistant, and explained his conversation with Jackson to him. "The last thing I want on my hands is a discrimination suit," Rutherford said to Mark. "I want you to get some data on promotions that have occurred in the last couple of years in our warehouse operations. Also, while you're at it, get the same information for our stores. Also, here are the names of three black employees given to me by Jackson. Pull their files and try to get any facts on what happened with their promotion requests." Mark replied, "I don't think it will be too difficult to pull together the information, Tom, now that we have finally gotten our personnel records centralized. But I'll probably have to talk with some of the department managers and supervisors also." Rutherford suggested that he interview the three black employees also. As Mark left his office, Rutherford began to think about the company's personnel practices and Jackson's allegations.

Background

Food Chain Supermarkets, Inc. is a regional chain of supermarkets located in the Midwest. Additionally, the company operates a central warehouse, bakery, and its own transportation system. Its main office, distribution center (warehouse), and a dozen stores are located in Reed County. Presently the company employs over 1,600 people in the county. According to recent census data, Reed County's labor force is about 22 percent black. The company has plans to refurbish its stores and to open an additional four stores over the next two years. Rutherford had been hired in anticipation of this growth to help better manage the company's personnel needs.

The distribution center has five departments: grocery, meat, frozen food, produce, and transportation. Each department has two shifts. The starting times of various employees on the same shifts are staggered. Both receiving and shipping functions are carried out at the warehouse. Order puller, order selector, order picker, and picker are synonymous terms for the same position. A warehouse crew leader is a working supervisor who assigns duties and performs the same duties as subordinates. Management positions in the stores consist of assistant produce manager, produce manager, grocery manager trainee, relief grocery manager, deli manager, relief assistant manager, assistant manager, head cashier, and assistant head cashier.

Personnel Practices

When Rutherford was hired four months ago, the President had explained that because of the physical dispersion of the stores, personnel policies were decentralized with a great deal of responsibility placed on the district managers. Promotion recommendations and decisions were made by supervisors of the different departments in the warehouse. In order to be promoted to a warehouse crew leader, an employee had to be on the same shift and in the same department as the opening. The factors utilized in promotion decisions at the warehouse were character, integrity, good sound morale, correct attitude, and initiative. The company felt that the supervisor was in the best position to judge whether or not an employee was promotable. There was no system for employees to apply for promotions. Written performance evaluations were limited to office employees, merchandisers, and store managers. At the retail stores, store supervisors made promotion recommendations to the district manager. Promotions were limited to persons recommended by the store managers. The district managers agreed with the store managers 90 to 95 percent of the time. The district manager decided who would be promoted, transferred, demoted, hired, or terminated for all positions up to the department head. Job vacancies were not routinely posted. Employees could be transferred from store to store as needed.

Rutherford recalled a conversation he recently had with one of the district managers, Joe Perkins: "We really don't need to post jobs since each district manager is usually aware of openings in his or her district and which employees are ready for promotion. Further, an employee doesn't have to ask in order to be considered for a promotion. Although we don't have a written evaluation system, the job performance of an employee is conveyed by word of mouth from one level of supervision to another."

Two Weeks Later

Rutherford had received the reports and data prepared by Mark on promotions within the warehouse and stores for the past two years (see Exhibit 2.6). Mark had also prepared summaries of what had happened to Jackson and the other three black employees mentioned by Jackson. As Rutherford began reading through the report, he wondered what changes would be needed at Food Chain. He certainly did not want to have another conversation like the one he had with Jackson two weeks earlier.

Questions

1. Analyze the table in Exhibit 2.6. What conclusions do you reach? Is there evidence of discrimination in promotion decisions?
2. Do you believe that Gemson, Thompson, LeBlanc, and Jackson were discriminated against?
3. What are some of the potential disadvantages of a "word of mouth" promotion system?
4. What should Rutherford do now?

Exhibit 2.6 Report on Promotion Rates

To:	T. L. Rutherford, Director of Personnel
From:	Mark Walters, Personnel Assistant
Re:	Promotions

I have collected the data you requested on promotion rates at our warehouse and stores for the last two years (see table). I have also summarized what I could learn about the Jackson situation and the other three promotion cases he mentioned.

PROMOTION RATES

Unit	Year	Total Employees		Total Promotions		Promotion Rates	
		White	Black	White	Black	White Rate	Black Rate
Warehouse/stores	1986	1603	284	171	21	10.66%	7.39%
Warehouse/stores	1985	1414	291	122	27	8.62	9.27
Warehouse	1985	223	192	18	21	8.07	10.90
Stores	1985	1191	99	104	6	8.73	6.10
Stores	1985	1192	111	129	8	10.80	7.20

Note: In 1986, blacks represented 5.8% of 137 store promotions and 9% of the work force. In the warehouse, 42 whites and 13 blacks were promoted to the crew leader job in 1986. In 1985, 94.6% of the managers were white and in 1986 it was 94.7%.

CLIFFORD GEMSON: Gemson was hired as a produce clerk in June of 1985. He had originally applied for a management position. He had three years of grocery store management experience including six months in produce management with another company. Gemson worked in two stores between June 1985 and April 1986. On several occasions Gemson asked his district manager (J. Perkins) and his store manager (C. Fagen) about promotion to vacant produce manager positions. The first vacancy was filled on October 8, 1985 by Bob Watkins, a white employee. Watkins, a produce clerk, had 18 months of experience with us. Watkins, who had no management experience was replaced by another white employee, Sheila Wilson, on November 8, 1985. Wilson was selected on the basis of her Food Chain experience as a produce clerk and an assistant produce manager for six months. Gemson was not considered for either vacancy.

continued

Exhibit 2.6 *continued*

ROY THOMPSON: Roy Thompson was hired by Food Chain at our warehouse on 9/18/84 as a maintenance (sanitation) employee. His duties included forklift driving, sorting damaged food, and rebuilding pallets. His prior work experience included supervisory duties and self-employment. Thompson trained a white employee of Food Chain (Neal Marcy, hired 5/12/85) who was promoted to crew leader of the maintenance (sanitation) department on 6/16/85. Before Marcy was hired, Thompson asked his supervisor (E. Jones) for the crew leader job to which Marcy was promoted. Jones told Thompson that he would never be a crew leader as long as he was supervisor. Jones denies saying this. According to Thompson, his supervisors had repeatedly told him that he had both excellent attendance and performance. On 8/15/86 a junior white employee, Earl Hanes (with less company experience than Thompson), was promoted to a sanitation crew leader for the same shift and in the same department that Thompson worked. According to Jones, Hanes was better qualified for the position because of his previous work experience.

LESLIE LeBLANC: Leslie LeBlanc was hired by Food Chain on 7/8/84 as a frozen food picker. Her next position was frozen food loader. LeBlanc was trained to act as a "fill-in" crew leader, and in fact did fill in as a crew leader until Ricky Anderson (white) was hired. LeBlanc trained Anderson in the duties of a "fill-in" crew leader. Anderson then assumed LeBlanc's place as "fill-in" crew leader. Anderson was offered a full-time crew leader's position, which he refused. LeBlanc was never offered this job. LeBlanc had previously informed Food Chain management of her prior experience as a shift leader at a textile mill.

WALTER JACKSON: Walter Jackson was employed by Food Chain on 4/14/84 at the warehouse in the meat department. Milk, dairy products, and meat are in the same department. Jackson's job duties prior to April 1986 included milk picking, unloading, and forklift driving. In the spring of 1986 a crew leader told Jackson that he was up for promotion to crew leader in the department. Terry Gibson (a white employee) received the job on June 7, 1986. Gibson was initially hired on 1/11/84, resigned 2/5/84 and was rehired 11/3/84. Jackson had more company and departmental experience than Gibson. However, he was never considered for the position. Gibson's prior duties were solely picking meat and Jackson had supervised Gibson when Jackson served as "fill-in" crew leader prior to Gibson's promotion. The supervisor asserted that Gibson had broader departmental experience than Jackson. Since that time two other employees in the meat department with less seniority and experience have been promoted over Jackson.

EXERCISE:
AGE DISCRIMINATION ROLE PLAY

I. *Objectives:*

    1. To understand the purpose and provisions of the Age Discrimination in Employment Act and its amendments.

    2. To help you realize how difficult it is to staff without bias from age stereotypes.

II. *Out-of-Class Preparation Time:* 1 hour

III. *In-Class Time Suggested:* 45 minutes

IV. *Procedures:*

    1. Read the entire exercise before class.

    2. Form groups of four (three members to role play and one to observe).

        a. Everyone should read the "Background" to the role-playing situation.

        b. Each role player in each group is to read his or her role: personnel director, younger candidate, and older candidate.

        c. The personnel director is to interview each applicant separately, in either order, for about 10 - 15 minutes.

        d. The personnel director must decide which applicant to recommend for a job and why. A second interview (5 minutes) is then conducted with each candidate to inform each of the decision and the criteria used.

        e. The observer takes constructive notes during the proceedings and reports observations on Form 1.

ROLE PLAYING

Background

Metropolitan Hospital is a large teaching institution in a Northeastern city. In recent years the patient census and occupancy levels have declined as a result of increasing competition and insurance incentives for the utilization of nonhospital services. Salary increases have been small (less than 5 percent) over the past four years and promotion opportunities few. While layoffs have been avoided, many middle-management positions and some clinical positions have not been filled when resignations have occurred.

As a result of a recent resignation, the position of Director of Nursing Services has recently become vacant. A successful individual in this position is able to relate to the medical staff, administration, and other clinical staff as well as the nursing staff itself. In addition to knowledge of the hospital and interrelationships among its component parts, tact and diplomacy are essential. In-depth knowledge of the various nursing functions and particular problems associated with each are essential. Administrative skills are generally more important than clinical skills in this position. A job description for the position is shown in Exhibit 2.7.

The hospital policy is to promote from within wherever possible and the personnel manager has narrowed the field down to two candidates. Both are head nurses in their respective departments.

The Personnel Director: Pat Grubis

You have been with the hospital for four years and feel you have done quite a good job. While you are concerned that the personnel function does not enjoy widespread support from the board or upper administration, you feel your own reputation within the facility is excellent. You have an M.A. degree in Human Resources Management and six years of experience in the personnel field. Your recommendations for various administrative positions have generally been accepted by upper administration and your candidates have performed well.

In the present case, you will be recommending one of the two candidates to the hospital administrator. You know the work habits of both applicants and feel either could do a good job. However, some things you have to consider are as follows:

1. Ann Smith (the older applicant) has not been hesitant to use the grievance procedure in the past. You fear she may appeal your decision internally if the promotion to Director of Nursing Service is denied. Worse yet, she may file suit for age discrimination under the Age Discrimination in Employment Act (ADEA).

2. The Director of Nursing Services must deal with complaints from nurses, physicians, and patients. Ann has been known to become "testy" when put under pressure.

3. Ann is well known and well liked in the hospital and has friends in "high places" as a result of her twenty-two years of service with the institution.

4. Linda Schaffer (the younger applicant) is a "fast track" individual. She has an M.S.N. degree in nursing service administration and finished second in her class. She is thirty-seven. By contrast, Ann is fifty-five and has a bachelor's degree in nursing, but no formal education in administration beyond a few in-service courses.

5. The position may be a career stepping stone for Linda. She feels ready to move upward, has many contacts in the nursing community, and will probably look elsewhere if the position is filled by someone else. Alternatively, Ann will probably stay if she is not promoted since she is eligible for retirement in three years after twenty-five years of service at the hospital.

6. The cost to the hospital will be different depending on the person you select. If it is Linda, the vacation is two weeks and sick leave is ten days. If it is Ann, her greater seniority will require the hospital to provide six weeks vacation and sick leave of twenty days.

7. Both applicants have good work records as head nurses. Linda scores a little better in terms of interpersonal relations with the nurses she supervises while Ann has more "political" contacts outside her own department. Linda has been absent from work more than Ann, in some cases because of sick children.

8. You are looking for a "win-win" strategy for both candidates since both are excellent employees who have made major contributions to the hospital. However, the reality is that you can only recommend one applicant for the position.

9. Establish criteria and objectives for your interview with each candidate and conduct a structured interview designed to determine whatever information you will need to make your recommendation.

Linda Schaffer: Younger Candidate

At age thirty-seven you feel an urge to move ahead in your career. You have been with the hospital for five years as head nurse and felt that you were passed over for the same position three years ago because of your relative youth. You have developed many contacts in the nursing community and are presently aware of several interesting openings in nursing service administration. This week you have agreed to be interviewed for one of these positions at another institution.

Although you have missed seven days of work during the past year due to children's illness and your own asthma condition, you are are well liked by your subordinates, interact well with physicians, are well organized, and have received excellent performance evaluations.

Ann Smith: Older Candidate

You have been with the hospital for twenty-two years and will be eligible for retirement in three years. At this point you are unsure about whether you will want to stay beyond that time. You are still healthy, although fatigue and stress have sometimes been a problem. Yet you can't imagine just sitting around with nothing to do since you are not married and work has been your whole life. At the same time, you feel you might like to "cut back" your work commitments at some point in the future.

Despite these inner concerns, you feel you have "earned" the position for which you are applying through years of excellent service to the institution. Moreover, your friends in the administration as well as elsewhere tell you they are supporting you. If you are not promoted, you will probably retire from Metropolitan Hospital in three years and seek some kind of a nursing administration position elsewhere. Depending upon who is appointed, you may also consider filing an age discrimination suit with EEOC since you attribute your previous failure to be promoted to Director of Nursing Services to be due to your age rather than your qualifications.

Exhibit 2.7 Job Description for the Position of Director of Nursing Services

JOB DESCRIPTION

JOB TITLE: Director of Nursing Services

DEPARTMENT: Nursing Services

JOB SUMMARY: The Director of Nursing Services is responsible for all aspects of nursing services delivered in the department including clinical quality, cost containment, goal-setting, employee motivation, planning, employee grievances, scheduling, evaluation, and other administrative functions which may be necessary for the smooth functioning of the department.

JOB RELATIONSHIPS:

1. Responsible to: The Associate Administrator
2. Employees Supervised: Directly supervises all head nurses, indirectly supervises all nurses in the department.

RESPONSIBILITIES AND DUTIES:

1. Interviews all nursing candidates for positions; provides input to head nurse and nursing supervisor regarding all applicants for nursing positions.
2. Approves all work schedules and changes in work schedules.
3. Develops budget proposals for the Department; controls costs to conform to the approved budget.
4. Plans work force requirements for the Department based upon the hospital's strategic plan and expected patient loads.
5. Evaluates performance of all head nurses and approves performance appraisals for all other nurses.
6. Conducts appraisal interviews with all head nurses.
7. Makes salary recommendations for all nursing personnel to the Associate Administrator.
8. Handles employee and patient complaints and grievances.
9. Communicates all hospital policies and procedures to nursing personnel.
10. Works on special projects at the request of the Administrator or the Associate Administrator.
11. The above statements reflect the general functions of the position and should not be construed as a detailed description of all the work requirements associated with the position.

continued

Exhibit 2.7 *continued*

QUALIFICATIONS:

Education: B.S. or M.S.N. degree in Nursing or Nursing Services Administration.

Experience: At least ten years of experience in Nursing and/or Nursing Service Administration.

Personal Qualifications: Must be able to work under pressure and time constraints; must be in good health and have a high energy level; must have good communication and interpersonal skills; and must exhibit tact, diplomacy, good judgment, and initiative.

Form 1 Observer Report

1. Who seemed to lead in each interview?

2. Was the Personnel Director adequately prepared for each interview? Were his or her objectives achieved?

3. Were proper questions asked? Did the personnel director refer to anyone's age? Was it a legal reference?

4. What should the interviewer do differently in the future? Did the personnel director achieve a "win-win" outcome?

continued

Form 1 *continued*

5. If the Personnel Director decided to recommend Linda Schaffer and Ann Smith sued the hospital under the ADEA, could the decision be defended? If so, how?

EXERCISE: IS THIS UNLAWFUL DISCRIMINATION?

I. *Objectives:*
1. To help you understand the application of the four major federal laws which regulate equal rights in employment. These laws are Title VII of the Civil Rights Acts of 1964 as amended by the Equal Employment Opportunity Act of 1972, the Equal Pay Act of 1963, the Age Discrimination in Employment Act of 1967, and the Vocational Rehabilitation Act of 1973.

bad, ineffective law

2. To help you understand the court's interpretation of these laws.
3. To help you understand the legal definition of discrimination and the burden of proof placed on defendants and plaintiffs.

II. *Out-of-Class Preparation Time:* 60 minutes

III. *In-Class Time Suggested:* 45 minutes

IV. *Procedures:*
1. Read the exercise and review the major laws before class.
2. The class should be divided into groups of 4.
3. Each group should read each of the incidents that follow and answer these questions:
    a. What legal statute(s) apply in this case?
    b. What issue(s) must the court decide in this case?
    c. If you were the judge, how would you rule? Did the employer discriminate unlawfully? Why or why not?

1. Gregory Pickens, a teacher in Webster County, was baptized into the Worldwide Church of God. The church's designated holy days caused Pickens to miss approximately six school days a year. The school board's collec-

tive bargaining agreement with the Webster County Federation of Teachers provides three days annual leave for observance of mandatory religious holidays. While the contract granted teachers three days of personal leave, personal leave could not be used for any religious activity or religious observance. In order to practice his religion, Pickens had to take unauthorized leave for which his pay was reduced accordingly. Pickens repeatedly asked (and was denied) the school board to allow him to use personal leave for religious observance or, as an alternative, to allow him to pay the cost of a substitute and receive full pay for additional days off for religious observances. Pickens filed a complaint in U.S. District Court alleging that the prohibition on the use of "personal leave" for religious observance discriminated against him because of his religion.

2. Edward Roberts, a black truck driver, in response to a newspaper ad applied in person for a tractor trailer driver position at a trucking company on March 31, 1986. Roberts' application listed twenty-two months of prior experience as a road driver. He had an additional ten years of experience which he did not list on the application due to a lack of space on the form. Roberts was neither interviewed nor contacted by the company about the status of his application. In June of 1986, Roberts saw an identical advertisement for tractor trailer drivers. Upon inquiry, Roberts learned that eight persons (all white) had been hired as truck drivers between April and June of 1986. All of the hirees had less than twenty-two months of driving experience. The company contended that Roberts was not hired because no opening existed when he applied. Roberts filed a discrimination complaint in district court.

3. John Santiago was employed as a security guard at Thompson's Ammunition Plant for a number of years. Due to the possibility of explosions, guards were placed at each of several gates to prevent employees from bringing in prohibited items. Female guards were also necessary to avoid a situation where male guards would be physically searching female employees. When faced with the need to reduce the work force, management reduced the guard force by discharging several male guards, including Santiago. All the female guards then employed were retained. Santiago had accrued more seniority than any of the female guards. Santiago filed a lawsuit charging "reverse discrimination" because he had lost his job when females with less job seniority kept their jobs.

4. James McFadden was a transsexual who, while still biologically male, announced to his employer (East Coast Airlines) that he intended to dress and act as a woman in preparation for "surgical sex reassignment." Mr. McFadden was subsequently fired from his pilot's job for refusing to comply with its requirement that he continue to dress and act as a man. McFadden subsequently filed a lawsuit in district court alleging that East Coast had conspired to discriminate against him on the basis of his sex (now to be female) and that he was treated differently from other women employed by the airline.

5. Elnora Williams, a black female teacher with ten years of classroom experience and partial completion of her doctoral degree in education, applied for several vacant middle and secondary principalships in the Knox County school system. Each time she applied she was told by the superintendent that "the school district believed that a 'male image' is necessary for a middle or secondary school principal." No females had occupied such principal positions in the school district. Williams subsequently filed a lawsuit in district court accusing the school system of discrimination.

6. Frank Foxworth was hired as a budget analyst in May of 1983 by Jackson County. During his first year as an analyst his work performance was rated satisfactory and above by his supervisor. In July of 1984, Foxworth learned that he had contracted AIDS (acquired immune deficiency syndrome). Foxworth was discharged in September from his $20,000 a year position. Foxworth filed suit alleging that the employer discriminated against him on the basis of his handicap (AIDS).

7. Harriet Klondike, Cyndy Patton, Helen Waters, and Margaret Double were employed as matrons at the Mailton County Jail. The county also employed male corrections officers and deputy sheriffs. The matrons guarded female inmates and spent the majority of their time on clerical duties while the corrections officers and deputy sheriffs spent the majority of their time guarding male inmates. The salary of matrons ranged from $525 to $886 per month while the salaries for the male guards ranged from $701 to $940 per month. The four matrons filed suit and alleged that they were paid lower salaries for work that was basically the same and that the pay differential was attributable to intentional discrimination.

8. The Harrisville Police Department required all police officers, both male and female, to satisfy a 5-foot, 6-inch minimum height requirement. Betty Johnston, thirty-three years old and 5 feet 3 inches tall, applied for a job as a police officer. She passed the city's physical examination and scored a 93 on the state civil service exam. Since the city maintained two eligibility lists (one female and one male), she was ranked as the number one candidate on the list for female officers. When two vacancies came open for female officers, Johnston and the second-ranked applicant were interviewed for the position but rejected because they did not satisfy the minimum height requirement. The third and fourth candidates were hired because they met the height requirement. Johnston later filed a suit against the city alleging that the height requirement was discriminatory toward women applicants because less than 20 percent of women in the United States reach the height of 5 feet 6 inches.

9. W. F. Barrow, fifty-one years of age, had been employed with the same company for seventeen years. After working as a salesperson for twelve years, he was promoted to Central Region Sales Manager. He had received an outstanding rating on his last performance evaluation and had consistently ex-

ceeded his targeted sales quota. He was terminated from his position two months after the evaluation. He was told by the vice president of sales that he was no longer needed and that the company had to make staffing changes in order to turn around declining sales on its major product lines. In less than a week, Barrow was replaced with a younger employee. Barrow and several other older sales employees who also had been terminated filed a complaint with the local EEOC office.

10. Officials of a city government charged with discrimination signed a consent decree agreeing to an affirmative action plan with specific promotion and hiring goals for increasing the number of miniority firefighters in the city's fire department. Four years later, when faced with severe budget problems, the city implemented a layoff plan aimed at protecting minority employees who were recently hired. Jerome Atwood, a white firefighter, was laid off even though he had greater seniority than many of the minority firefighters who retained their jobs. Atwood filed a lawsuit charging reverse discrimination.

INCIDENT:
THE EMPLOYEE WITH AIDS

It was another hectic day for Mary Landschulz, Cafeteria Manager for a department store located in the city of New York. She had just received a call from one of her employees, Cathy, stating that she would not be able to come to work that day. When she asked Cathy why, Cathy reluctantly stated that yesterday her doctor had informed her that she had AIDS (acquired immune deficiency syndrome). She did not know when she would return to work but knew that it wouldn't be soon. She said she would call next week.

Hanging up the telephone, Mary sat motionless in her office. She was stunned by what she had just heard. Cathy was an excellent employee and had served food on the cafeteria line for five years. Cathy had been sick recently for several days, but Mary had thought Cathy just had the flu or a cold. Now she knew the truth, and it was not a pretty picture. "Oh my gosh!" she exclaimed to herself, "What am I going to do?"

As Mary pondered this question, the alarm on her watch "beeped," reminding her that she had to attend a meeting with her employees. Slowly, she got out of her chair and walked down the hall to the meeting room. When she entered the room she found it buzzing with talk about Cathy. Mary headed for the nearest seat hoping that the topic of discussion would change. As she and the others sat down around the large oval table, one of the cafeteria workers turned to her and asked, "What's wrong with Cathy? She told Frank she might not ever be back to work." Suddenly, a hush fell over the room as everyone awaited Mary's reply.

Questions

1. As a result of the incident, should the company develop a specific AIDS policy?
2. How should Mary respond to Frank's question?
3. Assuming that the employees ultimately learn that Cathy has AIDS, how should Mary deal with their fears? What should she do if the employees refuse to work with Cathy when she returns?

INCIDENT:
THE EMPLOYEE'S PREGNANCY

Mr. Carson is the supervisor of a department in a small manufacturer of precision tools. The machinery in the fourteen-person department is competently operated by people all younger than he. All but four operators are men. Clara, one of the women, is five months pregnant. She had been there when Carson was hired and has maintained an excellent work record.

Carson had told the operators that they had complete responsibility and control of what happened on their machines when on duty. The work is of a highly technical nature and requires great concentration to keep the machines utilized to their fullest capacity.

The jobs require very little physical exertion, and most of the time employees simply have to push buttons. Occasionally, however, it is necessary to lift boxes associated with the work. Clara's fellow workers had been doing this for her during most of her pregnancy, but one day all were extremely busy and no one had time to help her. Thus, a bottleneck was created. Carson reprimanded Clara for not keeping the work flowing steadily.

The next day Clara walked into Carson's office and told him that she had read that lifting heavy objects might cause a miscarriage. She requested that he assign other workers to do all of the lifting for her. She also wanted the other workers to refrain from smoking for fear it might harm her baby. Carson was caught off guard by her requests and did not know how to respond. He knew the company had no policy which he could follow. He wondered what Clara's co-workers would say if he asked them to do her lifting and to quit smoking. He wondered if the lifting and smoke would be in fact harmful to the fetus and what legal issues might be involved. In addition, he wondered if other solutions wouldn't be more appropriate. Perhaps, she should be sent home on an unpaid leave of absence, or maybe he could transfer her to a different job where lifting wasn't required. He knew, however, that any job transfer would reduce Clara's pay by $5 - $6 per hour. All of these thoughts raced through his head as he stared up at the ceiling in his office hoping a solution would magically appear. After a few more moments of silence, Carson slowly looked at Clara and said, "I had better check with my boss on this one."

Questions

1. If you were Carson's supervisor, how would you respond to Clara's request?
2. Should Carson have allowed Clara's co-workers to lift boxes for her?
3. Was Carson at fault for allowing Clara to keep working after becoming pregnant?
4. Should Carson have reprimanded Clara for not keeping the work flowing steadily?

SKILL BUILDER: DATA ANALYSIS FOR AFFIRMATIVE ACTION PLANS

I. *Objectives:*
1. To enhance your understanding of how to prepare a utilization/availability analysis for affirmative action plans.
2. To teach you the data analysis requirements under affirmative action guidelines.

II. *Time Required to Complete:* 2 - 3 hours

III. *Instructions:* You work for a manufacturing firm located in Charlotte, North Carolina, and your company has just been awarded its first federal contract of $250,000. This contract is to supply one of your major products over a two-year period to the Department of Defense. You have been asked by your boss, the plant manager, to perform the utilization/availability analyses required under Executive Order 11246 as input in developing an affirmative action plan (AAP) for the Office of Federal Contract Compliance Programs (OFCCP).

You have reviewed the guidelines from the OFCCP on the requirements (see Exhibit 2.8). You have also pulled together labor market data in addition to compiling a detailed breakdown of the company's work force by job category, sex, and race (see Exhibits 2.9, 2.10, 2.11, 2.12, and 2.13).

REQUIRED

Using the relevant data, complete Form 1. Be sure to list any assumptions you make about the relevant labor market for each job category. Also be sure to indicate the job categories where women and minorities are underutilized. Make any other recommendations you deem necessary to the plant manager.

Exhibit 2.8 OFCCP/AAP Guidelines

DEFINITION

An affirmative action program is a set of specific and result-oriented procedures to which a contractor commits to supply every good-faith effort. The objective of those procedures plus such efforts is equal employment opportunity. An acceptable affirmative action program must include an analysis of areas within which the contractor is deficient in the utilization of minority groups and women, and further, goals and timetables to which the contractor's good-faith efforts must be directed to correct the deficiencies and thus to increase materially the utilization of minorities and women at all levels and in all segments of the work force where deficiencies exist.

UTILIZATION ANALYSIS

An AAP must contain a utilization analysis—a comparison of the percentages of women and minorities in each job category (work-force analysis) with the percentages available in the relevant labor market (availability analysis). The work-force analysis is a listing of the number of employees in the organization by job categories. For each job category the total number of male and female incumbents in each of these groups (blacks, Hispanics, American Indians, and Orientals) is assessed (see Exhibit 2.9).

An analysis of all major job groups and the extent to which minorities or women are underutilized is also requested. Underutilization is having fewer minorities or women in a particular job category than would reasonably be expected, according to their availability in the relevant labor market. When making the utilization analysis, eight points must be considered:

1. Minority population in the labor area around the organization.
2. Size of minority and female unemployment force in the area.
3. Percentage of minority and female work force as compared with the total work force in the immediate labor area.

continued

Exhibit 2.8 *continued*

4. Availability of minorities and women with requisite skills in immediate area.
5. Availability of promotable and transferable minorities and women within the employer's work force.
6. Existence of training institutions capable of training in the required skills.
7. Availability of minorities and women with skills in areas where the employer can recruit.
8. Degree of training the employer is able to undertake as an avenue for making all job classes available to minorities and women.

Based on 41 C.F.R. Chapter 60, Office of Federal Contract Compliance Programs, Department of Labor.

Exhibit 2.9 Work-Force Analysis

Job Categories	Overall Totals (Sums of Columns B thru K)	Number of Male Employees					Number of Female Employees				
		White (Not of Hispanic Origin)	Black (Not of Hispanic Origin)	Hispanic	Asian or Pacific Islander	American Indian or Alaskan Native	White (Not of Hispanic Origin)	Black (Not of Hispanic Origin)	Hispanic	Asian or Pacific Islander	American Indian or Alaskan Native
	A	B	C	D	E	F	G	H	I	J	K
Officials and managers*	154	138	2	0	0	0	13	1	0	0	0
Professionals	137	126	1	0	0	0	10	0	0	0	0
Technicians	76	61	2	1	1	0	6	2	0	3	0
Sales workers	77	65	4	0	0	0	7	1	0	0	0
Office and clerical	188	21	3	0	1	0	144	17	2	0	0
Craft workers (skilled)	150	120	15	1	2	0	9	3	0	0	0
Operatives (semiskilled)	294	200	58	2	10	2	16	4	0	2	0
Laborers (unskilled)	655	504	82	5	10	1	38	10	3	2	0
Service workers	89	17	49	5	1	2	2	9	2	0	2
TOTALS	1,820	1,252	216	14	25	5	245	47	7	7	2

*Includes supervisors

45

Exhibit 2.10 Population by Race and Sex, 1980,
Charlotte, Gastonia, Rock Hill, NC-SC, SMSA[1]

	Number		Percent Distribution	
	Total	**Female**	**Total**	**Female**
TOTAL	869,264	448,482	100.0	100.0
White	686,194	352,477	78.9	78.5
Black	170,301	89,481	19.6	19.9
American Indian, Eskimo, and Aleut	2,185	1,114	0.3	0.2
Asian and Pacific Islander	3,727	1,826	0.4	0.4
Hispanic	6,857	3,584	0.8	0.8

[1]North Carolina portion only (SMSA = Standard Metropolitan Statistical Area)

Source: 1980 Census of Population.

Exhibit 2.11 Civilian Labor Force by Sex and Race, 1986[1]

Sex and Race	Civilian Labor Force	Employed	Unemployed
Both Sexes			
TOTAL	514,796	489,574	25,222
White	417,540	400,260	17,280
Black	90,270	82,710	7,560
American Indian, Eskimo and Aleut	1,093	1,048	45
Asian and Pacific Islander	2,193	2,066	127
Hispanic	3,700	3,490	210
Female			
TOTAL	233,298	220,545	12,753
White	184,190	175,420	8,770
Black	45,970	42,150	3,820
American Indian, Eskimo and Aleut	495	467	28
Asian and Pacific Islander	993	938	55
Hispanic	1,650	1,570	80

[1]Based on 1980 census proportions.

Source: Employment Security Commission of North Carolina, Labor Market Division.

Exhibit 2.12 Occupations of the Civilian Labor Force by Sex and Race, 1980, Charlotte, Gastonia, Rock Hill, NC-SC SMSA[1]

Occupation	Total[2]	Total White	Total Black	American Indian	Asians	Hispanic	White Not Hispanic	Black Not Hispanic	Total Minority
TOTAL									
All industries	447,254	364,832	78,955	1,348	1,837	3,165	362,595	78,302	84,659
Managerial and professional specialty	87,018	77,673	8,482	119	689	589	77,211	8,410	9,807
Technicians	10,077	8,557	1,415	20	80	53	8,517	1,407	1,561
Sales occupations	45,837	42,341	3,241	84	141	287	42,115	3,203	3,772
Administrative support including clerical	72,927	62,762	9,857	115	173	387	62,438	9,814	10,489
Service workers	47,097	29,970	16,627	225	249	429	29,765	16,429	17,332
Farming, forestry, and fishing	5,483	4,301	1,103	53	19	26	4,282	1,103	1,201
Precision production and craft	59,987	51,716	7,830	282	130	477	51,341	7,757	8,646
Operators and fabricators	92,707	69,331	22,678	344	251	713	68,884	22,515	23,823
Handlers, equipment cleaners, helpers, and laborers	26,121	18,181	7,722	106	105	204	18,042	7,664	8,079

[1]North Carolina portion only.

[2]Racial and ethnic group columns may not be additive to total due to "race or ethnic group not classified" in census response.

Source: 1980 Census.

Exhibit **2.13** Occupations of the Female Civilian Labor Force by Sex and Race, 1980, Charlotte, Gastonia, Rock Hill, NC-SC SMSA[1]

Occupation	Total[2]	Total White	Total Black	American Indian	Asians	His-panics	White Not Hispanic	Black Not Hispanic	Total Minority
TOTAL									
All industries	202,039	160,509	40,184	524	702	1,436	159,524	39,821	42,490
Managerial and professional specialty	36,447	30,864	5,346	48	167	260	30,682	5,290	5,765
Technicians	4,667	3,716	923	7	16	23	3,706	915	961
Sales occupations	20,006	17,652	2,211	53	71	170	17,524	2,181	2,482
Adminsitrative support including clerical	55,628	48,504	6,928	86	95	280	48,269	6,898	7,359
Service workers	28,122	17,269	10,557	134	143	261	17,159	10,425	10,963
Farming, production and fishing	1,166	877	278	6	5	0	877	278	289
Precision production and craft	5,778	4,488	1,256	13	14	51	4,450	1,250	1,328
Operators and fabricators	43,556	32,601	10,588	169	165	344	32,375	10,503	11,181
Handlers, equipment cleaners, helpers, and laborers	6,669	4,538	2,097	9	26	47	4,507	2,081	2,162

[1]North Carolina portion only.

[2]Racial and ethnic group columns may not be additive to total due to "race or ethnic group not classified" in census response.

Source: 1980 Census.

Form 1 Utilization/Availability Report

Job Category	Sex		Race				
	Male	Female	White	Black	Hispanic	Asian	American Indian
Number of employees							
Percentage of employees (utilization)							
Percent available							
Underutilized:							

Note: A table will be needed for each job category.

Part 3

Planning for
Human Resources

Planning for human resources is one of the first activities of personnel/human resource management. Human resource planning is the process of defining future human resource objectives and the strategies for achieving those objectives. Human resource planning is a complex activity consisting of two key elements: forecasting and program planning. Forecasting involves predicting future human resource supply and demand. Program planning involves developing a set of integrated activities to meet human resource objectives. In recent years there has been a growing awareness of the need to better integrate human resource planning and overall strategic planning. Strategic plans determine human resource needs, but at the same time the quality and quantity of human resources available determine the strategic objectives an organization is able to pursue.

The three cases in this section, "Employee Layoffs at St. Mary's Hospital," "Strategic Human Resource Management," and "The Bank Merger," focus on a number of issues related to major changes in an organization's environment, objectives, and strategies and their impact on personnel/human resource management. The exercise "Which Employee Should Be Terminated?" involves you at a personal level in downsizing decisions. The second exercise, "Writing Job Descriptions," allows you to perform an important prerequisite activity for effective human resource planning in organizations—job analysis. The incident, "The New Work Schedule," underscores the importance of accurate employment planning. The skill builder in this section requires you to forecast an organization's human resource demand.

CASE:
EMPLOYEE LAYOFFS
AT ST. MARY'S HOSPITAL

St. Mary's Hospital is a medium-sized, 400-bed hospital in a northwestern city. It was established in 1908 by the Sisters of the Sacred Heart, an order of Catholic sisters. The facility has grown gradually over the years and is now the third largest hospital in the city. It is entirely nonunion and has never experienced an employee layoff since its inception.

Sister Mary Josephine has been the Chief Executive Officer of the hospital for eleven years. Eight years ago she hired Ms. Sharon Osgood as Director of Personnel. Ms. Osgood has an M.A. in Human Resources Management and has been instrumental in formalizing the institution's human resources policies and procedures.

Occupancy rates in the hospital had run between 76 and 82 percent from 1970 to 1982. However, since then, occupancy has fallen to 57 percent. Such declines have not been ususual for this industry during this time period as a result of changing reimbursement policies, emphasis on outpatient services, and increasing competition. However, the declining occupancy rate has affected this hospital's revenues to such an extent that it ran a deficit for the first time last year. The only response to these changes thus far has been a tightening of requirements for equipment or supply purchases.

At the most recent quarterly meeting of the Board of Directors, Sister Mary Josephine presented the rather bleak financial picture. The projected deficit for the coming year was $3,865,000 unless some additional revenue sources were identified or some additional savings found. The Board's recommendation was since there was an immediate crisis and short-term savings needed to be generated, employee layoffs were the only realistic alternative. They recommended that Sister Mary Josephine consider laying off up to 10 percent of the hospital's employees with an emphasis on those in "nonessential" areas.

Sister Mary Josephine responded that the hospital's employees had never been laid off in the history of the institution. Moreover, she viewed the employees as part of the "family" and would have great difficulty in implementing such a layoff. Nevertheless, since she had no realistic alternative for closing the "revenue gap," she reluctantly agreed to implement a layoff policy which would be as fair as possible to all employees, with a guarantee of reemployment for those laid off, and to find additional revenue sources so that layoffs would be unnecessary in the future.

Sister Mary Josephine called Sharon Osgood into her office the next morning, shared her concerns, and asked her to prepare both a short-term plan to save $3 million over the next year through employee layoffs as well as a long-term plan to avoid layoffs in the future. Her concerns were that the layoffs themselves might be costly in terms of lost investment in some of the laid-off employees, lost efficiency, potential lawsuits, and lower morale. She was concerned that the criteria for the layoffs not only *be* equitable, but also *appear* to be equitable to the employees. She also wanted to make sure that those to be laid off received "adequate" notice so they could make alternative plans or so that the hospital could assist them with finding alternative employment.   Since the hospital had no previous experience with employee layoffs and no union contract constraints, her feeling was that both seniority and job performance should be considered in determining who would be laid off.

Sharon knew the hospital's performance appraisal system was inadequate and needed to be revamped.   While this task was high on her "to do" list, she also knew she had to move ahead with her recommendations on layoffs immediately. The present performance appraisal system uses a traditional checklist rating scale with a summary rating.   Since there is no forced distribution, the average ratings of employees in different departments varies widely.

Exhibit 3.1 shows the summary ratings of employees in each department.   Most supervisors in all departments rate most of their subordinates either "average" or "outstanding."   Sharon has done a quick review of those employees whose overall ratings were "unsatisfactory" or "questionable."   Most are employees with less than three years of seniority, whereas the "average" employee has worked for St. Mary's approximately seven years.   Sharon is preparing to submit her recommendations to Sister Mary Josephine and has come to you for advice.   Exhibit 3.2 provides a summary of the distribution of employees and payroll expense by department for the most recent year.

Questions

1. Develop a plan for implementing employee layoffs over the next year which will generate $3 million in savings.   Give specific details concerning departments affected, the use of seniority vs. merit, the amount of notice, and out-placement activities.   What additional information (if any) will you need? Provide a rationale for each recommendation, together with reasons why other alternatives were not chosen.

2. How would you propose to avoid/minimize the problems identified by Sister Mary Josephine?

3. What long-term solutions do you see for the hospital once it gets its cash flow problems under control and eliminates its deficit?   What can it do to increase revenue so that future layoffs will not be necessary?

4. What difficulties exist in using "performance" as a criterion for layoffs?   How can such difficulties be overcome?

Exhibit 3.1 Percentage Distribution of Performance Appraisal Summary Ratings
by Department at St. Mary's Hospital

Department	Unsatisfactory: Needs to Improve Substantially	Questionable: Needs Some Improvement	Satisfactory: Meets Normal Expectations	Outstanding: Substantially Exceeds Norms
Nursing	6.4	6.4	54.2	33.0
Allied Health	5.7	6.2	47.8	40.3
Central Administration	2.7	3.1	67.5	26.7
Dietetics/ Nutrition	2.1	6.2	68.3	23.4
Housekeeping/ Maintenance	7.8	12.4	54.6	25.2
Medical Staff	1.1	6.2	63.8	28.9

Exhibit 3.2 The Distribution of Employment and Payroll Expenditures
at St. Mary's Hospital

Department	Number of Employees	Payroll ($)
Nursing	602	$15,050,000
Allied Health Departments	261	5,742,000
Central Administration	154	6,160,000
Dietetics/Nutrition	65	1,430,000
Housekeeping and Maintenance	36	540,000
Medical Staff	32	1,680,000
TOTAL	1150	$30,602,000

CASE:
STRATEGIC HUMAN RESOURCE MANAGEMENT

The College of Business Administration at Old State University is one of twelve state-supported collegiate business schools in a midwestern state. It is located in a city with a population of 400,000 with a diversified industrial base. Old State is the only state-supported institution in town. One small private college provides competition to the college.

Recently, the college has experienced a leadership transition. Dr. George Barnes who had been Dean of the College since 1968, retired. During his administration, the enrollment had increased from 1,202 undergraduates and 76 M.B.A. students in the 1968-69 academic year to 2,065 undergraduate and 218 M.B.A. students in the 1988-89 academic year.

Dean Barnes was well liked by students, faculty, and the central administration of Old State. However, he had not led the college in any new directions and had basically concentrated on "doing the same things better." The "same things" meant an emphasis on traditional programs (accounting, marketing, finance, etc.), teaching undergraduate students in the age range of 18-22 in daytime programs, and teaching a small number of full-time M.B.A. students. The latter have been mostly graduates of the college's undergraduate program who decided they were willing to spend two more years on campus to obtain the second degree.

Dean Barnes had also been successful in upgrading the proportion of faculty with terminal degrees from 56 percent in 1968 to 85 percent in 1988. Exhibit 3.3 provides faculty and student enrollment data for the college for selected years during the nineteen-year period of Barnes's tenure.

During the 1987 - 88 academic year, the Dean's Search Committee (consisting of faculty, students, alumni, central administration, and local business representatives) met frequently, screened over one hundred applicants, and personally interviewed six. While the committee arrived at no consensus, the majority supported Mr. Jack Blake for the Deanship. An offer was made and after several weeks of negotiation, Blake accepted the Deanship. His background was an M.B.A. from a prestigious Ivy League business school and executive leadership positions in a variety of U.S. corporations in the area of marketing. He left the position of Vice President of Marketing at one of the "Fortune 500" companies to accept the Deanship.

During the screening interviews with the Search Committee, Mr. Blake had made it clear that, if he were selected, the college would be "moving in new directions and exploring new markets." It was very clear Blake did not want to be "paper pusher," but did want to be an innovator and an entrepreneur. When pressed for specifics, he had indicated he "would have to study the situation in more detail."

When the new Dean arrived on campus in Fall 1988, he immediately convened a Strategic Planning Committee to (1) evaluate the college's external environment, opportunities, constraints, competitive advantages, and internal environment and (2) recommend a new set of long-term missions, goals, objectives, and programs. The committee consisted of two senior professors, the university's Vice President for Academic Affairs, one graduate student, one undergraduate student, two prominent alumni, and two local business leaders.

The committee recommended that the college focus upon the "adult learner" since demographic analysis suggested the age group 18-22 was shrinking and would be a declining market over the next decade. Specific recommendations included (1) more evening courses for both undergraduate and graduate students; (2) structuring the schedule so that both degrees could be earned entirely in the evening; (3) offering credit courses in some suburban locations; (4) offering requested noncredit practitioner courses at the college, at the employer's work site, and in various underserved small cities around the state; (5) exploring the possibility of offering degree programs at these locations; and (6) offering new M.B.A. degree concentrations in such areas as management of the arts, health care management, and public sector management.

The new Dean enthusiastically endorsed the report and distributed copies at the last faculty meeting of the fall semester. Several questions were raised, but it didn't appear serious opposition existed. However, at a follow-up meeting of department Chairs, the Dean indicated that his top priority for the 1988-89 academic year was to fill the nine vacant positions with new faculty who would be supportive of the new directions in which the college was moving. Specifically, he asked them to keep several criteria in mind while recruiting and selecting new faculty. These included previous managerial work experience, a willingness to teach night courses, a willingness to travel to other cities to offer coursework, and an ability to work with management practitioners on special projects.

In addition, he suggested that the Chairs consider those criteria when evaluating the performance of existing faculty and recommending salary increases. Finally, he indicated that one of the faculty positions would be used to recruit a new Assistant Dean for External Affairs who would be his link to the practitioner community. The latter would be involved with helping practicing managers identify their needs, work with faculty to meet these needs, and negotiate contracts for these services.

When word of the Dean's faculty recommendation spread through the "rumor mill," the reaction was swift and negative. Many of the "old guard" faculty felt they were hired primarily to teach full-time students on campus during the day. Consequently, they were threatened by the new evaluation criteria. They were also concerned that the Dean was interjecting "nonacademic" criteria into their departmental faculty recruitment processes and diverting resources to nonacademic activities. These faculty felt the inevitable result would be a declining quality of education in the college.

A group of these faculty have asked to meet with the Dean to discuss his proposals. The Dean is preparing a justification for both his strategy and his human resources management (faculty) recommendations.

Questions

1. How and why do strategic decisions affect human resources management policies? Can human resources policies or constraints ever affect strategy? Why or why not?
2. Evaluate Dean Blake's strategy and human resource policies. Did the strategy make sense with the internal and external environment of the college? Do the human resource strategies support and reinforce the organizational strategy? Why or why not?
3. Evaluate the process by which Dean Blake implemented the strategic and human resources changes. Can you suggest any improvements?
4. What should he do now?

Exhibit 3.3 Faculty and Student Enrollment Data for the College of Business Administration in Selected Years, 1968-89

Academic Year	Faculty	Faculty with Ph.D.	Student Enrollment		
			B.S.	M.B.A.	Total
1968-69	54	30	1202	76	1278
1970-71	58	36	1289	98	1387
1975-76	66	46	1654	134	1788
1980-81	74	57	1913	154	2067
1985-86	81	64	2216	198	2414
1986-87	80	65	2108	206	2314
1987-88	78	66	2065	221	2286
1988-89	80	68	2089	218	2307

CASE:
THE BANK MERGER

Jack Duncan Ramsey, Senior Vice President of Personnel at Northeastern Bank & Trust Company, reread the memo calling a meeting of top management to discuss the merger agreement signed with First Bank & Trust Company. First Bank & Trust Company was one of the largest commercial banks in Connecticut (see Exhibit 3.4) and this would be one of the largest mergers they had ever undertaken. First Bank & Trust enjoyed a strong market position throughout the state and over the years had exhibited above-average profitability. First Bank & Trust Company was a heavy personal and real estate lender. About 45 percent of its earning assets represented personal and real estate loans while about 10 percent were commercial and industrial loans.

In contrast, Northeastern is a big commercial lender offering a diversified range of financial services, with about 35 percent of its earning assets in corporate loans. Although Northeastern Bank & Trust Company had been basically put together through mergers, usually the mergers were with much smaller banks and involved mostly converting the acquired bank's operational procedures for loans and deposits to their system. Most of the banks that were purchased did not have centralized operating or administrative functions. The major personnel actions involved putting employees of the acquired bank on the payroll and conducting a short orientation program to inform them about benefits and bank policies and procedures. Typically, no employees lost a job because of the merger and any adjustments needed were handled through normal turnover and attrition.

Ramsey felt that this merger would be quite different and would require a more complex process to implement. First Bank & Trust Company was a statewide bank with over 80 branches in 38 cities and over 1,800 employees. As is often the case in banks of this size, First Bank & Trust Company had centralized support functions such as operations, personnel, audit, and accounting. Ramsey knew that consolidating the support functions and, in some cases, the line functions would be a major challenge in this merger.

The Planning Meeting

Larry McDonald, Chairman and Chief Executive Officer of Northeastern Bank & Trust Company, opened the meeting with the top officers, Jack Ramsey, Pat Stevenson (Senior Vice President of Operations), and Thomas "Buddy" Kent (President):

McDonald: Our merger with First Bank & Trust Company is a natural fit. We are located in sister states with very similar social, cultural, and political heritages. We already have a large corporate customer base in Connecticut and our advertising has covered many of its markets for years. I called this meeting today because we want this to be one of the smoothest mergers in our history. We need to come up with a plan to complete and implement the merger. I think we need to start now even though the merger is still pending Board and shareholder approval.

Ramsey: Larry, from the personnel side I can already anticipate some concern from First Bank & Trust about protecting their employees. There are probably already all kinds of rumors circulating and a lot of anxiety about what this merger is going to mean in terms of job security for their employees. We may have very few changes in personnel on the line side of the bank but some problems may crop up if there are major changes on the staff side.

Stevenson: I also think we're going to have to make some decisions about consolidating computer systems and getting their people up to speed on using our equipment and technology. The economies of scale here are a real plus and we should definitely keep that in the forefront of our thinking and planning.

Kent: We also probably need to come up with a combined business plan which should help us in getting First Bank & Trust Company management committed to our goals. We need to capitalize on our geographical proximity and similar cultures in developing a business plan.

McDonald: We must remain true to our own corporate philosophy. We have recognized for years that our customers will be treated well if our employees are treated well. This strategy has worked for us and we want to carry it over to all our bank employees. We can't guarantee them a job because we are going to take advantage of the economies of scale and consolidate many positions, but we should at least try to do everything possible to absorb and maintain as many good people as possible.

Ramsey: I agree with you, Larry. I think our hardest task is going to be managing the people side of this merger, especially the communication part. We've done the operations part many times before and have had good results. I really believe a successful merger is 10 percent planning and 90 percent communication.

The Steering Committees

Shortly after the meeting, three steering committees were formed to guide the merger process over the next year to 18 months. The Business Planning Committee consisted of the President of Northeastern Bank Corporation, the President of First Bank & Trust Company, and the top managers from the operations, personnel, and line functions of each bank. The committee compared bank products, decided how to handle the transition period, made pricing decisions, and decided how to phase in the merger. The committee developed a one-year profit plan and a three-year business plan for the combined banks. The business plan spelled out the bank's objectives for each of its major activities and an overall market strategy. The planned strategy was around the theme "Your Southern New England Bank." A major outcome of this planning was a decision to consolidate most of the bank's support functions at the headquarters of Northeastern Bank in Boston. These and other projected consolidations would save about $16 to $18 million a year. Once the overall business plans were formulated, the postmerger organization structure was developed for each major division of First Bank & Trust to reflect which jobs would remain. For example, the pre- and postmerger organization chart developed for the Connecticut Trust Center is shown in Exhibit 3.5. A profile of the employees in that Division is given in Exhibit 3.6.

The Operations Committee developed detailed work plans to operationally merge the banks. These plans included procedures for the conversion of loans, deposits, check processing, and other operational activities. The committee included managers from every major unit in the Operations Group of each bank as well as managers from support functions throughout both banks.

The Personnel Steering Committee, headed by Jack Ramsey, consisted of personnel staff from both banks. The committee was charged with developing a strategy for implementing personnel policies, practices, and procedures for placing employees whose jobs might be eliminated in other positions. During initial meetings differences in personnel philosophy emerged. First Bank & Trust Company traditionally had taken a more conservative, by-the-book approach to applying personnel policies. Northeastern Bank tended to be more flexible and would often consider the particular employee's circumstances and situation before making personnel decisions. At the time of the merger, First Bank & Trust Company did not have formal job descriptions and because of its smaller size did not have the same level of employee benefits as Northeastern. The turnover rate at First Bank & Trust was around 10 percent annually, somewhat higher than Northeastern's. One of the first things done by the committee was to draw up a list of major personnel issues to be managed over the next year or so:

1. Staff reductions and transfers.
2. Maintaining employee productivity during the merger transition period.
3. Communication flow to employees to minimize unwarranted rumors.
4. Socializing employees to Northeastern's "culture and philosophy."
5. Designing appropriate training programs.
6. Balancing EEO/Affirmative Action Goals.

Two months after the merger announcement, Ramsey received a memorandum (see Exhibit 3.7) from the Business Planning Committee requesting that a plan of action be developed to deal with expected staff displacement. Jack was somewhat alarmed at the number of employees who were being displaced—almost 20 percent of First Bank & Trust's work force. He also learned that there were a number of officer positions in the total.

Two days after receiving the memo, Jack's assistant, Ed Flanders, burst into his office with news that he had received several phone calls from employees of First Bank & Trust. The callers had heard that a big layoff was about to occur, and they wanted to know how they could keep their jobs. Ed wanted to know how he should respond to the employees. Ramsey simply said, "I knew this one would be different."

Questions

1. Evaluate the bank's approach to implementing the merger.
2. Are there personnel issues other than those listed by the Personnel Steering Committee that emerge when two companies merge?
3. Do you agree with Ramsey's comment that a successful merger is 10 percent planning and 90 percent communication? Why or why not?
4. Develop a plan of action for handling the projected labor surplus. What factors need to be considered?
5. How should the Personnel Steering committee handle the needed reduction of staff in the Trust Center?

Exhibit 3.4 Profile of Northeastern Bank and First Bank & Trust Company

	Northeastern	First Bank & Trust
Net Income	$101.3 million	$18.7 million
Return on assets	0.71%	1.08%
Return on equity	13.92%	15.09%
Total assets	$13.5 billion	$1.6 billion
Total deposits	$9.6 billion	$1.2 billion
Number of employees	7,560	1,857
Number of branches	201	83

Exhibit 3.5 Trust Center, First Bank & Trust Company, Pre- and Postmerger Organization Chart

Premerger Organization Chart

```
                            Trust Center
                         Trust Center Manager
                                  |
   ┌──────────────┬──────────────┬──────────────┬──────────────┬──────────────┐
Employee       Corporate      Personal Trust   Personal Trust      Tax          Real Estate
Benefits        Trust         Administrator    Business         Department      Department
Department     Department                      Development       Head           Head
Head           Head                            Department
                                               Head
   |              |                                  |              |              |
┌──┴──┐        ┌──┴──┐                  ┌────┬────┬──┴─┬────┐    ┌──┴──┐        ┌──┴──┐
New    Admin-  New    Word              Hartford Stamford      Fiduciary Tax   Hartford Stamford
Business istration Business Processing  Bridgeport New London            Service
                                        Hartford Stamford
                                        Bridgeport New London
```

Expected Postmerger Organization Chart

```
                      Trust Executive
                            |
   ┌──────────────┬──────────────┬──────────────┬──────────────┐
Investments   Corporate Trust  Trust Support   Personal Trust
   |              |                 |               |
Portfolio     ┌───┴────┐      ┌─────┴─────┐    ┌──┬──┬──┬──┬──┐
Manager    Corporate Employee Tax      Real Estate
           Securities Benefits Department Department
              |
           Corporate
           Trust
```

Exhibit 3.6 First Bank & Trust Company, Employee Profile (Trust Center)

Name	Position	Sex	Race	Age	Tenure	Last Performance Rating[a]
Douglas Reid	Trust Center Manager	M	W	52	20	5
Harriet Jones	Employee Benefits Department Head	F	W	40	18	4
Bryan Dinkins	Employee Benefits New Business	M	W	37	8	4
Diva Brown	Employee Benefits Administration	F	B	32	5	3
Carol Cushman	Employee Benefits Administration	F	B	28	4	4
Diane Reeves	Employee Benefits Administration	F	W	41	7	3
Kathy Neel	Employee Benefits Administration	F	W	50	17	3
Bob Watson	Corporate Trust Department Head	M	W	54	19	5
Henry Jeffrey	Corporate Trust New Business	M	W	44	10	4
Margaret Neale	Corporate Trust Administration	F	W	29	3	4
Barbara Westin	Corporate Trust Word Processing	F	W	31	2	3
Vivian Hawkins	Personal Trust Administrator	F	B	37	10	4
Victor Dale	Personal Trust Hartford	M	W	49	12	4
William Devoe	Personal Trust Stamford	M	W	39	7	5
Leslie Hill	Personal Trust Bridgeport	F	W	33	4	4
Donald Phillips	Personal Trust New London	M	W	59	23	4
Arthur Barnett	Personal Trust Business Development Head	M	W	62	25	5
Alonzo Alvarez	Personal Trust Business Development Hartford	M	H[b]	35	8	4
Kendrith Hanks	Personal Trust Business Development Stamford	M	W	27	4	3
Robert Davidson	Personal Trust Business Development New London	M	W	28	5	5
Jennifer Degen	Personal Trust Business Development Bridgeport	F	W	47	9	5
Cynthia Fuchs	Tax Department Head	F	W	38	10	5
Michael Gridley	Fiduciary	M	W	34	4	3
Rosalind Smith	Tax Services	F	B	26	3	4
Leonard Clay	Real Estate Department Head	M	W	57	15	4
Katherine Stern	Real Estate Hartford	F	W	27	2	3
Terry Henderson	Real Estate Stamford	M	B	40	9	5

[a] The company uses a rating scale of 1 (poor) to 5 (outstanding).
[b] Hispanic

Exhibit 3.7 Memorandum on Postmerger Staffing

MEMORANDUM

DATE: September 15, 19xx

TO: Jack Duncan Ramsey, Chair
             Personnel Steering Committee

FROM: Buddy Kent
             Business Planning Committee

RE: Postmerger Staffing

Approximately 375 individuals will be displaced in the next 6 to 12 months—almost all of these in Hartford. We will be unable to deal with this total number via reassignments and normal turnover. A plan of action must be developed to handle this situation. One such reduction needs to occur in the Trust Center where we must cut that staff from 27 to 19. In addition to a general plan of action, we would also like to see a run-through on a proposal for handling the situation in the Trust Center. I believe your committee has the necessary data.

EXERCISE:
WHICH EMPLOYEE
SHOULD BE TERMINATED?

I. *Objectives:*
    1. To make you aware of the difficulties involved in making termination decisions.
    2. To familiarize you with possible criteria a manager can use in making termination decisions.
    3. To give you practice in conducting termination interviews.
II. *Out of Class Preparation Time:* 10 minutes to read exercise and decide which employee should be terminated.
III. *In-Class Time Suggested:* 40 - 50 minutes

IV. *Procedures:* Either at the beginning of or before class you should read the exercise and determine which title examiner should be fired.

To start the exercise, the instructor will ask five students to play the role of title examiners. One of you will play the role of Rick Feinberg, another the role of Jeff Simon, and so on. These individuals will be asked to leave the classroom and prepare to play their role. They should study carefully the material contained in this exercise and determine how to respond if in fact they are the one chosen to be terminated.

The instructor will divide the remaining students into groups of four to six. Each group should discuss which one of the five title examiners should be terminated and why. After the group has reached a consensus, it should select one spokesperson to communicate the decision to the appropriate title examiner.

After all groups have finished performing the preceding tasks, the role play begins. One at a time, each group's spokesperson announces to the class which title examiner his or her group believes should be terminated. The instructor then brings that person into the room and asks him or her to sit down in the front. The spokesperson sits down opposite the title examiner, tells that person that he or she is terminated, and gives the rationale behind the decision. The title examiner then responds in any realistic way which he or she deems appropriate. This process continues until all groups' spokespersons have had an opportunity to present their decision. A critique of the role plays and a discussion of the difficulties involved in terminating an employee then follow.

SITUATION

The Stanton Title Insurance Company was founded in 1964 by Harvey Stanton to sell title insurance policies to buyers of real estate. The company works closely with a group of about thirty-five lawyers who, although they do not actually buy the title insurance policies, encourage their clients (the property purchasers) to do so. When the company was originally established, Mr. Stanton was its only employee. As company sales increased, new employees were hired, and now twenty-three individuals are working in various capacities for the firm. Mr. Stanton has always followed the policy of making all major decisions himself. This includes making all personnel decisions such as determining who should be hired and how much they should be paid.

Five of the employees work primarily on examining titles at local government offices. In recent weeks, Harvey has noticed that the workload of these five employees has declined considerably. In part this is due to the recent election of three "no-growth" candidates to the city council. In addition, a competing firm has recently opened an office in town and is successfully taking business away. Harvey has reluctantly decided that he must terminate the employment of one of the title examiners. He cannot simply transfer one of them to a new position. His only question is, which one?

A summary of Harvey's evaluation of each title examiner is in Exhibit 3.8; a profile of each of the five title examiners appears below:

Rick Feinberg: Forty-five years old; white; married with three children; twenty years with the company; graduated from a community college; knows how to resolve difficult title policies due to his extensive experience; is difficult to get along with; antagonizes other employees at main office; hates to fill out company reports not related to title examination and refuses to do so on occasion; will not work overtime under any condition which puts a burden on others.

Jeff Simon: Twenty-three years old; black; married; attending college; one year with the company; wife works at main office as a computer programmer; works very hard and is eager to learn; well liked by all employees and is highly dependable; is never absent and will gladly work overtime to meet emergencies; with more experience he should be an outstanding title examiner; is highly loyal and dedicated; moved recently to a new apartment across the street from the government office where he works.

Kathy Wallace: Twenty-four years old; college degree; black; working on M.B.A. at night; three years with company; well liked by employees; very active in community affairs; capable of moving up to a top management position with the company; often misses work due to school and community activities.

Doris Matthews: Thirty-six years old; white; attended community college but did not graduate; ten years with company; niece of Harvey Stanton; has had eye problems and headaches which affected work quality this year and may continue to do so; has been very helpful in getting new business for the company; is well known and highly respected by law firms.

Anthony Pope: Sixty-three years old; white; 15 years with company; no college; hard working and well liked by employees; three children in college; a solid, stable employee who is able to remain calm and solve problems in crisis situations; excellent at resolving conflicts between employees; well known to local government officials; very slow but highly accurate worker.

		Work Quality	Work Quantity	Knowledge of Job	Dependable	Cooperativeness	+	X
RF	19,000	Excellent	G	EX	G	Poor	15	144
JS	14,000	Good	G	F	Ex	Ex	16	288
KW	18,000	Good	Fair	G	Fair	Ex	18	144
DM	16,000	Poor	G	E	Good	Good	14	108
AP	17,000	Good	P	R	Ex	EX	16	192

Exhibit 3.8 Harvey's Evaluation of Individual Job Performance for Title Examiners for Last Year

Title Examiner	Current Salary	Work Quality	Work Quantity	Knowledge of Job	Depend- ability	Coopera- tiveness
Rick Feinberg	$19,500	Excellent	Good	Excellent	Good	Poor
Jeff Simon	$14,000	Good	Good	Fair	Excellent	Excellent
Kathy Wallace	$18,500	Good	Fair	Good	Fair	Excellent
Doris Matthews	$16,000	Poor	Good	Excellent	Good	Good
Anthony Pope	$17,000	Good	Poor	Excellent	Excellent	Excellent

EXERCISE:
WRITING JOB DESCRIPTIONS

I. *Objectives:*
  1. To familiarize you with the job analysis process and with job descriptions.
  2. To give you practice in writing job descriptions.

II. *Out-of-Class Preparation Time:* 30 minutes

III. *In-Class Time Suggested:* 45 minutes

IV. *Procedures:*
  1. Before beginning this exercise, you should (a) review carefully, if you have not already done so, the different methods organizations use to conduct job analyses and (b) review the Job Analysis Questionnaire (in Exhibit 3.9).
  2. Students should be divided into pairs. Each person should then interview his or her partner with reference to a job about which the partner is very familiar. Use the Job Analysis Questionnaire for the interview. The questionnaire can be used to help determine the major responsibilities and tasks of the job and the required knowledge, skills, abilities, and personal characteristics needed to perform the job.
  3. After each of you has interviewed his or her partner and vice versa, write a job description covering your partner's job. Remember to use action verbs when describing the employee's tasks, duties, and responsibilities. It is also important that specific duties be grouped and arranged in descending order of importance. The completed job description should follow the format shown in Exhibit 3.10. The completed job description should be shown to the partner to determine whether additional information is required or whether changes need to be made.

Your instructor may require that you turn in a final copy of the completed job description at the next class period.

4. If time permits, the entire class discusses the various uses of job descriptions and the effectiveness of the interview as a method of job analysis.

Exhibit 3.9 Job Analysis Questionnaire

A. Job Responsibilities and Duties
   1. Job title
   2. Department title and/or division title
   3. Title of immediate supervisor
   4. Description of duties (Describe the duties in enough detail to provide a complete and accurate description of the work.)
      a. Provide a general overall summary of the purpose of your job.
      b. What are the major results or outputs of your job?
      c. Describe the duties and tasks you perform daily. Weekly. Monthly.
      d. Describe duties you perform irregularly.
   5. List any machines, instruments, tools, equipment, materials, and work aids used in your job. Indicate percent of time used.
   6. Describe the nature of your responsibility for nonhuman resources (money, machinery, equipment, etc.). What monetary loss can occur through an error?
   7. What reports and records do you prepare as part of your job? When are they prepared?
   8. What is the source of instructions for performing your job (e.g., oral or written specifications)?
   9. Describe the nature and frequency of supervision received.
   10. How is your work reviewed, checked, or verified?
B. Reporting Relationships
   11. How many employees are directly under your supervision? What are their job titles?
   12. Do you have full authority to hire, terminate, evaluate, and transfer employees under your supervision? Explain.
   13. What contacts are required with other departments or persons other than your immediate department in performing your job? Describe the nature and extent of these contacts.
C. Working Conditions
   14. Describe the working conditions present in the location and environment of your work such as cold/heat, noise, fumes, dust, etc. Indicate frequency and degree of exposure.
   15. Describe any dangers or hazards present in your job.
D. Job Qualifications (Be certain not to list the incumbent's qualifications, but what is required for performance by a new employee.)

continued

Exhibit 3.9 *continued*

16. Describe the kind of previous work experience necessary for satisfactory performance of this job.
17. What is the amount of experience required?
18. What kinds of knowledge, skills, and abilities (KSAs) are needed to perform the job?
19. What is the minimal level of education (grammar, high school, two-year college, four-year college, etc.) required?
20. Are any special physical skills and/or manual dexterity skills required to perform the job?
21. Are there any special certification, registration, license, or training requirements?

Exhibit 3.10 Sample Job Description

JOB TITLE: Shift Supervisor

POSITION PURPOSE: The purpose of this position is to maintain a safe and efficient plant operation through directing the activities of the operation's personnel and providing a management support function for the plant superintendent.

TYPICAL JOB DUTIES:

1. Directs the activities of the operations personnel and coordinates the activities of the maintenance personnel.
2. Issues written communication to employees concerning personnel policies and operational concerns.
3. Administers maintenance request program through collecting requests, scheduling, and recording maintenance activities.
4. Administers the plant tagging procedure.
5. Conducts the training and safety programs for shift employees.
6. Schedules shift assignments to reflect workload and vacation schedules.
7. Performs administrative tasks such as recording workers' time, maintaining records concerning operational activities, and updating written procedures.
8. Prepares annual budget for assigned plant area and maintains the inventory level on these items.
9. Appraises performance of shift employees annually.
10 Counsels employees on disciplinary problems and job-related performance.
11 Assumes plant superintendent's duties when assigned.

PHYSICAL REQUIREMENTS: Walking and climbing stairs

continued

Exhibit 3.10 *continued*

REPORTING RELATIONSHIPS: The shift supervisor reports directly to the plant superintendent. The shift supervisor directs the control room operator, two or more utility operators, trainees, and other assigned personnel. Also coordinates the activities of the maintenance personnel present on shift.

QUALIFICATIONS:

Education: Associate degree or equivalent training (e.g., management training classes), OR five (5) years of management experience.
Related Experience: Minimum of three (3) years as a control room operator for a coal-fired boiler operation.

JOB KNOWLEDGE/SKILLS REQUIRED:

1. Comprehensive understanding of plant systems.
2. Fundamental understanding of electrical systems and motor control centers.
3. Thorough knowledge of boiler chemistry.
4. Comprehension of flow, logic, and electrical prints.
5. Ability to perform elementary mathematical and algebraic calculations.
6. Communication and human relations skills.
7. Ability to operate CRT, Spectrometer, PH meter, and conductivity meter.
8. Managerial skills.

INCIDENT:
THE NEW WORK SCHEDULE

Walt Myers, Assistant City Manager, was somewhat dismayed by the headlines that appeared in the latest edition of the local newspaper: "Sanitation Workers Form New Employee Committee." He found himself thinking about the events of the past few months.

He had been surprised by the amount of dissatisfaction expressed by sanitation workers toward the new work schedule instituted three months ago. Many felt that the new schedule was instituted without consulting workers. The schedule changed twice-a-week backyard garbage service to once-a-week backyard collection with once-a-week pickup at curbside. The work force shrank from 416 employees to 316 to service the 100,000 garbage collection customers in the city. The sanitation department with the approval of the city council had changed the system to save money. The reduction in service would save the city almost $1.5 million a year. While backyard pickup service averages 5 minutes per house, curbside pickup averages only 3 minutes per house. On the average, each worker picks up 7,000 to 9,000 pounds of garbage and trash a day. It was hoped that improvements in collection routes and equipment would boost worker productivity.

In order to meet the new schedule garbage must be picked up five days a week, including holidays. During bad weather garbage pickup is postponed and resumed when the weather gets better, even if that means working Saturdays. Before the schedule change, sanitation employees worked five days a week from 7 A.M. to 3 P.M. (40- hour week). Since the change their schedule has become more erratic. Some days the trucks return to the sanitation yard by 3 P.M. Other days the workers don't get off until 5 p.m. or later. The sanitation workers, who earn an average of $15,493 a year, argue that they should be paid more because the change in schedule has put undue pressure upon them for higher productivity. They also want to receive double overtime for holiday work. This demand has become a big issue because many have given up second jobs because of the unpredictable length of the workday.

The new schedule had not been well received by customers either. The city received thousands of phone calls from residents complaining about unpicked up garbage and confusion about the new schedule.

Myers' thoughts were quickly jolted back to the present by the ringing of his telephone. The call was from the Mayor informing him that he had arranged a meeting with the employee committee and wanted Myers to attend the meeting. He asked that Myers review the work plans developed for the new schedule and possible alternatives for resolving the problems. He reminded Myers that election day was less than two months away, and he wanted to have the problems settled quickly.

Questions

1. Did the sanitation department correctly forecast the number of sanitation workers needed to carry out the new schedule?
2. What factors did management overlook when planning the new work schedule?
3. What options are available to Myers for addressing the concerns of the workers?

SKILL BUILDER:
HUMAN RESOURCE
FORECASTING ASSIGNMENT

I. *Objectives:*

    1. To give you practice in forecasting an organization's human resource needs.

    2. To familiarize you with some of the factors which affect an organization's future human resource needs (growth, automation, turnover).

    3. To familiarize you with the complexities involved in making human resource forecasts.

    4. To point out that all human resource forecasting is based on assumptions and that these assumptions are critical to the accuracy of the forecast. Incorrect assumptions lead to erroneous forecasts.

II. *Time Required to Complete Assignment:* One to two hours

III. *Instructions:* Read the "Situation" that follows and determine (1) turnover for the main office, old branches, and new branches for each of the next three years and for each of the major personnel categories, (2) the number of new employees the bank will need to hire for each major personnel category for each of the next three years, and (3) the total number of employees who will be working for the bank as of the end of each of the next three years. Assume that you are making the projection in December for subsequent years ending December 31.

SITUATION

The National Bank and Trust Company currently employs approximately 1,100 employees. It presently has fifty branch offices located throughout the metropolitan area, each of which employs approximately fourteen individuals (four supervisory personnel and ten tellers or clerical employees). The bank expects to add ten branch offices during the next twelve months, twelve the following year, and sixteen in the third year. Branches within the bank differ considerably in size so the figures given above represent averages.

During the past month, the bank has placed an order for thirty automated teller machines which will be placed in its old branch offices. These machines are scheduled to be in operation December 31, one year from now. The bank has found that for each new machine purchased, one fewer teller is needed, on the average.

During the past few years the bank has experienced very high turnover at its branches (approximately 30 percent for tellers and clerical employees and 20 percent for managerial personnel). Turnover at the bank's main office (headquarters) has been about 10 percent. The bank expects that these rates will continue during the next three years.

Part 4

Recruiting and Staffing

Once adequate human resource planning has taken place to determine how many people and the types of skills needed to further the organization's objectives, staffing activities must be considered. The materials in this section cover the two major activities in staffing: recruitment and selection. Recruitment refers to the process of attracting a pool of candidates to apply for the organization's available positions. The selection process involves making judgments necessary to best match job requirements with applicant knowledge, skills, and abilities. Staffing is a costly and complicated process that has a strong impact on organization effectiveness. Staffing is often viewed as one of the most critical personnel/human resource management functions, and a valid and reliable staffing process is essential in today's legal environment.

The first case in this section, "Recruiting Recreational Vehicle Surveyors," focuses on designing a recruitment plan for jobs that may be viewed as less than attractive by potential job candidates. "The Professor Who Almost Did Not Make It" centers on the staffing process used in promotion decisions. "Selecting Patient Escorts" highlights the need for understanding exactly what is involved in developing and maintaining valid selection procedures. The last case in this section, "A Solution for Adverse Impact," requires you to apply the *Uniform Guidelines on Employee Selection Procedures* to ensure fair employment practices in a federal government agency. The three exercises in this section require you to evaluate recruitment effectiveness, make selection decisions, and conduct a selection interview. The incident and skill builder provide opportunities for you to examine the legality and validity of preemployment inquiries.

CASE:
RECRUITING RECREATIONAL
VEHICLE SURVEYORS

Liberty Engineering Co. is located in a large suburb of Cleveland, Ohio. The company was founded during the 1940s and does considerable drafting and design work for the major automotive companies and their suppliers. When sales in the auto industry are high, Liberty Engineering experiences a significant volume of work. However, when recessions hit the automotive marketplace, work at Liberty also decreases sharply.

In an attempt to stabilize revenues, the President of Liberty Engineering decided it would be prudent to diversify the company by bidding on government contracts. The company had little experience in these areas, but the President felt that this would not preclude it from bidding on contracts and obtaining them.

Within a six-month period the company had bid on and lost two contracts. However, a third bid pertaining to the safety and use of recreational vehicles proved to be successful. The contract was for several hundred thousand dollars and was granted on a cost-plus basis. The government was interested in obtaining information regarding how people actually use recreational vehicles such as pickup truck campers, motor homes, and various kinds of recreational trailers. Ultimately, the purpose of the study was to determine what additional safety rules, if any, should be established relating to the manufacture and use of recreational vehicles. Among the pieces of information desired by the government were how much weight citizens place in their recreational vehicles, what kinds of trailer hitches are in use, whether recreational vehicles have proper suspension systems, and to what extent citizens are aware of the safety features of their recreational vehicles.

In Liberty's proposal to the government, the company stated that it would recruit, select, and train qualified individuals to survey over 1,000 recreational vehicles. The surveying would be done at three different sites: a desert location, a seashore site, and a mountainous locale. At a meeting with government officials, three locations were selected: Cape Hatteras, North Carolina; Smoky Mountains National Park, Tennessee; and Lake Mead, Nevada. Two other important decisions were also made at the meeting: So as to ensure consistency of data collection, all surveyors would be trained together at a campground at Smoky Mountains National Park; then the employees would be divided and sent to their respective job sites. It was also decided that each survey crew would consist of one leader and four surveyors and that two crews would be sent to each data collection site.

All responsibility for recruiting and training the required thirty employees (six leaders and twenty-four surveyors) fell on the shoulders of Bob Getz, the new Personnel Director. Bob had worked as a designer for Liberty for twenty years prior to being transferred to Personnel. At the same time a project Bob had been working on for two years ended, the old Personnel Director had quit, so Bob was a logical choice. In addition, Bob was well liked by most of Liberty's older employees and knew a great deal about the company's policies and procedures. Bob's major shortcoming was that he knew little about personnel activities.

Before recruiting potential job applicants, Bob knew that he would first need to develop a set of job descriptions for all thirty employees. Since crews would be doing essentially similar jobs, albeit at different locations, Bob needed only to develop job descriptions for each of four survey positions and that of the leader. Hence, Bob obtained the list of data which was to be collected on each vehicle, determined the tasks required to collect the data, and divided the tasks into four job positions. The resulting job descriptions were as follows:

Surveyor I: Responsible for taking pictures of recreational vehicle with a camera. Interview driver and record information received.

Surveyor II: Read and record scale weights for each recreational vehicle tire. Take tire pressures and measure tread depth. Record make, size, and air capacity of each tire.

Surveyor III: Unhook trailer hitch, if present, and record make of hitch, ball diameter, and whether levelers are present. Determine type of suspension on recreational vehicle and count number of leaf springs if present.

Surveyor IV: Stop recreational vehicle as it enters campground, explain to driver the purpose of the study, ask the driver to participate in study. When survey of recreational vehicle is complete, discuss the findings with the driver.

The leader's responsibilities would be to plan daily work activities, motivate the employees to do the surveying, complete all forms, and do occasional troubleshooting.

With job descriptions in hand, Bob met with Norm Larson, Vice President of Liberty, and the one ultimately responsible for conducting the recreational vehicle surveys. During the meeting Bob learned that all thirty employees were to meet at Smoky Mountains National Park on June 10. They were to be trained on the job for four days, and the company would provide them with lodging and food while they were there. All employees were to provide their own transportation to the park and to their subsequent job sites and ultimately back home. The company would pay them for travel time but would not provide any mileage allowance, lodging, or food. Upon arrival at the job site, employees would need to find accommodations for July and August and would receive no lodging or food allowance from the company during their stay. Once work commenced at each job site, employees would be responsible for providing their own transportation to and from the campground.

All employees were to be paid $4.75 per hour. No vacation benefits, sick days, or other major benefits would be provided. The company would, however, provide benefits mandated by law such as social security and workers' compensation. No one under the age of 18 would be hired because of safety reasons.

After the meeting with Norm, Bob decided he should check with the campground management at the different job sites. He learned that most recreational vehicles leave campgrounds early in the morning and enter late in the afternoon. Few arrive or depart between 10 A.M. and 4 P.M. In order to survey a maximum number of vehicles, therefore, crews would need to work from 6 A.M. to 11 A.M. and from 3 P.M. to 8 P.M., a total of 10 hours a day. Therefore, each crew could work a four-day-on and a four-day-off schedule. Bob was told that temperatures at Cape Hatteras would range between 65 and 95 degrees, while at Lake Mead they would range between 85 and 115 degrees. Neither of these locations would provide employees with any shade; hence employees at these sites would need to work in the sun and wear uniforms, including hats. The Smoky Mountains National Park location would be cooler than the others and surveying could be done in shaded areas. When Bob asked the campground managers whether they knew of any people who would be interested in working on the survey project, their response was, "You've got to be kidding." The manager at Lake Mead campground flatly told Bob that he couldn't conceive of any person being willing to drive from Lake Mead to Tennessee and back under the conditions Bob outlined. He suggested that Bob put a want ad in the Cleveland newspaper.

After talking with the campground managers, Bob was quite depressed. He knew that he had to hire thirty employees within the next few weeks. He knew that six of them had to have sufficient leadership skills to get the job done while not antagonizing the employees so much that they would quit. He further realized that the twenty-four surveyors would have to enjoy the outdoors and be willing to tolerate extreme heat. He realized, too, that the ideal surveyor would be one who had above-average knowledge of auto mechanics, legible handwriting, reasonable communication skills, and an ability to work well with others under adverse conditions. What Bob didn't know was how he could recruit and hire thirty people who would fit these descriptions.

Questions

1. If you were Bob, how would you recruit the needed employees?
2. If Bob is unable to recruit the needed employees, what change in the working conditions, pay, or benefits would you make first to attract more employees?
3. Evaluate the Lake Mead campground manager's suggestion that Bob recruit employees by placing a want ad in the Cleveland newspaper.

CASE:
THE PROFESSOR WHO ALMOST
DID NOT MAKE IT!

When I joined the Management Department of Southeastern Central University (SCU) in 1982, I found myself in a happy environment. I was the third woman to join the College of Business as an assistant professor in a tenure track position. There was a balanced mix of emphasis on teaching and research which I liked. While research was valued in the College of Business, one did not experience the "publish or perish" syndrome in operation. On an average, one referred publication per year was all that was expected of faculty as a minimum, even though the Department of Management faculty did publish much more than that and the department had some nationally known researchers in several areas of management. When I interviewed at SCU, I got the feeling that the thirteen-member faculty team of the Management Department offered a healthy, collaborative, friendly atmosphere in which cooperation and team spirit were highly valued and actively encouraged. I saw opportunities to work with several faculty members, and it is not surprising that I had nothing but good feelings when I joined the Department of Management at SCU in the fall of 1982.

One of the nice things going for me was the opportunity to interact and collaborate with Usha Sastri, an Indian faculty member who had graduated from Berkeley in 1977 and had joined SCU the same year. Usha was an older woman who had obtained her M.B.A. and Ph.D. degrees after twenty years of organization work experience. She totally immersed herself in teaching and research, and her life-style facilitated this. Her husband worked for an insurance company in Philadelphia, and her children were employed on the West Coast. Living by herself in the small university town, Usha put all her time and energy into her job and had become reputed in the college for her teaching and research abilities and skills. I had often wondered why Usha had joined the little-known SCU rather than some other prestigious university which would be more than happy to have someone of her calibre. I understood later that despite graduating at the top of her class in record time and having glowing recommendations from her dissertation chair, many universities were skeptical about even asking her to come over for an interview because of her foreign background. Usha mentioned once that she had overheard some conservative deans and chairpersons telling her dissertation chair at a conference that their students would not understand or respect a foreign woman. Three universities, however, did at least extend her an interview just as she was finishing her dissertation, and all three offered her the job. She said she was finally happy to be in a position to exercise some choice and joined SCU because of its research reputation. "This is a good place for fresh Ph.D.s interested in learning about and doing good research," Usha often said.

Contributed by Mua Narakes.

I admired Usha a lot. She was a quiet achiever. In the nine years since her graduation (as of the time of this case writing), she seemed to have established a national reputation as an avant-garde researcher in the areas of international management and careers. She averaged about five referred publications per year in the last four or five years, and had also published three books during this time. Her reputation as a teacher was that she was a very concerned and knowledgeable instructor who had high standards of expectations of her students. What I really enjoyed about Usha was her professionalism, her unassuming nature, and her quiet efficiency. Sometimes, however, she seemed to be frustrated when the faculty just would not listen to what she had to say in the faculty meetings and seemed to completely ignore her inputs. I was often amused to observe another faculty member express exactly the same ideas that Usha would have stated just a few minutes earlier, and get an enthusiastic response from the group as if they had heard some original creative thoughts on the subject for the first time!

To understand the happenings narrated in this case, a background of the department is necessary.

Background of Department of Management Faculty

The Department of Management has some excellent people. The three full professors who were in the department when I joined are all nationally reputed figures and each is unique in his own right. Two of them held leadership positions in the Academy of Management (the major professional organization for business professors) and while one was a prolific writer and researcher in the policy area, the other had written textbooks in the management and organizational behavior areas which were adopted by schools all across the country. The third professor who was an expert in the communications area was a big name as an organizational communication consultant for top firms on the East Coast and in the Midwest and had published several books on communication.

Among the associate professors, several were publishing in prestigious top journals in their areas. Two or three, however, gave me the impression that research was not their cup of tea. We were four assistant professors in the department, I being the most junior. We were all anxious to do research and at the time of writing this, each one of us had at least a couple of articles accepted for publication. The senior professors and the juniors collaborated as their interests fitted and the environment was, for the major part, one of healthy cooperation.

Shifting Norms

Over the past three years, there has been an imperceptible shift in values that has slowly been developing in the college. Two or three senior professors in the various departments of the college who were not really research oriented but had made a name for themselves through publishing textbooks, suddenly started to focus their vision on the international arena. They had a powerful impact on the new Dean who came on board in 1983 and influenced him to think that the way for the college to move was in the lucrative area of international service, imparting executive and management education to organizations in developing countries. As a matter of fact, these professors made several trips and spent their sabbatical teaching in foreign universities, acting as liaison persons in establishing university-level contacts between SCU and several foreign universities.

With greater attention being focused in the so-called international service area, the research efforts of faculty members came to be less rewarded and though nobody was given any clear idea or direction, some of the associate professors were casually told by the Dean that they had to devote more time to "outreach" ac-tivities and less time to research. The merit raises which were hitherto attached basically to research productivity and teaching effectiveness were now also tied to a nebulous concept called "outreach service" — a service which was expected to ex-tend beyond the regular university, college, and departmental committee work. During performance appraisal meetings, the chair gave some faculty at the as-sociate professor rank the feedback that they have to do more "outreach" work, without defining what that meant. Fortunately, I was not affected by these chang-ing norms since I was still an untenured assistant professor who was supposed to concentrate on research. I could, however, hear the disgruntlement and com-plaints from the senior associate professors who said that they did not understand what was going on, and nobody, including the Dean, was clarifying anything for them. People like Usha just continued to do their research and served on many campus committees.

The Jolt

In 1985, Usha felt that her teaching, research, and service credentials were strong enough to go up for promotion to full professor. Planning to submit her promo-tion dossier as per the college guidelines in early October, she sought out the opinion of three full professors in the department as early as March 1985 to see if they thought she was ready for promotion. Two of the three felt that her research was without doubt superior and her other credentials were very good. The third organization behavior (OB) professor, who was in the same area as she was, however, gave her the feedback that she had to demonstrate leadership by taking on offices in the Academy of Management before she could think of going up for promotion. In April, most unexpectedly and fortunately for Usha, it so happened that she was requested to be on the doctoral consortium panel of one of the divisions of the academy, and another division sought her out to be on certain im-portant committees. Delighted by these unanticipated pleasant turns of events, Usha once again started to think seriously about her promotion. She went to the Dean to discuss the matter, but he told her that the OB professor had already indi-cated to him that she was not ready for the promotion. She told the Dean that since then she had been offered leadership positions in the academy, but that new information did not seem to elicit any encouraging responses from the Dean.

The Smart Move

Frustrated by the Dean's reactions, Usha made a smart move. She sought the views of several unbiased external opinion leaders in her field when she went to the National Academy meetings in August. Seeing her vita, all the four leading researchers and nationally renowned scholars she talked to felt that her vita was strong enough to go up for full professor and get promoted. When she expressed that some may feel that her service record may not be as strong as would be normally required for promotion to full professor, they laughed and said that the resume indicated that she had been on at least twenty different university, college, and departmental committees over the past nine years, and nobody could ask for more. One of them, an expert in the careers field, said that he was not aware of any university which requires the holding of national academy offices as a prerequisite for promotion to full professor and indeed considered the notion amusing! "Maybe people are just threatened by your becoming a full professor, Usha," he said laughingly. Emboldened by these positive remarks and encouraged by the other two professors in her department, as well as by her chair who thought she had a solid vita, Usha decided to push her promotion dossier through. Unfortunately, however, the chair who was supportive of her was leaving in August to take the Dean's position at another university, and the person chosen as the acting chair and Usha had a long history of an unhealthy competitive relationship. According to Usha, both had joined the department at the same time, and while he treated her with little respect during the first four years, he totally avoided her after both got promoted to associate rank at the same time in their fourth year. It was rumored that he never forgave Usha for negotiating successfully to get a thousand dollars more as starting salary than he did when they both joined SCU in 1977.

Having decided to pursue her goal, Usha thought it prudent to communicate her decision to the Dean and to the professor in her department who was against her going up for promotion. She told them that she had consulted various top people at the academy who felt she was ready for promotion, and since she was now entrusted with several important assignments at the academy, she decided to go up for promotion. While the Dean did not vehemently oppose her decision, he did not hold out more than a 50-50 chance for her success. He suggested that it would perhaps be better if she waited another year. The OB professor, however, still strongly disagreed with her judgment saying that the new positions at the academy were not an adequate measure of leadership and that she was little known within the college itself—a statement that took her completely by surprise. He also advised her that since the department would have an acting chair that year and we would not recruit a new person before the year was out, she should not think of going up for promotion for the next two years at least. He stated that it would be unfair to the acting chair and the new chair if she were to push her promotion dossier through them. Terribly discouraged by such remarks and knowing that the professor's clout with the Dean might substantially jeopardize her chances, Usha spent several sleepless nights before she finally decided to start putting together her dossier.

Mustering the Highest Recommendations

Usha generated a list of nationally known professors from top ranking schools who would evaluate her teaching, research, and service credentials. If they were not impressed with her work or even tended to be lukewarm in their reactions to her credentials, her fate would be sealed. Usha spent several days carefully assembling the relevant materials for the persons who would be evaluating her teaching, research in two significant areas, and service. Each set of materials went out with a succinct, one-page listing of her significant contributions to the respective areas. The evaluation packets were sent to twenty outsiders and five insiders. She was gratified when all but one highly applauded her contributions and recommended her promotion. The one local professor who had reservations was more concerned about the elapsed time since her last promotion which was just a little over four years.

However, Usha's gratification from reading the highly commendatory letters was not easily attained since the acting chair, contrary to the existing norms of the college, refused to share the evaluations with her when they arrived addressed to him. When she knew that several responses were pouring in and she was not even told that they were being received, she asked her chair about it, only to be told that she was not to be privy to the responses. When she pointed out that such had not been the practice until now, he refused to listen to her and commented that she was being unduly demanding. When she went to the Dean to seek his intervention in the matter, he concurred with the chair's statement that the evaluations were not to be shared and that even the chair's and Dean's letters of recommendation were not to be shared with the candidate. Usha was astounded that the Dean, who had been in the university system for three years, would be ignorant of the policies with regard to promotion and tenure documents. She pointed out to him that his statement was incorrect, that the philosophy of the college had always been that the dossier is a presentation of the candidate and that the candidate had to sign off saying that he or she had seen everything contained in the dossier before it could be reviewed by the departmental committee.

The Dean was vehement in his assertion but agreed to check up and find out the correct procedures. In the meantime, Usha unearthed the policy document, underlined the portions that substantiated her statements and took the document to the Dean. In the meantime, the Dean had checked with others and found that he was wrong and had just informed the chair about the correct procedures. It was only after all this hassle that Usha had access to the letters, which the chair let her see at his convenience and not when they were received.

The Departmental Verdict

When the three full professors met to vote on the dossier with the acting chair present, the vote was, as expected, two in favor and one against. Obviously, much was debated and argued, and despite the fact that outstanding schools had indicated that the dossier would merit promotion without any hitch, the OB professor absolutely refused to vote in favor. The two reasons, as slipped through the grapevine, were that Usha had just been promoted to associate four years ago and that she had not rendered outstanding service to the department or the college. The professor who voted against Usha's promotion left the next week to teach at a foreign university during his sabbatical. The closing paragraph of the acting chair's letter of evaluation stated, "In sum, my recommendation for Dr. Usha Sastri's promotion from associate to full professor is a supportive yes with strong reservation as it pertains to the leadership issue."

Usha was definitely shaken by the chair's statement about her service. She wanted to make sure that the college committee to whom the dossier would be next passed on did not overlook the fact that she was serving on eight university, college and departmental committees that very semester. Hence, she asked the chair for her dossier so that on the service part she could highlight on the first page of the summary statement the eight committees that she was serving on currently. The college committee would then have all the facts about her service record on the very first page. The chair vehemently refused to let her do this and complained about the matter to the Dean. The Dean, as usual, sided with the chair and coming to her office, literally yelled at Usha for her "demanding disposition." Again, when Usha showed him the policy document where it was clearly indicated that the candidate could add anything after the chair's evaluation and before the dossier went to the college committee, he reluctantly allowed her to add what she wanted but remarked with anger pointing a finger at the dossier that her "troubles went deep beyond her service in the eight committees." All these experiences were very painful to Usha, who felt that she was being unduly harassed by the system.

The College Committee's Verdict

The College Committee, which consisted of one senior professor from the department with no voting rights, one senior professor from each of the other three college departments, and two senior professors from different colleges in the university, met and *unanimously* voted in favor of the promotion. This was in no small measure due to the department professor making a strong presentation of the case, highlighting Usha's strong service record. He emphasized that Usha was serving on eight committees that very semester (three of them ad-hoc) and could not possibly be asked to take on more responsibilities. It was later whispered that this professor also told the committee that in the light of the prevailing animosity between the Management Department's acting chair and the candidate, the chair's recommendation had to be read with caution.

The Dean's Evaluation

The Dean in his letter of recommendation started off by saying that Usha merited the promotion based on all three areas of research, teaching, and service, but qualified the last one by adding that Usha had to attend to some developmental needs with respect to institutional leadership. He added that the developmental concern related to the quality of the service role, especially at the departmental level. He further opined that committee leadership, in itself, did not constitute the top-level senior faculty member's contributions to the department and the college, both of which depend on the senior and associate professors for academic leadership.

All's Well That Ends Well

Sometime in April 1986, Usha received a congratulatory letter from the Vice President of Academic Affairs at SCU informing her about her promotion to full professor. "Your activities at SCU are warmly regarded and appreciated and your continued contributions will substantially strengthen and preserve the university's vitality in carrying out its mission as a comprehensive university dedicated to teaching, research and service," the letter said.

Quenching My Curiosity

When matters had settled down, I was curious to see the dossier of all four professors who had gone up for full professor and were promoted. Contrary to my expectations, I did not find any of the other three professors to be particularly outstanding in terms of service. Usha had indeed served on more committees, and only the communications professor had served on more university committees than Usha had. Of course, all three had held offices in the National Academy of Management or comparable organizations. The professor who had tried to block Usha's promotion did not have half the number of publications that Usha's record showed.

I am wondering what I should be doing. My time for promotion and tenure will arrive sooner than I care to think, and fate may not be any kinder to me than it was to Usha. A less strong person than Usha would have been devastated by the horrible experiences. "Be smart and obtain the respect of the biggies in the field," Usha advised me after her promotion, adding, "They could not hold me down only because they were afraid of being ridiculed by significant others in the academic world if they had not promoted me. How can they justify the fact that Stanford and USC would have promoted me but here at SCU they could or would not? It would have smacked too much of discrimination!"

Two years ago there was an anonymous survey conducted by the Affirmative Action Committee on campus asking respondents, among other things, if they or anyone known to them experienced any discrimination with the department, college, or university because of race, gender, or other minority concerns. My response at that time was a big NO. If the same survey were conducted again today, I honestly do not know if my response would still be the same. I am not yet clear whether it was discrimination or something else that was going on that gave Usha all the problems that she really should not have had to go through during the promotion process! I am wondering what kind of a game I should play!

Questions

1. Discuss the Management Department's handling of Usha's promotion.
2. What problems can occur when an organization fails to have explicit promotion criteria?
3. Was Usha a victim of discrimination or a victim of an inadequate promotion process?

CASE:
SELECTING PATIENT ESCORTS

on test what I would do — + why what I would not do — why

City Hospital is located in the heart of a large midwestern city. It is one of five major hospitals in the area and has recently built a small addition for treating well-known patients such as professional football players, top company executives, and singing stars. Visiting or local celebrities always choose City Hospital if they need treatment.

City Hospital has about 1,200 hospital beds and employs 4,500 individuals, including about forty patient escorts. The job of patient escort is a rather simple one, requiring only minimal training and no special physical talents. When patients need to be moved from one location to another, patient escorts are summoned to assist in the move. If the move is only a short distance, however, a nurse or orderly could move the patient. Of particular importance is the fact that patient escorts almost always take patients who are being discharged from their hospital room to the front door of the hospital. A wheelchair is always used, even if the patient is able to walk unassisted. Thus, the typical procedure is for the nurse to call for a patient escort; the escort gets a wheelchair and goes to the patient's room, assists the patient into the wheelchair, picks up the patient's belongings, wheels the patient down to the hospital's front door or to his or her car in the parking lot, and returns to the work station.

The job of patient escort is critical to the hospital since the escort is always the last hospital representative the patient sees, and hence has a considerable influence on the patient's perception of the hospital. Of the approximately 40 escorts, about three-fourths are men, and one-fourth are women. Most are high school graduates in their early twenties. Some, particularly those on the early morning shift, are attending college at night and working for the hospital to earn money to pay college expenses. Four of the escorts are older women who had previously served as hospital volunteers and then decided to become full-time employees instead. Turnover among patient escorts is quite high and has averaged 25 percent in recent years. In addition, upward mobility in the hospital is quite good, and as a result, another 25 percent of the escorts typically transfer to other jobs in the hospital each year. Thus, about half of the patient escorts need to be replaced annually.

The hospital follows a standard procedure when hiring patient escorts. When a vacancy occurs, the Personnel Department reviews the file of applications of individuals who have applied for the patient escort job. Usually the file contains at least twenty applications because the pay for the job is good, the work easy, and few skills are required. The top two or three applicants are asked to come to the hospital for interviews. Typically, the applicants are interviewed first by Personnel and then by the patient escort supervisor. The majority of those interviewed know some other employees of the hospital, so the only reference check is a call to these employees. Before being hired, applicants are required to take physical exams given by hospital doctors.

Every new escort attends an orientation program the first day on the job. This is conducted by a member of the hospital's Personnel Department. The program consists of a complete tour of the hospital, a review of all the hospital's personnel policies, including a description of its promotion, compensation, and disciplinary policies, and a presentation of the hospital's mission and philosophy. During this orientation session, employees are told that the hospital's image in the community is of major importance and that all employees should strive to maintain and enhance this image by their conduct. After orientation, all patient escorts receive on-the-job training by their immediate supervisor.

During the last two-year period the hospital has experienced a number of problems with patient escorts that have had an adverse effect on the hospital's image. Several patients have complained to the hospital administration that they have been treated rudely, or in some cases roughly, by one or more patient escorts. Some complained that they had been ordered around or scolded by an escort during the discharge process. Others stated that the escort had been careless when wheeling them out of the hospital to their cars. One person, in fact, reported that an escort had carelessly tipped him over. All escorts are required to wear identification tags, but patients usually can't remember the escort's name when complaining to the hospital. Additionally, the hospital usually has difficulty determining which escort served which patient because escorts often trade patients. Finally, even when the hospital can identify the offending escort, the employee can easily deny any wrongdoing. He or she often counters that patients are generally irritable as a result of their illness and hence are prone to complain at even the slightest provocation.

At the hospital administrator's request, the Personnel Manager asked the chief supervisor of patient escorts, the head of the Staffing Section within the Personnel Department, and the Assistant Personnel Director to meet with him to review the entire procedure used to select patient escorts. It was hoped that a new procedure could be devised that would eliminate the hiring of rude, insulting, or careless patient escorts.

During the meeting a number of suggestions were made as to how the selection procedure might be improved. Criticisms of the present system were also voiced. The chief supervisor of patient escorts argued that the problem with the hospital's present system is that the application blank is void of any really useful information. He stated that the questions that really give insights into the employee's personality were no longer on the application blank. He suggested that applicants be asked about their hobbies, outside activities, religious affiliations, and their personal likes and dislikes on the application blank. He also suggested that each applicant be asked to submit three letters of recommendation from people who knew the applicant well. He wanted these letters to focus on the employee's personality, particularly the employee's ability to remain friendly and polite at all times.

The Assistant Personnel Director contended that the hospital's interviewing procedure should be modified. He observed that during the typical interview little attempt is made to determine how the applicant reacts under stress. He suggested that, if applicants were asked four or five stress-producing questions, the hospital might be in a better position to judge their ability to work with irritable patients.

The head of the Staffing Section noted that patient escorts require little mental or physical talent and agreed that the crucial attribute escorts need is the ability always to be courteous and polite. He wondered whether an "attitude" test could be developed that would measure the applicant's predisposition toward being friendly, etc. He suggested that a job analysis could be done on the patient escort position to determine those attitudes that are critical to being a successful patient escort. Once the job analysis was complete, questions could be developed that would measure these critical attributes. The test questions could be given to the hospital's present patient escorts to determine whether the test could accurately distinguish the best from worst escorts. The staffing head realized that many of the questions might need to be eliminated or changed, and that, if the test appeared to show promise, it would probably need to be revalidated in order to meet government requirements. He felt, however, that a well-designed test might be worth the effort and should at least be tried.

The meeting ended with all four participants agreeing that the suggestion of trying to develop an "attitude test" was probably the most promising. The Assistant Manager and chief supervisor of patient escorts stated that they would conduct a thorough job analysis covering the patient escort position and develop a list of attitudes that are critical to its success. A second meeting would then be held to prepare the actual questions that would appear on the test.

Questions

1. Critique each of the alternative approaches suggested for solving the problem of selecting patient escorts.
2. Recommend a procedure for recruiting and hiring patient escorts.
3. Besides improving its selection procedures, what other actions could the hospital potentially take to improve the behavior of the patient escorts?

CASE:
A SOLUTION FOR
ADVERSE IMPACT

A federal government agency was in need of assistance regarding its staffing practices. Recently, some of the job applicants had complained that the selection
procedures for one of the entry-level law enforcement jobs were discriminatory.
The personnel specialists, who had previously ignored this possibility, were now
alerted to the potential problem of adverse impact against women and minorities.

Bob Santa was a personnel specialist for the agency and had been employed
with the staffing division for almost three years. He had kept up with the laws and
regulations on discrimination and equal employment opportunity. About two
months ago, he had attended a training seminar on the *Uniform Guidelines on
Employee Selection Procedures*. Upon returning to the agency, Bob decided that
an evaluation of their current staffing practices was necessary as they had been
developed over ten years ago and prior to the adoption of the *Uniform Guidelines*
in 1978. These guidelines were designed to provide a proper framework for determining the proper use of selection procedures. They indicated how organizations
should evaluate their selection rates using the four-fifths rule and also specified
the standards organizations should use to validate their procedures.

The Selection Process

The selection of entry-level agents for the law enforcement job involved a two-step
multiple-hurdle process. Applicants were first required to pass a cognitive ability
test, a similar but somewhat easier test than the Scholastic Aptitude Test (SAT).
The exam was made up of twenty-five verbal items and twenty-five quantitative
items. A candidate was required to receive a passing score of 70 (35 of the items
correct) in order to be eligible for the second step of the selection process, an interview. A three-member panel of supervisors asked each applicant questions on
how they would deal with various hypothetical job situations. After an initial
period of questions regarding the applicant's education and experience, the applicant was given a situation and then asked to respond to the situation. Typically,
after each candidate's initial response, further questioning would ensue from the
panel to determine the full response of the candidate. The interview would last
about one-half an hour. At the end of the interview, the three interviewers would
rate the candidate on ten dimensions such as attitude, motivation, communication,
etc. Candidates receiving high scores on most of the dimensions would pass the
interview. After a physical examination and a security check, the candidate was
hired and asked to report to training.

This case was prepared by Ronald J. Karren, School of Management, University of Massachusetts at
Amherst.

The Determination of Adverse Impact

Bob knew that the guidelines required employers to make adverse impact determinations at least once a year. Although records had been kept, the agency had not calculated the selection rates over the past three years. Bob thought that it was long overdue and decided to have this done as soon as possible.

A week later the selection rates were tabulated. The data are presented in Exhibit 4.1.

After calculating the adverse impact for both the test and the interview, Bob decided that a discussion with the Personnel Psychologist in the agency would be necessary. A meeting was arranged between Bob, his supervisor and head of the staffing division, and the Personnel Psychologist for the agency, Ron Burden. A discussion ensued regarding the validation requirements of the *Uniform Guidelines*. It was decided that the original job analysis was poorly done and that very little documentation had been retained by the agency. Although there was a task inventory, the major tasks or job duties had not been rated for importance, frequency, difficulty, and trainability. Ron pointed out that this documentation would be critical if they ever needed to defend the selection procedures in court. At the end of the meeting it was decided that it would probably be a good idea to do another job analysis that was in accordance with the new *Uniform Guidelines*. Ron felt that the selection procedures would have to be modified to fit the results of the job analysis. Ron was asked to determine how the job analysis would be done while Bob would coordinate the project in the field.

Job Analysis

The *Uniform Guidelines* recognize that there is no one best way of analyzing the job. Since there was little documentation available, Ron had to decide on a method or technique that would generate from the agents and supervisors the important work behaviors and the tasks associated with them. After much deliberation, he decided to use the critical-incident technique. Ron knew that if the agency wanted to continue using situational questions in the interview, the critical-incident job-analysis technique readily lends itself to the development of this type of question. The method involves collecting reports of behaviors that are "critical," in that they distinguished between successful and unsuccessful work performance. Instructions to the agents and supervisors were to include (1) the circumstances that preceded the incident, (2) the setting in which the incident occurred, (3) what the agent did that was effective or ineffective, and (4) the consequences of the incident.

Ron asked a sample of agents to develop three critical incidents and to indicate the task associated with each critical incident. Upon receipt of the critical incidents, Ron and Bob derived an inventory of work behaviors. This list of work behaviors was then sent back to the agents, and they were asked to rate the importance of the behavior, how frequently it was performed, and the amount of training that was required to learn that behavior.

When this information was collected, Ron and Bob generated a list of major job tasks or job duties. They then assigned all the important work behaviors to the tasks they were associated with. This list of tasks and work behaviors was then sent out to a group of supervisors who were asked to review the list. This same group of supervisors were also asked to meet for a two-day conference later in the month. This group of experts was to determine the important knowledge, skills, abilities, and other characteristics (KSAOs) required to perform these behaviors. Ron also planned for these experts to select the critical incidents that would be used for the new interview.

Supervisory Conference

At the conference the supervisors were given the inventory of tasks and their corresponding work behaviors. They were asked to derive the KSAOs and then to rate how important the skill or ability was for the performance of the work behaviors. The most important knowledge, skills, abilities, and other characteristics are shown in Exhibit 4.2.

The job experts were asked to evaluate the current staffing practices in light of this list of KSAOs. Ron, Bob, and the supervisors agreed that the content of the exam would have to be changed to reflect the first three KSAOs. Ron proposed a reading comprehension exam in which the content would be a small sample of the procedures, laws, and regulations that are taught at the training academy. Applicants would read a section and then answer questions regarding the laws and regulations taught in that section. This type of test has been called a miniature training and evaluation test. All the parties agreed that this would be a very job-related and a good way of assessing the first three KSAOs.

The job experts wanted to retain the interview. Ron and Bob thought that this was fine as long as the following conditions were met:

1. All the questions in the interview would have to be job-related.
2. Critical incidents from the job analysis would be selected to assess the last five KSAOs.
3. Sample answers to each critical incident would be determined in advance. Interviewee responses would be rated on a five-point scale defined explicitly in advance.
4. The same scoring method would be used for each applicant. All procedures would be consistently used for each applicant so that all applicants had the same chance of being selected.
5. All interviewers would be required to attend a training session to learn how to administer and assess the structured interview.

The supervisors agreed to these conditions. However, they did not want the interview to be completely structured. They felt that the interview should begin with a few questions regarding the applicant's past education and experience. Bob and Ron agreed to this with the stipulation that this information should not bias how the candidate would be assessed and scored at the end of the interview.

When Bob and Ron returned to the agency, they were happy over what had transpired at the supervisory conference. The question that remained was the type of validation to be used on the newly developed selection procedures. Ron felt that they should validate the selection procedures with a criterion-related validity strategy. They would collect the scores for both the interview and the test and later compare them to either success in training or their performance appraisal at the end of the first year. Since Ron was familiar with these procedures, he felt that this was a preferred strategy over a content validity strategy. On the other hand, Bob felt that a predictive validity study was too costly and unnecessary. Since their newly developed procedures were job-related, a content validity approach was sufficient. Instead of arguing over which type of validation strategy to use, they decided to discuss the matter with Bob's supervisor and meet again later in the week.

Questions

1. Is there any evidence of adverse impact against any race, sex, or ethnic groups?
2. If the total selection process for a job has no adverse impact, should the individual components of the selection process be evaluated for adverse impact?
3. Which type of validation would you use? Why? What are the differences between content and criterion-related validity studies?
4. Evaluate the job-analysis procedures used in this case. Is it necessary to do such a thorough analysis?
5. If you are doing a criterion-related validity study, should your criterion be success in training or on-the-job performance?

Exhibit 4.1 Tabulation of Selection Rates

	Pass Rates for the Test		
Group	**Number Who Took Test**	**Number Who Passed**	**Pass Rate**
Whites	282	134	47.5%
Blacks	36	10	27.8
Hispanics	102	44	43.1
Asians	0	0	0
American Indians	0	0	0
Men	385	170	44.2
Women	35	18	51.4
TOTAL	420	188	44.8

continued

Exhibit 4.1 *continued*

Pass Rates for the Interview

Group	Number Interviewed	Number Who Passed	Pass Rate
Whites	112	87	77.7%
Blacks	8	5	62.5
Hispanics	40	22	55.0
Men	148	109	73.6
Women	12	5	41.7
TOTAL	160	114	71.2

Note: The number interviewed for each group is less than the number who passed the test. The difference represents individuals who did not wish to continue through the second part of the selection process.

Exhibit 4.2 KSAOs Derived from the Task/Behavior Inventory

1. Knowledge of federal law
2. Knowledge of procedures and regulations
3. Reading and verbal comprehension
4. Ability to deal effectively in dangerous situations
5. Ability to communicate effectively
6. Skill in interpersonal relations
7. Judgment ability
8. Ability to solve problems quickly and effectively

EXERCISE:
EVALUATING THE
RECRUITING FUNCTION

I. *Objectives:*

   1. To make you aware of the necessity of evaluating the efficiency and effectiveness of various recruitment sources.

2. To provide you with practice in analyzing data, drawing conclusions, and planning a strategy to remedy identified problems or deficiencies.
3. To make you aware of the linkages among staff turnover, recruitment sources, recruitment methods, and adequate staffing.

II. *Out-of-Class Preparation Time:* 2 hours

III. *In-Class Time Suggested:* 45 minutes

IV. *Procedures:* Read the entire exercise, including the "Background" on St. Vincent's Hospital. Then, using the data provided in Exhibit 4.3, do the calculations on Form 1. A yield ratio is the number of applicants necessary to fill vacancies with qualified people. It is the relationship of applicant inputs to outputs at various decision points. For example, the yield ratio for all recruitment sources in Exhibit 4.3 shows that 273 nurse applicants were generated over the three-year period from 1986 to 1988. Since only 221 were classified as potentially qualified, the yield ratio is 273/221 or 1.24 to 1. Yield ratios at other steps in the process are also shown for all recruitment sources on Form 1. These data show that the hospital needs to start with more than five times as many applicants as it needs to fill job openings and more than thirteen times as many applicants as it hopes to have as "above average" performers.

Do the calculations for Form 1 on your own prior to class. Think about the implications of these data for future recruitment at the hospital. Then look at Exhibit 4.4 in conjunction with the background description and think about the implications for the recruiting process. During the class period, form groups of three to five, which will act as a consulting team for the hospital. Discuss and answer the "Questions" in your group. At the end of the class period have a spokesperson for each group discuss the group's answers and rationale with the entire class.

BACKGROUND

St. Vincent's Hopsital is an 80-bed hospital in a northeastern city affiliated with the Roman Catholic church. The administrator is Sister Claire, a fifty-six-year-old member of the Daughters of Charity religious order.

During the last decade the hospital operated with a nursing staff of between fifty and sixty registered nurses and experienced a nursing turnover rate of about 25 percent. The turnover rate was average for that city during the time period. The turnover rate actually declined to about 20 percent during the first two years of the current decade. However, it picked up to 25 percent again by mid-decade, and then accelerated to an average of 35 percent over the current three-year period.

These higher turnover rates have put additional pressure on the recruiting process to provide larger numbers of qualified candidates. However, Sam Barnett, Director of Human Resources, has reported more and more difficulty locating qualified nurse candidates over the three-year period. Barnett's office has prepared the recruitment data shown in Exhibit 4.3. The data show that 273 applicants (from all sources) had to be screened to produce 52 qualified candidates who accepted a job offer. One year later 19 of these 52 had left the hospital. The last column shows the direct and indirect costs of recruitment by source, including clerical time, supervisor time, and direct costs such as travel and postage. The Human Resource Department has also conducted a telephone survey of all the nurses they could locate who did *not* accept a job offer from the hospital during the most recent three-year period. Reasons for such rejections are shown in Exhibit 4.4.

Sister Mary Louise, the sixty-two-year-old Director of Nursing Service, has been conducting all the off-site recruitment for many years. This includes both the nursing Job Fair and the State Nursing Association meeting. She has begun to feel "burned out" because of all her external recruiting and internal evaluation of candidates over the years.

At a recent meeting, she suggested that an outside group (your group) be brought in to analyze the whole recruiting process, identify problems and opportunities, and suggest improvements. Sister Claire and Barnett both readily agreed to an outside consultant because they are aware of predictions of severe nursing shortages in the next decade due to declining nursing school enrollments. St. Vincent's itself contributed to this enrollment decline by closing its own School of Nursing due to fewer applications for admission and the high cost of operation.

Since recruitment of new nurses has begun to fall behind turnover of nurses employed at St. Vincent's, the vacancy rate has begun to increase. In the middle of the current decade only 11 percent of staff nursing positions were unfilled. Now, this percentage has increased to 23 percent. One result has been an increasing workload on the existing nursing staff. In addition to increased turnover, the symptoms of staff burnout (i.e., stress, conflict, absenteeism) are becoming more evident.

Questions

1. How would you evaluate the nurse recruiting strategy currently being used by the hospital? Is the hospital using too few or too many recruiting sources? Why?
2. If you presently feel the hospital is using too many recruitment sources, which ones would you emphasize and why?
3. What stage or stages in the recruitment process seem to be most amenable to improvements? What specific improvements would you suggest to decrease the yield ratios. Why?
4. On the basis of data in Exhibit 4.4, as well as the "Background" section, what changes (if any) in the recruitment process would you suggest? Why?

Exhibit 4.3 Data on Recruitment Sources for Registered Nurses at St. Vincent's Hospital, 1986-88

Recruitment Source	Number of Applicants	Potentially Qualified	Invitation for Interview	Qualified and Offered Job	Accepted Job	One-Year Survival	Above-Average Rating	Total Recruitment Cost
1. Direct applications								
write-ins	53	42	30	20	13	8	4	$1550
walk-ins	64	47	38	24	11	6	2	1500
2. Employee referrals	13	12	7	5	4	3	2	400
3. Newspaper ads	24	16	8	4	2	1	0	750
4. Journal ads	19	18	10	8	4	2	2	450
5. Educational institutions								
junior colleges	16	13	11	6	2	2	1	1200
hospital-based schools	8	8	3	2	1	0	0	800
university programs	24	24	16	14	10	8	7	1300
6. Private employment agency	9	9	8	5	2	2	1	700
7. Public employment agency	8	4	2	1	1	0	0	300
8. Direct mail	15	14	4	3	1	0	0	450
9. Job fair	13	7	5	3	1	1	1	900
10. State Nursing Association meeting	7	7	4	3	0	0	0	1150
TOTALS	273	221	146	98	52	33	20	$11,450

Form 1: Yield Ratios at Each Step in the Recruitment Process and Recruitment Cost per Nurse Hired, St. Vincent's Hospital, 1986-88

Recruitment Sources	Yield Rates						Average Cost Per Nurse Hired
	Potentially Qualified	Accepted Interview	Offered Job	Accepted Job	One-Year Survival	Above-Average Rating	
1. Direct Applications write-ins walk-ins							
2. Employee referrals							
3. Newspaper ads							
4. Journal ads							
5. Educational institutions junior colleges hospital-based schools university programs							
6. Private employment agency							
7. Public employment agency							
8. Direct mail							
9. Job fair							
10. State Nursing Association meeting							
Averages for all sources	1.24	1.87	2.79	5.25	8.27	13.65	

Exhibit 4.4 Reasons for Nurse Rejection of a Job Offer
from St. Vincent's Hospital, 1986-88

Reason	Number	Percent
Recruitment Processes		
Job attributes not communicated	2	4.3
Negative perception of recruiter	12	26.1
Negative perception of hospital	2	4.3
Lack of timely follow-up	13	28.3
Perceived lack of honesty in recruitment process	1	2.2
Negative information from recruiter	1	2.2
Job Attributes		
Location of hospital	3	6.5
Salary offer	2	4.3
Hours of work	2	4.3
Promotional opportunities	0	0.0
Fringe benefits	0	0.0
Working conditions	3	6.5
Perceived poor job "match"	5	10.9
TOTALS	46	99.9

EXERCISE:
SELECTION DECISIONS

I. *Objectives:*
   1. To make you aware of the complex criteria often used to select candidates for administrative positions.
   2. To help you develop skills in planning and implementing semistructured interviews.
   3. To give you practice in preparing for, participating in, or evaluating the selection interview.
II. *Out-of-Class Preparation Time:* 2 hours
III. *In-Class Time Suggested:* 45 minutes

IV. *Procedures:*

1. Read the entire exercise including the "Background," "Questions for the Semistructured Interview," and the various forms. During the previous class period, the instructor should have divided students in the class into groups of seven: four executive committee members, two applicants, and one observer.

2. Prior to class, prepare for your role in the group. Committee members should fill in the first two columns of Form 1 and the interviewer questions on Form 2 in pencil or on a separate sheet of paper. This will facilitate committee discussion, reduce the amount of class time needed for interview preparation, and save the forms themselves for the *final* list of criteria (Form 1) and interview questions (Form 2). Committee members should be prepared to play their roles (Form 2) as they would expect the described individuals to behave in real life. The observer for each group should read Form 3 in advance. Then fill it out during the interview and be prepared to discuss it at the end of the class period.

   The two applicants in each group should review their resumes in either Exhibit 4.5 or Exhibit 4.6 and be prepared to elaborate on any of the data in the resume as well as provide supplementary information if they wish to the committee.

3. During the class period, each committee should spend ten to fifteen minutes comparing notes and designing a *final* set of criteria and weighting system for Form 1 and interview questions for Form 2. Neither the applicants nor the observers should be present during these discussions. When the committee is ready, the applicants should be called from outside the room one at a time. In the meantime, the applicants should be doing final preparations for their interviews, including consideration of how they will respond to hypothetical questions which may be asked.

   Possible selection criteria the committee may want to consider are previous experience as a hospital CEO, educational background, ability to "fit" into the organization in terms of personal views and goals, knowledge of Brookdale Hospital and its problems, ideas for solving the hospital's problems, interpersonal skills, communication skills, and administrative skills.

4. Each candidate is then interviewed for ten to fifteen minutes. After each interview, board members fill out the remainder of Form 1 including the rating of each candidate on each criteria, the total score for each, and any additional comments. The observer will take notes and make an evaluation on Form 3 during the interviews. At the conclusion of these interviews, the committee compares notes and makes a decision concerning which candidate should be recommended for the position and why.

5. When all the groups have finished the interview and assessment process, the instructor asks each group to report to the entire class in the following order: the committee decision and rationale, the performance of the two applicants, and the observer's report. Lessons concerning the selec-

tion interview process are presented by both interviewers and interviewees. Depending on class size, this "wrap-up" phase should take ten to fifteen minutes.

BACKGROUND

Brookdale Hospital is a 420-bed proprietary (for-profit) hospital located in a large midwestern city. The hospital was originally founded by a group of local physicians in 1948. In 1982, they sold out to one of the national hospital chains and are now part of a large system of hospitals involving forty-nine hospitals with about 12,000 beds in eighteen states (mostly in the Midwest). The corporation follows a policy of decentralization. Consequently, while support services have been provided, the hospital has continued to operate with a great deal of autonomy.

Recently, the hospital has begun to experience declines in occupancy rates and increased annual deficits. John Rhodes has been the Chief Executive Officer for the past eight years. Two months ago he suffered a stroke and, at the advice of his physician, has decided to retire at age fifty-five.

The Board of Trustees has appointed the Associate Administrator, Terry Bradford, as the Acting Administrator and Chief Executive Officer while a search for Rhodes' replacement is made. The Executive Committee of the Board has advertised the position widely over the past six weeks in a variety of professional publications, including the *Wall Street Journal*.

As a result of the resumes generated through this recruitment process, the Board has selected the two top candidates for the position: Terry Bradford and Chris Smith, an administrator of a small sixty-bed hospital in a nearby city. Resumes for each are shown on Exhibits 4.5 and 4.6. The committee has also developed a job description for the position as shown in Exhibit 4.7.

The process for hiring a new CEO requires a formal vote by the entire Board as well as concurrence by the President of the corporation. However, the latter two steps have always been formalities. The critical decision is the recommendation of the Executive Committee. This committee consists of the following four individuals: Sam Gordon, Amanda Simpson, Steve Bailey, and Jane Sears.

Gordon is a physician and the Chief of the Medical Staff (a salaried position) and has been with the hospital for thirteen years. He is fifty-eight years old and has a specialty in general surgery. He has been concerned about what he views as the eroding power of physicians vis-à-vis administrators and outside regulators over the past few years. Consequently, he would like the committee to recommend someone who can work well with physicians, understand their needs, and generally support their desires to provide high-quality patient care.

Simpson is President of the City Council and was selected for both the Board and the Executive Committee because of her political contacts. Her goals are to make sure the hospital survives, keeps its costs under control, and continues to provide some care for indigents. Since Brookdale is one of the major hospitals in the city serving her constituents, Simpson naturally is concerned that the corporation may shut its doors due to the deficits it has been experiencing. She feels the hospital has to be more innovative in developing and marketing new services to off-set the declines in inpatient services.

Bailey is President and Chief Executive Officer of Applied Electronics, a very successful company which he founded eighteen years ago. He admits he still doesn't know much about health care, but has been a member of the Board for twelve years due to his entrepreneurial talents and his business contacts. His view is that the hospital needs to become more "businesslike" and focus on services which are profitable. He also believes that the hospital has not done enough to raise funds through private philanthropy.

Sears is the president of a local bank. She has an M.B.A. from the Wharton School and has been in banking for twenty-two years. Her major concern is the deteriorating financial position of the hospital. In her view, the new CEO should have excellent financial management skills as well as an ability to work well with physicians. She views the previous CEO (Rhodes) as deficient in these areas.

The committee has invited both Bradford and Smith to interview for the position of CEO. The outline for the selection process is shown on Form 1 and the form for questions to be developed by the committee is on Form 2.

QUESTIONS FOR THE SEMISTRUCTURED INTERVIEW

In its purest form, a structured interview occurs when the interviewers bring to the interview a list of predetermined questions to ask the interviewee. The advantage is that the interviewers have previously discussed and agreed upon the relevant criteria. During the interview, all interviewers focus upon these criteria. Weighting of these criteria is often used as well. This systematic process usually results in higher levels of consistency among interviewers than is the case with unstructured interviews.

However, structured interviews do not allow the interviewee to discuss a topic of his or her choice or to provide additional information on areas which require further explanation. An unstructured interview emphasizes creating a supportive climate and helping the interviewees discuss values, goals, objectives, and career plans.

A compromise which retains the benefits of a structured interview while also creating the openness of the unstructured interview is the semistructured interview. Here the interviewers not only develop a set of structured questions to evaluate the candidate based on the agreed-upon criteria but also ask open-ended questions, such as "What are your long-term career goals?" and "Why is that important to you?"

Develop a list of up to ten questions to ask the two applicants and decide which committee members should ask which questions. Be sure to consider the criteria identified on Form 1 as well as some open-ended questions designed to learn more about the applicant. Write these questions on Form 2.

Exhibit 4.5 Resume 1

TERRY A. BRADFORD
119 Brook Hollow Lane
Columbus, Ohio

JOB OBJECTIVE

To secure a position as Chief Executive Officer for a large proprietary hospital in the Midwest.

EDUCATION

1962 - 1966:   Oberlin College, Oberlin, Ohio
        Major: Sociology
        Degree: B.A., June 1966, <u>Cum laude</u>, G.P.A. 3.52

1972 - 1973:   Ohio State University, Columbus, Ohio
        Major: Business Administration,
        Emphasis: Organization Behavior
        Degree: M.B.A., June 1973, G.P.A. 3.86
        Member: Beta Gamma Sigma (national scholastic
        honorary in Business)

Other: After completing my M.B.A. degree, I have taken two additional graduate courses in accounting and one additional course in finance at Ohio State University.

EMPLOYMENT HISTORY

February 1983 - Present: Associate Administrator; Brookdale Hospital, Columbus, Ohio
    Duties: liaison between the CEO and the medical staff, nursing staff, and other major hospital departments; represents administrator at various functions; strategic planning and marketing; reviews financial and occupancy data.

June 1976 - February 1983:   Assistant Administrator; Oakland Hospital, Oakland, Ohio
    Duties: worked with the Administrator and Assistant Administrator on a variety of administrative functions in finance, personnel, marketing, and public relations.

continued

Exhibit 4.5 *continued*

August 1973 - June 1976:   Personnel Assistant; Bayview Municipal
                                  Hospital, Bayview, Ohio
                                        Duties: designed personnel appraisal
                                        form, conducted selection interviews,
                                        designed and taught courses for super-
                                        visors, and designed advertisements
                                        for positions.

June 1966 - September 1972:   Various sales and administrative positions in
                                  a variety of organizations.

PERSONAL

Date of Birth: September 6, 1944
Height: 5'8"   Weight: 150 lbs.
Marital Status: Divorced, no children
Hobbies: Music, travel, and swimming

Exhibit 4.6 Resume 2

CHRIS A. SMITH

Home Address: Office Address:
2057 Hickory Street   Administrator
Anytown, Ohio   Morningside Hospital
                                                       204 Jefferson Street
                                                       Anytown, Ohio

Personal: Married, two children

Educational Background:
B.S. — Heideberg College, Tiffin, Ohio (1967)
M.B.A. — Cleveland State University, Cleveland, Ohio (1971)

Experience:

Morningside Hospital, Anytown, Ohio   November 1979 - Present
        Administrator   June 1983 - Present
        Associate Administrator   November 1979 - June 1983

continued

Exhibit 4.6 *continued*

Eastside Hospital, Hometown, Ohio
    Financial Manager   June 1976 - November 1979

McLains Department Store, Hometown, Ohio
    Financial Manager   January 1974 - June 1976
    Financial Trainee   June 1971 - January 1974

City of Hometown, Ohio
    City Planner   July 1967 - August 1969

<u>Member:</u> Rotary Club

Exhibit 4.7 Job Description: Chief Executive Officer, Brookdale Hospital

DESCRIPTION OF WORK

General Statement of Duties: Supervises and coordinates administrative work of a complex nature involving the entire hospital and all its components; represents the hospital to outside stakeholders.
Supervision Required: Receives policy guidance from the Board of Directors.
Supervision Exercised: Plans, organizes, motivates, coordinates, and directs a staff of administrative and clerical personnel. Total direct supervision involves over fifteen indivduals.

EXAMPLE OF DUTIES

1. Initiates and coordinates activities related to long-range planning and marketing of the hospital's services.
2. Develops and enforces policies and procedures related to administrative functions.
3. Coordinates major staff services, including budget, personnel, medical services, nursing services, dietetics, and housekeeping.
4. Develops and compiles administrative reports as required by the Board or external regulatory agencies.
5. Performs related work as required.

continued

Exhibit 4.7 *continued*

REQUIRED KNOWLEDGE, SKILLS, AND ABILITIES

Extensive and broad knowledge of complex management systems (internal and external) in a health-care environment. Skill and ability in planning, personnel management, and budgetary control. Ability to relate to external stakeholders, including the Board of Directors.

QUALIFICATIONS FOR APPOINTMENT

Education: Graduation from a college or university with major coursework in business administration, public administration, or health administration.
Experience: Ten years or more of progressively responsible experience in administration or management.

Form 1 Criteria for Selecting a Chief Executive Officer and Ratings of Applicants Based on These Criteria

Criteria: Major dimension of the CEO job based upon the job description and personal characteristics desired	Weight of the Criteria (1-5)	Job Applicant Rating on the Criteria (1-10)		Total Score (Weight X Rating)		Comments About Each
		Bradford	Smith	Bradford	Smith	
1.						
2.						
3.						
4.						
5.						
6.						
7.						
8.						
9.						
10.						
Total Scores						

Form 2 Questions for Interview

1.

2.

3.

4.

5.

6.

7.

8.

9.

10.

Form 3 Observation Sheet

1. How well did the committee establish rapport with each applicant?

2. How well did each of the candidates respond to the committee's questions? What improvements would you suggest? Why?

3. Approximately what percentage of the fifteen minutes interview time was spent listening to the applicant and what percentage consisted of committee questions and/or comment? How appropriate was this breakdown?

4. Did the committee overemphasize negative information, show bias based on irrelevant factors, or otherwise treat either applicant unfairly?

5. Did the committee probe unclear areas, or did it allow short answers which did not provide necessary information?

6. What is your overall assessment of the success of the committee in eliciting relevant information for making this selection decision? Why?

EXERCISE: SELECTION INTERVIEW ROLE PLAY

I. *Objectives:*
    1. To help you develop skills in conducting selection interviews.
    2. To provide you with practice in basic principles of effective interviewing.
II. *Out-of-Class Preparation Time:* 30 to 90 minutes, depending on role played (students who play the interviewee will need to prepare a resume).
III. *In-Class Time:* 45 minutes
IV. *Procedures:* The class should be divided into groups of three: an interviewer, interviewee, and observer. Roles should be assigned ahead of time so you will have time to prepare your role. This is especially important for those of you who will play the role of interviewee since you are to use your own resume and qualifications during the role play. Read the scenario that follows and the role description provided by the instructor. Participants should assume that the interview is taking place in a campus placement office. The role play begins when the interviewee arrives for the interview and ends when both individuals have accomplished their objectives. At the end of the role play the interviewer completes the interviewer's report (Form 1) and shares it with the interviewee. Next, the observer provides feedback on his or her observations to the group (Form 2). The group then identifies and discusses the hardest part of the interview from both the interviewer's point of view and the applicant's perspective. If time permits, the entire class then discusses the reliability and validity of the interview as a method of selecting applicants for jobs.

SCENARIO

The director of college recruiting for Duro Insurance Company is presently recruiting college students for its administrative trainee program. The one-year training program involves a combination of on-the-job training and formal classroom training. Upon successful completion of the training a candidate is assigned a position as assistant department supervisor.

Duro Insurance Company ranks in the top 15 percent of life insurance companies nationally with in-force insurance in excess of $6 billion. Duro markets all forms of insurance, bonds, and pension products on an individual and group basis. More recently, the company added diversified financial services, including discount brokerage services, real estate financing, and mutual funds. The company is divided into 6 major divisions (Employee Benefits, Commercial Insurance, Individual Life, Automobile, Homeowners, and Diversified Financial Services) and functionally into several major operating departments: Sales, Underwriting, Administrative, Loss Prevention, Actuarial, Claims, Legal, Financial and Investments, Advertising and Public Relations, Personnel, and Research and Policy Development. Duro has over 25,000 employees and more than 300 field offices throughout the country. The company has enjoyed a pattern of steady growth and expansion over the years.

Job Description for Administrative Trainee

1. Handle day-to-day administration of field office, including the supervision of office clerks.
2. Plan and oversee the use of space, furniture, and equipment on a continuing basis and recommend changes as necessary.
3. Supervise computer processing operations for issuing and servicing insurance policies.
4. Implement and maintain accounting and collection procedures.

The trainee works closely with the department head in learning these duties.

Job Qualifications

1. B.S./B.A. with business management background.
2. Ability to communicate effectively.
3. Ability to handle detail.
4. Ability to plan and direct activities of subordinate personnel.
5. Demonstrated leadership potential.
6. Knowledge of computers.

Additional Job Data

1. The trainee position reports directly to a department head.
2. Expected career progression is to assistant department supervisor (1 - 2 years) and, with continued development, to department head (4 - 5 years after supervisory assignment).
3. The position requires relocation.
4. The company offers competitive salaries and benefits, including a tuition repayment plan and in-house career planning and development.

Form 1 Interviewer's Report

APPLICANT_____ POSITION _____
DATE_____ INTERVIEWER _____

Rate the applicant's background and behavior, taking into consideration the factors listed for each area. Circle a rating for each factor. Give an overall rating also.

1.   Presentation (appearance, manner, oral communication skills, interest, motivation):

Poor 1 2 3 4 5 Excellent

2.   Education (major, intellectual abilities, academic achievement, knowledge of field):

Poor 1 2 3 4 5 Excellent

3.   Work experience (related experience, skill and competence, job performance, interpersonal skills, leadership):

Poor 1 2 3 4 5 Excellent

4.   Summarize candidate's strengths:

5.   Summarize candidate's weaknesses:

6.   Overall evaluation and recommendation:

Poor 1 2 3 4 5 Excellent

Recommendation: ( ) Invite for field visit   ( ) Do not invite

Comments:

Form 2 Observation Sheet

1. What was the quality of the interaction between the interviewer and interviewee?

2. What type of interview did the interviewer use (structured versus non-structured)? How well did it work?

3. Were the questions job-related?

4. What did the interviewer do to put the applicant at ease?

5. Did the interviewer listen? Did the interviewer spend too much time talking?

6. Did the interviewer follow up on questions not completely answered?

7. Did the interviewer gain enough information to make a decision about the interviewee?

8. General observations.

INCIDENT:
THE CAMPUS INTERVIEW

After four years of college, Sylvia Taylor was excited and looking forward to pursuing a career as a CPA in one of the big-eight accounting firms. During her four years she had maintained a 3.7 average in her accounting classes and had been treasurer of the Accounting Students Association. Although somewhat older than her fellow classmates, she had worked well with them. She had registered with the Campus Placement Service and had several interviews scheduled during the semester. She had taken full advantage of all the services offered by the placement office and felt that she was well prepared for presenting herself to potential employers.

Her first interview with one of the big-eight firms was going quite well until the interviewer, Mr. Abrams, asked her, "Sylvia, I see here on your application materials that you have a five-year-old son. What are you going to do about him if you get the job?" Sylvia was caught off guard by the question. But mustering all of her wits, she responded, "Gee, do you mean I have to get rid of him if I get the job?" Mr. Abrams' face turned red. He quickly thanked Sylvia for her time and ended the interview.

As Sylvia left the placement office, she wondered if she had handled the situation correctly. She also wondered if she should take any further actions.

Questions

1. Discuss Sylvia's handling of the interviewer's question. Are there any other ways she could have handled the situation?
2. Are there any general rules applicants can follow in dealing with potentially unlawful interview questions?

SKILL BUILDER: EVALUATING JOB APPLICATION FORMS

I. *Objectives:*

1. To familiarize you with the criteria for selecting questions on an application form.

2. To give you practice in evaluating the questions on different application blanks.

II. *Time Required to Complete:* 2 hours

III. *Instructions:* Obtain samples of job application forms from two different organizations. You should thoroughly review the legal requirements for pre-employment inquiries and other relevant information on application forms found in the text, and if necessary, through library research. Use the guide below to evaluate the questions in the application blanks obtained. Prepare a report summarizing your findings for each application form and any recommendations for improving the form.

QUESTIONS TO BE ASKED IN EVALUATING APPROPRIATENESS OF APPLICATION BLANK ITEMS

1. Is this question job-related?
2. Will answers to this question have an adverse impact in screening out minorities and/or women (i.e., disqualify a significantly larger percentage of members of one particular group than of others)?
3. Is this question really needed to judge an applicant's qualifications and suitability for the job?
4. Does the question constitute an invasion of privacy?
5. Can the applicant's response to this question be verified?

Source: Adapted from Robert D. Gatewood and Hubert S. Feild, Human Resource Selection (New York: Dryden Press, 1987), p. 279.

Part 5

Compensation and Salary Administration

An organization's compensation policies play a major role in its ability to compete in labor markets, to retain experienced employees, to motivate high quality performance, and to support organizational strategic objectives. In this context organizations must make their compensation systems both attractive and equitable. In designing pay systems, organizations attempt to achieve three types of equity: external, internal, and individual. Balancing the three types of equity is critical to the long-term effectiveness of pay systems. The importance of compensation is highlighted by the fact that it represents approximately 50 percent of a typical organization's total costs.

The materials in this section focus on a number of important compensation issues. The first case, "The Overpaid Bank Tellers," explores the issue of external equity and the impact of wage and salary surveys on pay level decisions. "Rewarding Volunteers" focuses on noneconomic rewards in a not-for-profit organization. The essential role of job evaluation in designing pay systems is underscored in the exercise, "Job Evaluation at Jenkins Power Company." "Wagesim" is an in-basket exercise which allows students to make the day-to-day decisions needed to administer a salary system. The incident, "Merit Increases," addresses the problems associated with the design and administration of performance-based pay systems. Finally, the skill builder gives students practice in applying the Fair Labor Standards Act.

CASE:
THE OVERPAID BANK TELLERS

The State Bank is located in a southwestern town of about 50,000 people. It is one of four banks in the area and has the reputation of being the most progressive. Russell Duncan has been the President of the bank for fifteen years. Before coming to State Bank, Duncan had worked for a large Detroit bank for ten years. Mr. Duncan has implemented a number of changes that have earned him a great deal of respect and admiration from both bank employees and townspeople alike. For example, in response to a growing number of Spanish-speaking people in the area, he hired Latinos and placed them in critical bank positions. He organized and staffed the city's only agricultural loan center so as better to meet the needs of the area's farmers. In addition, he established the states first "uniline" system for handling customers waiting in line for a teller.

Perhaps far more than anything else, Mr. Duncan is known for establishing progressive personnel practices. He strongly believes that the bank's employees are its most important asset and continually searches for ways to increase both employee satisfaction and productivity. He feels that all employees should continually strive to improve their skills and abilities and hence cross-trains employees and sends many of them to courses and conferences sponsored by banking groups such as the American Institute of Banking.

With regard to employee compensation, Mr. Duncan firmly believes that employees should be paid according to their contribution to organizational success. Hence, ten years ago he implemented a results-based pay system under which employees could earn raises each year from zero to 12 percent, depending on their job performance. Raises are typically determined by the bank's Personnel Committee during February and are granted to employees on March 1 of each year. In addition to granting employees merit raises, six years ago the bank began giving cost-of-living raises also. Mr. Duncan had been opposed to this idea originally but saw no alternative to it.

One February another bank in town conducted a wage survey to determine the average compensation of bank employees in the city. The management of the State Bank received a copy of the wage survey and was surprised to learn that its tellers, as a group, were being paid an average of 55 cents an hour more than were tellers of equal seniority and job performance at other banks. The survey also showed that employees holding other positions in the bank (e.g., branch managers, loan officers, and secretaries) were being paid wages similar to those paid by other banks.

After receiving the report, the Personnel Committee of the bank met to determine what should be done regarding the tellers' raises. They knew that none of the tellers had been told how much their raises would be but that they were all expecting both merit and cost-of-living raises. They also realized that, if other employees learned that the tellers were being overpaid, friction could develop and morale might suffer. They knew that it was costing the bank over $25,000 extra to pay the tellers. Finally, they knew that, as a group, the bank's tellers were highly competent, and they did not want to lose any of them.

Questions

1. If you were on the bank's Personnel Committee, what would you do regarding raises for the tellers?
2. How much faith should the Personnel Committee place in the accuracy of the wage survey?
3. Critique the bank's policy of giving merit raises which range from zero to 12 percent, depending on job performance.
4. Critique the bank's policy of giving cost-of-living raises. Should they be eliminated?

CASE:
REWARDING VOLUNTEERS

Background

Northern University is a large university in a small college town in the Northwest. After several years of political pressure, internal conflicts, and negotiations, the university applied for, and was granted, an FCC license for a new public radio affiliate. The general goals of the station were to provide quality noncommercial alternative broadcasting with an emphasis on local and national news, jazz, and classical music. The station would have no paid commercials, but would broadcast public service announcements and cultural events.

A short-term objective was to assemble and train a volunteer staff (mostly students and faculty) until funds could be provided for an all-professional administrative staff. A longer-term objective was to develop an all-professional announcing staff.

Exhibit 5.1 shows the organization structure of the radio station. The General Manager, Chief Engineer, News Director, Administrative Assistant, and Program Director were all full-time paid positions. All of the other positions were either part-time employees, part-time work-study students, or unpaid part-time volunteers.

The largest segment of the staff were the volunteers who were primarily college students, faculty, or faculty spouses. The students volunteered to get training and experience which they hoped would propel them into careers in the media. Faculty volunteered either for new experience or because they liked playing particular types of music. The others volunteered to help the station and to meet new people. Volunteers were trained and used as both announcers and in "behind the scenes" positions such as board operators. Many of the board operators were told they could become announcers in the future.

The Program Director's responsibilities included developing the on-air program schedule, developing a volunteer training program (including both equipment operation and on-air announcing), and scheduling/supervising the volunteers and work-study students. The Program Director also did some on-air announcing and worked as the internal liaison coordinating the various departments.

Problems

The person hired initially as Program Director had a leadership style that did not fit well in a volunteer-oriented organization. Specifically, he was task-oriented and had few skills in managing others. This leadership style contributed to conflicts within the organization, and the Program Director left the organization by mutual consent after nine months on the job. The position of Program Director remained unfilled for nine months.

During that time period, the General Manager and the Administrative Assistant split the work ordinarily done by the Program Director, including recruitment, selection, training, and scheduling of the volunteers. However, none of these activities were ever institutionalized in terms of written policies and procedures. For example, there were no written job descriptions for volunteers explaining duties and responsibilities for particular positions. Nor was there any formal feedback system for evaluating volunteer performance and receiving volunteer input. Opportunities for volunteer training were also reduced during this period.

After nine months, a new Program Director was hired. He had previous experience as a Program Director at another public radio station and came highly recommended. His initial statement was one of amazement at the high quality of announcing among the volunteers. In fact, he sent out a memorandum to that effect during his second week on the job. However, as time passed more and more of the volunteer announcers were told by the Program Director that their services were no longer required as announcers. They were offered the opportunity to work behind the scenes as board operators with no on-air announcing. Most chose to simply quit.

When challenged by the volunteers, the Program Director stated that there was too much voice variation among the volunteers and an all-professional sounding station needs more uniformity. Since there was no money to hire full-time professional announcers, the Program Director (as well as several other paid staff) began to do more and more of the on-air announcing. The Program Director himself was working more than sixty hours per week. No new volunteers were being trained. Most of the old volunteers had either quit or been demoted. The five still doing on-air announcing then requested a meeting with the General Manager.

At the meeting, these volunteer announcers indicated their displeasure concerning the decisions of the Program Director. They indicated they had contributed not only their time but had also made monetary contributions to the station and had encouraged others to do so. The General Manager thanked the announcers for their contributions of time and money, but indicated he had given the Program Director control of the programming including personnel matters. They were still welcome to do volunteer work at the station and could continue announcing "for the time being." The volunteers were not happy with this response and promptly submitted their resignations.

The General Manager now had an even more severe problem. The paid staff were already spread too thin and stretched to the limit even before the latest volunteer resignations. The station was committed to twenty hours of programming each day and pre-recorded tapes could not fill the entire programming gap since they also required staff time to produce. The station was clearly in a crisis situation.

Questions

1. What specific mistakes were made by (a) the Station Manager and (b) the Program Director?
2. What types of rewards are most appropriate for volunteers? To what degree were these provided to volunteers at the radio station?

Exhibit 5.1 Organizational Structure of the Station

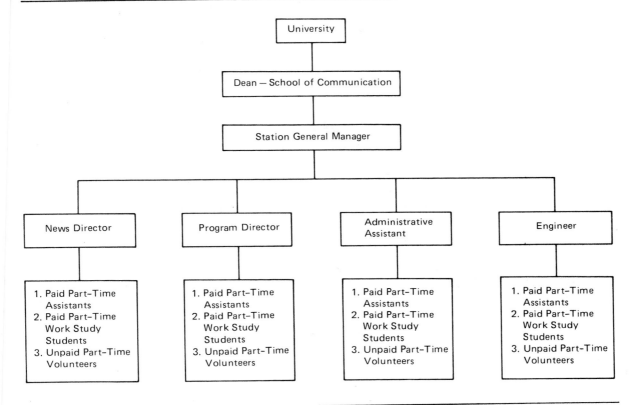

EXERCISE:
JOB EVALUATION
AT JENKINS POWER COMPANY

I. *Objectives:*
1. To give you practice in evaluating jobs using a point system.
2. To help you learn the advantages and disadvantages of the point method of job evaluation.

II. *Out-of-Class Preparation Time:* 30 minutes

III. *In-Class Time Suggested:* 45 minutes

IV. *Procedures:*

1. Review the Job Evaluation Manual (Exhibit 5.2) and the job descriptions (Exhibit 5.3) before class.
2. The class should be divided into groups of four or five to complete the exercise.
3. Read the scenario below and follow the instructions given.

JENKINS POWER COMPANY

You have been selected to serve on the Job Evaluation Committee at Jenkins Power Company. The new plant manager has been receiving a number of complaints about the wage rates in the plant. Upon closer examination, the plant manager has learned that most complaints center on situations where employees feel there are gross discrepancies among salaries in the plant. The plant manager has decided to alleviate the complaints by establishing a systematic salary structure. To begin the restructuring, the plant manager has selected four key production jobs to be evaluated. Your committee has been given a job evaluation manual for production jobs (Exhibit 5.2) and descriptions for the four jobs (Exhibit 5.3). This manual uses eight factors for determining the point value of jobs. Use the job evaluation manual to evaluate each job and determine its point value. Use Form 1 to record your point ratings. At the completion of the exercise, your instructor will ask each group to write their total points for each job on the board. The entire class will then discuss the results and the advantages and disadvantages of the point method of job evaluation.

Exhibit 5.2 Job Evaluation Manual

A. *Education*: Measures the basic knowledge or formal training to learn the job duties. Job knowledge or background may have been acquired either by formal education or by training or a combination thereof.

Degree		Points
1	Elementary school with knowledge of basic arithmetic and ability to read instruments and other gauges	14
2	Junior high school with knowledge of multiplication, division, decimals and fractions; simple use of charts, tables, and drawings	28
3	High school diploma or equivalent; or one to three years trades training; knowledge of mathematics and complex charts, tables and drawings	42

continued

Exhibit 5.2 *continued*

4	High school plus two-year technical college degree; knowledge of advanced mathematics and detailed specifications	56
5	Four-year technical college or university degree with knowledge of higher mathematics and engineering principles	70

B. *Experience*: Measures the amount of experience needed to perform the job at a competent level.

Degree		Points
1	Six months or less	20
2	Greater than six months, but less than one year	40
3	At least one year, but less than three years	60
4	At least three years, but less than five years	80
5	Five years or more	100

C. *Complexity and Judgment*: Measures the use of independent action and judgment in making of decisions and the amount of resourcefulness and planning the job requires.

Degree		Points
1	Little or no judgment or independent action	14
2	Some judgment to comply with instructions; minor decisions	28
3	Average use of judgment to analyze and make decisions	42
4	Considerable use of judgment to analyze and make decisions	56
5	Outstanding use of judgment; major independent decisions to solve complex problems	70

D. *Physical Demands*: Measures the kind, amount, and frequency of physical effort associated with job duties.

Degree		Points
1	Little physical effort required	10
2	Light physical effort required	20
3	Average physical effort required	30
4	Considerable physical effort required	40
5	Heavy continued physical effort required	50

continued

Exhibit 5.2 *continued*

E. *Mental Demands*: Measures the mental effort associated with performing a task and the degree of concentration needed.

Degree		Points
1	Occasional mental attention; work flow intermittent	5
2	Frequent mental attention required	10
3	Continuous mental attention; repetitive work flow	15
4	Concentrated mental attention to perform complex work	20
5	Intense and precise mental concentration needed	25

F. *Supervisory Requirement*: Measures the responsibility for number of employees supervised.

Degree		Points
1	1 - 3 employees	15
2	4 - 7 employees	30
3	8 - 14 employees	45
4	15 - 20 employees	60
5	More than 20 employees	75

G. *Responsibility*: Measures the amount of responsibility for equipment, material or product, and safety of others. Consider probable loss resulting from improper performance.

Degree		Points
1	Little or no responsibility	15
2	Some responsibility	30
3	Moderate responsibility	45
4	Considerable responsibility	60
5	Very considerable responsibility	75

H. *Working Conditions*: Measures job surroundings and environmental influences such as atmosphere, ventilation, noise, and congestion. Consider the extent to which physical conditions are disagreeable and uncomfortable.

Degree		Points
1	Absence of uncomfortable elements	10
2	Limited exposure to uncomfortable elements	20

continued

Exhibit 5.2 *continued*

3	Frequent exposure to uncomfortable elements	30
4	Continuous exposure to several uncomfortable elements	40
5	Intensive/continuous exposure to several uncomfortable elements	50

Exhibit 5.3 Job Descriptions for Four Key Production Jobs

JOB DESCRIPTION: EQUIPMENT OPERATOR

GENERAL PURPOSE: To perform site inspection of plant system and remote control operation.

SUPERVISION RECEIVED: Reports directly to the shift supervisor.

SUPERVISION EXERCISED: Provides technical direction to the utility operator and trainee.

JOB DUTIES: Monitors plant operation through visual inspection; operates the graver demineralizer; isolates equipment for maintenance repairs and tags equipment parts; inspects, reports on status, and activates remote control mechanisms on plant system; monitors and maintains oil levels for plant equipment; fills cooling tower chemical treatment tanks; performs light maintenance activities on off shifts; serves as member of fire fighting brigade; assists in transference of acid and caustic solution to plant system; performs all plant water chemistry tests.

JOB KNOWLEDGE/SKILLS/ABILITIES REQUIRED: Thorough understanding of plant system: start-up, shutdown, and trip procedures; thorough knowledge of boiler chemistry; comprehension of flow prints; ability to operate spectrometer, Ph meter, conductivity meter, graver demineralizer, fork truck, and front loader; knowledge of emergency procedures and understanding of electrical system and motor control.

PHYSICAL REQUIREMENTS: Performance of duties requires walking and climbing ladders and stairs; light lifting, working (occasionally) in dark, high-temperature environment; and working with hazardous materials.

EDUCATION/EXPERIENCE REQUIRED: Associate degree in technical area; two years of related experience in plant operations in a coal-fired boiler operation; *OR* equivalent combination of education and experience.

continued

Exhibit 5.3 *continued*

JOB DESCRIPTION: LABORER

GENERAL PURPOSE: To keep plant area clean and to perform miscellaneous tasks as assigned.

SUPERVISION RECEIVED: Reports directly to the shift supervisor.

SUPERVISION EXERCISED: None

JOB DUTIES: Cleans control room, rest rooms, offices and lab; empties all trash cans; cleans boiler fronts and floors; cleans baghouse and ID fan area; inspects and cleans drain trench as needed; cleans coal-handling areas; keeps roadways cleaned off; cleans drain ditch around coal pile; waters grass and performs miscellaneous tasks as directed by shift supervisor.

JOB KNOWLEDGE/SKILLS/ABILITIES REQUIRED: Ability to comprehend and implement oral instructions; ability to use power-scrubbing and polishing equipment.

PHYSICAL REQUIREMENTS: Walking and climbing (ladders and stairs); lifting up to 60 lbs.; working (occasionally) in dark, high-temperature environments; working with hazardous cleaning materials.

EDUCATION/EXPERIENCE REQUIRED: Knowledge of basic arithmetic.

JOB DESCRIPTION: CONTROL ROOM OPERATOR

GENERAL PURPOSE: To ensure safe and efficient plant operation through constant monitoring of plant systems and correcting system deviations.

SUPERVISION RECEIVED: Reports directly to the shift supervisor.

SUPERVISION EXERCISED: Coordinates the work of the fuel operator, utility operator, and trainee.

JOB DUTIES: Monitors plant steam and process steam, feedwater system, boiler ducts and flues, waste water treatment, turbine lube oil system, main steam temperature and pressure, coal-handling system and other major systems through computer output; determines origin of system deviation through activating control mechanisms; maintains log of daily operation; records hourly amount of electrical generation and usage; communicates with coal dispatcher concerning production and load requirements; provides training and technical instruction to equipment operator, fuel operator, and helper.

continued

Exhibit 5.3 *continued*

JOB KNOWLEDGE/SKILLS/ABILITIES REQUIRED: Comprehensive understanding of plant system; understanding of electrical systems and motor control centers; knowledge of boiler chemistry, comprehension and interpretation of flow prints; ability to operate CRT; communication and human relations skills; ability to perform mathematical and algebraic calculations; ability to analyze problem situations.

PHYSICAL REQUIREMENTS: Manual dexterity to operate console; normal color vision.

EDUCATION/EXPERIENCE REQUIRED: Associate degree in a technical area; minimum of three years of experience in power plant system control environment; *OR* any equivalent combination of education and experience.

JOB DESCRIPTION: SHIFT SUPERVISOR

GENERAL PURPOSE: To maintain a safe and efficient plant operation through directing the activities of the operation's personnel and providing a management support function for the plant superintendent.

SUPERVISION RECEIVED: Reports directly to the plant superintendent.

SUPERVISION EXERCISED: Directs the control room operator, equipment operator, fuel operator, two utility operators, two laborers, and two trainees.

JOB DUTIES: Directs the activities of the operation's personnel; coordinates the activities of the maintenance personnel; issues written communication to employees on personnel policies and operational concerns; conducts training and safety programs for shift employees; schedules shift assignments; performs administrative tasks such as recording workers' time; prepares annual budget for assigned plant areas; maintains inventory level; appraises performance of shift employees; counsels employees on disciplinary problems and job-related performance.

JOB KNOWLEDGE/SKILLS/ABILITIES REQUIRED: Comprehensive understanding of plant systems; knowledge of start-up, shutdown, and trip procedures for boilers and turbines; knowledge of emergency procedures; comprehensive understanding of electrical systems and motor control systems; comprehension and interpretation of flow, logic, and electrical prints; ability to operate CRT; communication, human relation, and managerial skills; ability to comprehend and prepare written communications; ability to present facts, conclusions, and recommendations (problem-solving skills); ability to perform college-level mathematical and algebraic calculations.

continued

Exhibit 5.3 *continued*

PHYSICAL REQUIREMENTS: Walking and climbing stairs.

EDUCATION/EXPERIENCE REQUIRED: College degree in engineering; six years of experience in power plant operation with a minimum of one year of supervisory experience; *OR* equivalent combination of education and experience.

Form 1 Rating Summary Sheet

Factors	Position			
	Equipment Operator	Laborer	Control Room Operator	Shift Supervisor
Education	56	14	56	70
Experience	60	20	80	100
Complexity and judgment	42	14	42	56
Supervisory requirement	15	1	15	45
Physical demands	20	30	10	10
Mental demands	10	5	15	15
Responsibility	45	15	60	60
Working conditions	20	20	10	20
POINT TOTAL	268	118	288	376

EXERCISE:
WAGESIM — A COMPENSATION ADMINISTRATION IN-BASKET

I. *Objectives:*
  1. To familiarize you with some of the problems involved in building and maintaining a compensation system.
  2. To provide you with alternative approaches for solving some typical compensation-related problems.
  3. To give you practice in writing memos to employees regarding compensation issues.
  4. To familiarize you with job evaluation procedures.

II. *Out-of-Class Preparation Time:* 20 minutes to read exercise plus one to two hours to discuss In-Basket items with group members and write memos

III. *In-Class Time Suggested:* 45 minutes to discuss all In-Basket items

IV. *Procedures:* You are to begin by reading all of the material presented in this exercise. Your team is to assume that it is responsible for developing and maintaining the Mack Organization's wage and salary system. Assume further that the person who previously had these responsibilities has just quit and left your team all of the items which follow in your In-Basket. Your team is to respond in writing to each employee who wrote a memo. Secondly, explain in writing on a separate sheet of paper what additional actions your team would take with reference to each item. For example, if your team believes that it should gather additional information before making a final decision on an item, explain what information your team would want. Or, if your team believes that additional memos or discussions with someone in the company are needed, explain this. Your team should bring both the memos and the "Additional Action" sheets to class. Be prepared to present and defend these materials during class discussion.

Situation

The Mack Organization is a large organization whose headquarters is located in the midwestern United States. It has offices located throughout the country and employs over 700 individuals. You may assume the organization is a chemical company, a manufacturing company, a hospital, a university, or virtually any large organization with which you are familiar.

   The Mack Organization's Personnel Department includes a Compensation Administration section that consists of two individuals, one of whom is you (your team). The company has several different wage structures, including one for executives and one for clerical personnel. For compensation purposes, all clerical employees are divided into five job classifications. The organization's current wage structure for clerical personnel is shown in Exhibit 5.4.

MACK ORGANIZATION
Compensation Policies
(Excerpts from policy manual)

How Salaries Are Determined

Employee salaries directly relate to the work they do and how well they do it. Two major factors work together to establish the salaries payable for various jobs—position evaluation and salary ranges.

Job Evaluation

Job evaluation is a method of measuring the relative work of each job in the organization compared to all the other jobs, based on an objective analysis of the duties and responsibilities of the position. The concept is not unique to us; determining the relative value of jobs within an organization is an integral part of any salary administration program, regardless of the company.

At the Mack Organization, job evaluation works like this:

First, a description is written for each job. The information for it comes from a questionnaire completed by the person performing the job. The description defines the function of the job and lists the major duties performed. Each description is then evaluated by a standing committee of people from various areas of the organization who have a broad knowledge of the jobs that exist throughout the organization. Their evaluation is based on "yardsticks," including knowledge required, freedom of action, accountability, contacts with employees and customers, physical effort required, unusual working conditions, research responsibilities, and supervision or management responsibilities. Based on these yardsticks, the job is assigned a point value. By listing all positions according to their point value, the relative worth of each position is established.

When a new job is developed, or duties change on an existing one, the job description is submitted to the position evaluation committee. The committee analyzes it, determines the overall point value, and assigns it to its proper place within the ranking structure. The result is an up-to-date listing of all the jobs at the organization from entry level to management. This is the first phase in determining salaries. The second phase is the assignment of jobs to grades and the establishment of salary ranges.

Grade Levels and Salary Ranges

Based on the total points received in job evaluation, jobs are assigned to a grade level. Each grade has an entry or minimum rate and a maximum salary payable for the jobs in that grade: the amounts between the entry rate and maximum comprise the salary range for the grade.

To ensure that the organization's salaries remain at a fair, competitive level, ranges and rates are checked continuously against those paid for similar positions in other organizations. Adjustments to the ranges are made periodically as area market rates change.

Usually employees begin at the bottom of each salary grade. Employees are considered for a merit increase after six months of satisfactory service. After this, they may receive an annual merit increase upon completion of satisfactory service. There are a total of six possible merit increases. Cost-of-living increases are granted periodically by the organization to all employees.

Payday

The Mack Organization's staff is paid on a biweekly basis, every other Friday. There are twenty-six pay periods each year. For pay purposes a normal week is Friday through Thursday.

Normally a full-time employee is quoted a weekly salary when hired. To compute the annual salary, multiply the weekly salary by 52, or the biweekly salary by 26. Their monthly salary equals their annual salary divided by 12.

All employees are paid by check. Attached to the check is a statement indicating gross pay, deductions required by law, any voluntary deductions, and net pay.

Full-time employees are paid up-to-date on payday — the amount they receive includes what they have earned through that payday. Any overtime or premium earnings are paid on a two-week delayed basis. Part-time employees are paid through the previous Thursday so that their hours may be properly credited.

Employees who have lost their checks or have had them stolen are requested to contact the Personnel Department, which issues a stop payment and prepares a new check.

Pay Advances

In extreme emergencies, it is possible for employees to be paid for those hours already worked during the current pay period. It is also possible for employees to receive a vacation advance before they go on vacation. All advances need the approval of an employee's supervisor. Six hours are needed to prepare checks.

Exhibit 5.4 Mack Organization's Wage Structure for Clerical Personnel

Class Title	Classified Salary	Number of Employees
Office Services Aide	$10,813 min $14,414 max	40
Office Services Assistant	$12,735 min $17,021 max	30

continued

Exhibit 5.4 *continued*

Secretary	$12,735 min $17,021 max	20
Senior Secretary	$13,827 min $18,522 max	40
Executive Secretary	$15,016 min $20,146 max	20

IN-BASKET ITEMS

Item 1
TO: Wage & Salary Division
FROM: Mary Wallace - Vice President
SUBJECT: Request for Promotion

This is to formally request your endorsement of my intent to promote Susan Anthony, an Office Services Aide in my office, to the position of Office Services Assistant. Ms. Anthony has taken the clerk typist test administered by your office and scored 55 wpm. Though I realize the requirement for Office Services Assistant is 70 wpm, Ms. Anthony possesses the necessary skills to perform all tasks in this office. Ms. Anthony has been with this office for five years and is a loyal and dedicated employee. I wholeheartedly encourage your endorsement of this recommendation. A vacant Office Services Assistant position is available in this office. Please advise as soon as possible.

Item 2
TO: Wage and Salary Section
FROM: Kelly Actor
SUBJECT: Promotion Request/Pay Increase

I have been with this company for ten years. My present position with this company is Senior Secretary, at the maximum pay level.

The Wispette Company has offered me a position which would give me a 9% increase in salary for similar duties.

Since I do enjoy my work, I hate to leave. However, my financial obligations to my family leave me no choice. My husband has recently been disabled, with no hope of employment for three years. As I mentioned, I have enjoyed my ten years with this company. My supervisors and I get along well. I have not missed any work during the ten years except for the two-week vacation during the summer.

If you will match the Wispette Company's offer, I would prefer to stay with your company. I understand there is no opening for an Executive Secretary — which would be a comparable position. I need an answer soon.

Item 3

TO: Wage and Salary Section
FROM: Jane Swenk, Supervisor
RE: Long-term employee wage dispute

M. O. Scott, a secretary, expressed concern that her daughter, also a secretary, was making an equal amount of money. M. O. has been employed for twenty-eight years, her daughter for five. Merit raises are given yearly only for the first five years, and M. O. has not gotten one in twenty-three years. I don't think this policy is fair. M. O. should get something for her longer service. Please respond so I can explain the situation to M. O.

Item 4

TO: Compensation Administration
FROM: Personnel Director
RE: Payroll Budget for Next Month

Please prepare a payroll budget for next month for clerical employees. Make whatever assumptions you feel are necessary in doing your calculations. Just let me know what the assumptions are. Many thanks.

Item 5

TO: Wage and Salary Section
FROM: Bob Franklin, Clerk Typist B
RE: Lost paycheck

Please issue me a new paycheck for the last pay period. I can't seem to find mine. I asked my wife if she had it or cashed it, and she doesn't remember. I don't think she did because I think she would have remembered it if she did cash it. My pay is $10,813 per year. Please do it as soon as possible.

Item 6

TO: Compensation Section
FROM: Betty Dyer, Supervisor
SUBJECT: Promotion for Tammy Tuff

Tammy Tuff is an excellent secretary in my office. She does an outstanding job with all assignments and performs beyond standards for a secretary in everything she does. She completes her assignments in half the time of other secretaries and voluntarily assumes extra duties after finishing her assignments.

In addition to her outstanding performance, Ms. Tuff has improved morale in the office since she entered on duty nine months ago. She always has a smile on her face and brightens the day for co-workers with her pleasant disposition. Best of all, she makes others feel important, and this has carried over to their work. Everyone seems to take pride in their work; consequently, performance and productivity are up.

Due to Tammy's influence, the turnover rate is zero, leaving her with no promotion potential in this office. Based on Tammy's excellent performance, skills that exceed the requirements of the job, and attitude that has improved morale, I feel that Tammy deserves a promotion within the office even though there is no Senior Secretary vacancy.

Item 7

TO: Wage & Salary
FROM: Hal Markley, Supervisor
SUBJECT: Early Issuance of Pay

I am leaving town in two hours and will be gone for four days on emergency business. Since I will be out of town on payday three days hence, it is essential that I receive my check before I leave.

Item 8

TO: W & S
FROM: McNamara, Department Manager

Mary White, an Office Services Aide, left two hours early yesterday, without permission, to attend a civil rights rally. Should she be paid for this time or not?

Item 9
TO: Wage and Salary Section
FROM: Sue L. Ross, Supervisor
SUBJECT: Promotion for Julie Tate

Julie Tate, Senior Secretary, has been temporarily assigned some of the duties of an Executive Secretary position. The position is temporarily vacant due to the Executive Secretary being on vacation.

Julie has been told by me that she may be assigned higher level duties on occasion, but she is not satisfied. She has threatened to take her complaint to the Personnel Office, insisting that she deserves financial compensation for absorbing some duties of an Executive Secretary. None of the additional duties is too difficult for Julie to handle, and she actually does an excellent job on all assignments when she stops complaining about her unfair treatment.

I am recommending that Julie be promoted to an Executive Secretary position so that I can assign her higher-level duties whenever my Executive Secretary is on vacation or sick leave. This way Julie would not complain about the grade level of her work, and the flow of work in the office would proceed smoothly without disruption.

Please respond to this recommendation.

Item 10
TO: Wage and Salary Section
FROM: Doris Pope
SUBJECT: Merit Pay Increase for Frances Brown, Secretary

I would like you to approve an extra 8 percent pay increase for my personal secretary, Ms. Frances Brown, to be effective immediately. Ms. Brown has served in this position throughout my eight-year tenure and that of my predecessor, for a total of twenty-five years. Ms. Brown will be presented with a letter of commendation at a departmental meeting this P.M. It would be helpful if you could complete the paperwork for this salary adjustment by 5:00 P.M. so that I can present it with the commendation.

Thanks,

Doris Pope

Doris Pope
Department Head

INCIDENT:
MERIT INCREASES

Dr. Carl Jones is Chairperson of the Department of Management in the College of Business Administration at a large state university in the East. He has been a member of the department for fourteen years and a full professor for five years. Last summer he was asked to assume the Chair after a screening committee conducted interviews and reviewed resumes for him and three other candidates.

Carl was very excited about the new challenges and has begun several innovative projects to enhance faculty research and consulting. The teaching function in the Department has always been first-rate while research has been somewhat weaker. Carl has continued to be very productive as a scholar, publishing three articles, two book chapters, and one proceedings article over the past year. He also made considerable progress on a management text which he is co-authoring. Finally, he has been active in his professional association, the Academy of Management, where he served as Chair of one of the professional divisions.

The University's policy is that all salary increases are based only on merit. Carl had developed a very sophisticated performance appraisal system for his faculty to help him quantify salary recommendations. His point system considers and weights different items in the areas of teaching, research, and service. Teaching and research were given weights of 40 percent each with service at 20 percent. For the coming academic year, his recommmended salary increases averaged 7 percent and ranged from 3 to 14 percent. Carl felt he had good documentation for all his recommendations.

Carl submitted his recommendations to Dean Edmund Smith and was pleased when all these recommendations were accepted. He then proceeded to schedule appointments to meet with each faculty member to discuss his recommendation, the reasons for the recommendation, and goals for the coming year. While a few of the faculty receiving lower increases indicated dissatisfaction with his weighting system, particularly the emphasis on research, these meetings generally went well.

Carl then submitted his own annual report detailing his accomplishments as Chair as well as his more personal accomplishments. From his perspective, he felt he deserved at least a 10 percent increase since his department had made major strides in a number of areas while the other departments had been standing still. Moreover, none of the other Chairs were professionally active on the national level and none had published in the past year. His teaching evaluations were also in the top 15 percent of faculty in the college.

Dean Smith sent out letters to all the Department Chairs in August. Carl was shocked to learn that his salary increase was just 7 percent. Information he received through the "grapevine" was that all the Chairs had received the 7 percent increase. He also learned from one of the other chairs that the Dean always gave the Chairs equal percentage increases each year. Contrary to the official university policy, there were no distinctions based on merit.

Carl was visibly upset about what he considered to be a major inequity. He then called the Dean's secretary to schedule an appointment to discuss the situation with Dean Smith.

Questions

1. Are "merit" salary increases always based on "merit"? Why or why not?
2. Why has Dean Smith had a policy of equal percentage salary increases for all department chairs despite the stated university policy?   Are all the chairs equally meritorious?
3. What should Dr. Jones say to Dean Smith at their meeting? What are the long-range benefits of a true "merit" program? What are the problems associated with the lack of such a "merit" system for department chairs? How likely is the discussion to change Dean Smith's decision and future behavior? Why? If the Dean does not change his policy, what are the long-run implications for the college?

SKILL BUILDER:
APPLYING THE FLSA—
IS THIS JOB EXEMPT?

I. *Objectives:*
   1. To familiarize you with the requirements of the Fair Labor Standards Act.
   2. To show you how to apply the law in determining whether jobs are exempt or nonexempt.

II. *Time Required to Complete:* 30-45 minutes

III. *Instructions:*
   1. Assume that you are working as a job analyst for your state. One part of your job involves determining whether administrative jobs are exempt from the wage and hour provisions of the Fair Labor Standards Act (FLSA).
   2. Read the excerpt from the FLSA provisions pertaining to exempt status for administrative positions (Exhibit 5.5). Your instructor may also require you to review pertinent state laws.
   3. Review the Federal Wage and Hour Exemption Determination Form completed for two different jobs in a state agency (Exhibits 5.6 and 5.7) and determine the exempt status of each job. Prepare a half-page summary of your findings and justification thereof.

Exhibit 5.5 FSLA Wage and Hour Exemptions for Administrative Personnel

EXEMPTIONS

Executive, administrative, professional, or outside sales personnel: An exemption from both the minimum wage and overtime pay requirements is provided in section 13(a)(1) of FLSA for any employee employed in a bona fide executive, administrative, professional, or outside sales capacity, as these terms are defined and delimited in regulations of the Secretary of Labor. An employee will qualify for exemption if he or she meets *all* of the pertinent tests relating to duties, responsibilities, and salary as stipulated in the applicable section of Regulations, 29 C.R.F. Part 541.

Administrative: In order to be exempt as a bona fide administrative employee, *all* of the following tests must be met:

(a) The employee's primary duty must be either:

  (1) Responsible office or nonmanual work directly related to the management policies or general business operations of the employer or the employer's customers; or

  (2) Responsible work that is directly related to academic instruction or training carried on in the administration of a school system or educational establishment; and

(b) The employee must customarily and regularly exercise discretion and independent judgment, as distinguised from using skills and following procedures, and must have the authority to make important decisions; and

(c) The employee must:

  (1) Regularly assist a proprietor or bona fide executive or administrative employee; or

  (2) Perform work under only general supervision along specialized or technical lines requiring special training, experience or knowledge; or

  (3) Execute under only general supervision special assignments; and

(d) The employee must not spend more than 20 percent of the time worked in the work week (no more than 40 percent if employed by a retail or service establishment) on work that is not directly and closely related to the administrative duties discussed above, and

(e) The employee must be paid on a salary or fee basis at a rate of not less than $155 a week (or $130 a week in Puerto Rico, Virgin Islands or American Samoa), exclusive of board, lodging, or other facilities, or in the case of academic administrative personnel in public or private schools, the salary requirement for exemption must be at least $155 a week or one which is at least equal to the entrance salary for teachers in the employing school system or educational establishment or institution.

continued

Exhibit 5.5 *continued*

Special proviso for administrative employees paid on a salary or fee basis of at least $250 per week: An administrative employee who is paid on a salary or fee basis of at least $250 a week ($200 per week in Puerto Rico, the Virgin Islands, or American Samoa), exclusive of board, lodging, or other facilities, will be exempt if:

(a) The employee's primary duty consists of either:

    (1) Responsible office or nonmanual work directly related to the management policies or general business operations of the employer or the employer's customers; or

    (2) Responsible work that is directly related to academic instruction or training carried on in the administration of a school system or educational establishment; and

(b) Such primary duty includes work requiring the exercise of discretion and independent judgment.

Source: U.S. Department of Labor, Employment Standards Administration, Wage & Hour Division, WH Publication 1281.

Exhibit 5.6 Federal Wage and Hour Exemption Determination Form A

Inventory Control Officer	*2054*	*9/5/8x*
Position Title (Classification)	Position Number	Date
Purchasing		*Mary Lincoln, Director*
Department or Office		Department or Office Head
Harry Phipps *(60) $15,070*		*Todd Jenkins, Asst. Director*
Incumbent Grade/Salary		Immediate Supervisor

JOB SUMMARY

State in general terms the overall purpose and/or function of the position: The responsibilities of the inventory control officer can be divided into three categories: (1) Taking the Annual Physical Inventory, (2) Tagging new equipment as it arrives, and (3) Direct responsibility for surplus property.

MAJOR DUTIES AND RESPONSIBILITIES

Summarize the major duties and responsibilities of the position and indicate the approximate percentage of time required for each:

continued

Exhibit 5.6 *continued*

1. Schedule inventories in advance.
2. Supervise the actual inventory-in-progress to insure that every precaution is taken to produce accurate inventory records.
3. Locate any items not accounted for.
4. Maintain accurate records of fixed assets.
5. Train inventory staff in the proper procedures for conducting the inventory.
6. Tag all new fixed assets.
7. Arrange for the disposal of surplus property.

(Percentage of time for responsibilities: physical inventory 70%; tagging new equipment 20%; and surplus property 10%.)

Answer the following questions regarding the position:

1. *Number of people directly supervised:*

Full-Time Supervision	Part-Time Supervision
_____ Administrative	_____ Administrative
_____ Clerical	__6__ Clerical
_____ Service	_____ Service

2. *Describe the responsibility for hiring, firing, promoting, etc. of subordinates:*
    None; handled by Director of Purchasing.

3. *Describe supervision and guidance received:*
    Most of the instructions for the job come from guidelines established by the State Fixed Assets System and the State Auditors.

4. *What special training, experience, or knowledge is necessary to perform the duties of the job?*
    No special training required or education. Must be knowledgeable of Fixed Assets System.

5. *Describe the use of discretion and independent judgment:*
    Some. Most procedures are routine, however.

6. *Describe any original and creative work you may do requiring invention, imagination, or special creative talents (if applicable). What percentage of time is spent on creative work and what percentage is spent on routine (non-creative, non-discretionary, or non-analytical) work?*
    Not applicable. Procedures are routine.

continued

Exhibit 5.6 *continued*

The above statements constitute an accurate and complete description of the duties of the position.

Harry Phipps

Incumbent Signature

Todd Jenkins

Supervisor Signature

Exhibit 5.7 Federal Wage and Hour Exemption Determination Form B

Director of Administrative Computing	*3159*	*9/5/8x*
Position Title (Classification)	Position Number	Date
Computing Services		*William Bern, Director*
Department or Office		Department or Office Head
Earl Atwood *75 $29,150/year*		*Vincent Pollard, Assoc. Director*
Incumbent Grade/Salary		Immediate Supervisor

JOB SUMMARY

State in general terms the overall purpose and/or function of the position: Direct systems and programming staff support for computer systems for Business Affairs. Includes accounts payable, purchasing, cash receipts, accounts receivable, general ledger, chart of accounts, security and traffic payroll, personnel, statewide reporting system, physical plant, fixed assets, internal auditing, and auxiliary services.

MAJOR DUTIES AND RESPONSIBILITIES

Summarize the major duties and responsibilities of the position and indicate the approximate percentage of time required for each:

1. Recruit and staff available positions at budgeted level.
2. Direct, supervise, and train programmers and analysts.
3. Evaluate staff performance and recommend promotions and other actions.
4. Maintain existing computing systems.
5. Develop new systems and direct development if user training and documentation.

continued

Exhibit 5.7 *continued*

6. Assist in establishing and implementing departmental objectives.
    (50 percent of time is spent on management and supervision of staff and
    the other 50 percent is spent on developing new systems, maintaining
    present systems and departmental planning.)

Answer the following questions regarding the position:

1. *Number of people directly supervised:*
    Full-Time Supervision   *Part-Time Supervision*

    __8__ Administrative   _____ Administrative
    __1__ Clerical   _____ Clerical
    _____ Service   _____ Service

2. *Describe the responsibility for hiring, firing, promoting, etc. of subor-
    dinates:*
    Full responsibility for the 9 employees who report to me.

3. *Describe supervision and guidance received:*
    Overall direction and priorities are provided by the Associate Director
    and Director of Computing Services.

4. *What special training, experience, or knowledge is necessary to perform
    the duties of the job?*
    Four-year college degree in Business Administration or Management In-
    formation Systems, with courses of study in Business, Computer
    Science, and Accounting; minimum of four years experience in systems
    design, programming and project management and/or advanced studies;
    and five years of experience in computer systems design, programming,
    and management including supervision of technical and professional
    employees; proficient in programming languages, especially COBOL.

5. *Describe the use of discretion and independent judgment:*
    The position involves a great deal of discretion and judgment in design-
    ing new systems, responding to user needs, and managing personnel in
    the department.

6. *Describe any original and creative work you may do requiring invention,
    imagination, or special creative talents (if applicable). What percentage
    of time is spent on creative work and what percentage is spent on
    routine (non-creative, non-discretionary, or non-analytical) work?*
    The majority of my work is analytical involving the design of new com-
    puter systems to handle various administrative needs at the agency.
    About 60 percent of my job is non-routine requiring intense mental con-
    centration and problem solving skills.

continued

Exhibit 5.7 *continued*

The above statements constitute an accurate and complete description of the duties of the position.

Incumbent Signature   Supervisor Signature

Part 6

Orientation, Training, and Development

The training and development of human resources is becoming increasingly important as organizations attempt to maintain their long-term competitiveness and productivity. Estimates indicate that U.S. organizations spend over $100 billion annually on training and development programs for employees. Training and development may be used to remove employee performance deficiencies, to prevent employee skill obsolescence as new technologies occur, to retrain displaced workers, to train employees in organizational safety requirements, to develop management personnel, and to manage employee career development. In recent years, the latter activity has gained greater emphasis because many organizations recognize career management as a critical component of strategic human resource management. Consequently, organizations are making greater efforts to better match employee career goals and interests to organizational human resource needs.

The materials in this section cover many of the contemporary human resource training activities found in organizations. The first case, "Career Development at Applied Electronics," addresses career development and its relationship to other human resource activities. The implementation problems associated with designing effective safety programs in organizations is explored in "The Safety Training Program" case. The incident, "Zan Marshall's Introduction to Grotto Fish," provides a provocative scenario for examining problems in organizational entry for new employees. The exercise, "Design and Evaluation of Training Programs," requires you to match training methods to training objectives and to determine appropriate methods of evaluating training programs. "On-the-Job Training" provides you with practice in conducting training. Finally, the skill builder enables you to learn how to use task analysis to identify training needs for a particular job.

CASE:
CAREER DEVELOPMENT
AT ELECTRONIC APPLICATIONS

Electronic Applications Corporation is a major producer of silicon chips for the computer industry. It is located southeast of San Francisco in an area of high technology firms. Since its founding in 1972, the company has grown rapidly in terms of sales and profits, thus enhancing its stock price many times over.

However, human resource policies have tended to lag behind company growth. Emphasis has been on reactive policies to meet the requirements of external organizations such as the federal government. Human resources have not been a high priority.

Recently, Harold Sweeney has been hired as Director of Human Resources for the company. Sweeney had previously served as an Assistant Personnel Director for a large "blue-chip" corporation in southern California. He took his present position not only because of an increase in pay and responsibility, but also because of what he termed "the challenge of bringing this company from a 1950s human resources mentality to one more compatible with the realities of the 1990s."

Sweeney has been on the job for four months and has been assessing the situation to determine the more significant human resource problems. One significant problem seems to be high turnover among electrical engineers who work in Research and Development. This is the core of the research function and turnover rates have averaged about 30 percent per year over the past three years.

In assessing the cause of the problem, Sweeney checked area wage surveys and found Electronic Applications paid 5 - 8 percent *above* the market for various categories of electrical engineers. Since the company did not have a formal exit interview system, he could not check out other possible explanations through that mechanism. However, through informal conversations with a large number of individuals, including the engineers themselves, he learned that many of the engineers felt "dead-ended" in the technical aspects of engineering.

In particular, the Research and Development Department had lost some of the younger engineers who had been considered to be on the "fast track." Most had gone to competitors in the local area.

One particular Research and Development employee who impressed Sweeney was Helen Morgan. Helen was twenty-nine years old, had a B.S. degree in Electrical Engineering from California Institute of Technology, and was studying for her M.B.A. at the University of Santa Clara at night. Helen had been employed for seven years, three in an entry-level engineering position and four as a section chief. The latter promotion was the highest position in Research and Development other than the position of Director of Research and Development.

Helen claimed that "the company doesn't really care about its good people." In her view, the present director, Harry James, doesn't want to allow his better people to move up in the organization. He is more interested in keeping them in his own department so he can meet his own goals without having to orient and train new people. Helen also claimed she was told she "has a bright future with the company" by both James and the former Personnel Director. Her performance appraisals have been uniformly excellent.

She went on to criticize the company for using an appraisal form with no section dealing with future potential or future goals, no rewards for supervisors who develop their subordinates, no human resources planning to identify future job openings, no centralized job information or job positioning system, no career paths and/or career ladders, and attitudinal barriers against women in management positions.

Sweeney checked out the information Morgan had provided him and found it to be accurate. Moreover, he heard through the "grapevine" that she is in line for an excellent position with a nearby competitor. Clearly, he has an even greater challenge than he had anticipated. He realizes he has an immediate problem concerning high turnover of certain key employees. In addition, however, he also has a series of interconnected problems associated with career development. But he is not quite sure what to do and in what order.

Questions

1. What additional questions should Sweeney ask or what additional information is be needed before proceeding toward a solution to this problem? Why?
2. What are the individual and organizational benefits of a formalized career development system?
3. If Sweeney decides to develop a formalized career development system at Electronic Applications, what components or types of services should be offered? Why?
4. Should the career development activities be integrated with other human resource management activities? If yes, which ones? Why?

CASE:
THE SAFETY TRAINING PROGRAM

Houghton Refrigeration Company builds refrigerators for other large refrigerator companies such as General Electric Co. It employs about 300 people, mostly assembly line workers, and is located in a small rural town in Utah. The company typically builds, on a contract basis, chest-type freezers and small bar-type refrigerators. On occasion, however, it also builds standard size refrigerators.

The president of the company is a former engineer, as are most of the other executives. These individuals are very knowledgeable about engineering, but have received little training in the basic principles of management.

During the summer months, volume at the factory increases significantly, and the company needs to hire about forty new employees to handle the heavy workload. Most of these new employees are college students who attend a small private college located about fifteen minutes from the plant. Some high school students are hired as well.

When a new employee is hired, the company asks him or her to complete an application blank and then to show up at the plant gate ready for work. Employees receive no orientation. The worker is shown to a work station and after a minimum amount of on-the-job training, the new employee is expected to start performing a job. Most of the jobs are quite simple, and hence, the training is typically completed within five to ten minutes. The first line supervisor usually shows the employee how to do a job once, then watches while the employee does the job once, leaves, and comes back in about twenty minutes to see how the employee is progressing. Typical jobs at the plant include screwing fourteen screws into the sides of a freezer, placing a piece of insulation into the freezer lid, and handing out supplies from the tool room.

Joe Gleason
remember this
guy

The company has had excellent experience with college students over the years. Much of the success can be attributed to the older workers coming to the aid of the new employees when trouble or difficulties arise. Most new employees are able to perform their jobs reasonably well after their on-the-job training is completed. However, when unexpected difficulties arise, they are usually not prepared for them and therefore need assistance from others.

The older workers have been especially helpful to students working in the "press room." However, Joe Gleason, the first-line supervisor there, finds it amusing to belittle the college students whenever they make any mistakes. He relishes showing a student once how to use a press to bend a small piece of metal, then exclaims, "You're a hot-shot college student; now let's see you do it." He then watches impatiently while the student invariably makes a mistake and then jokingly announces for all to hear, "That's wrong! How did you ever get into college anyway? Try it again, dummy."

One summer the company experienced a rash of injuries to its employees. Although most of the injuries were minor, the company felt it imperative to conduct a series of short training programs on safe material-handling techniques. The company president was at a loss as to who should conduct the training. The personnel director was a sixty-four-year-old former engineer who was about to retire and was a poor speaker. The only other employee in the Personnel Department was a new nineteen-year-old secretary who knew nothing about proper handling techniques. Out of desperation the president finally decided to ask Bill Young, the first-line supervisor of the "lid-line," to conduct the training. Bill had recently attended a training program himself on safety and was active in the Red Cross. Bill reluctantly agreed to conduct the training. It was to be done on a departmental basis with small groups of ten to fifteen employees attending each session.

At the first of these training sessions, Bill Young nervously stood up in front of fourteen employees, many of whom were college students, and read his presentation in a monotone voice. His entire speech lasted about one minute and consisted of the following text:

> Statistics show that an average of thirty persons injure their backs on the job each day in this state. None of us wants to become a "statistic."
>
> The first thing that should be done before lifting an object is to look it over and decide whether you can handle it alone or if help is needed. Get help if there's any doubt as to whether the load is safely within your capacity.
>
> Next, look over the area where you're going to be carrying the object. Make sure it's clear of obstacles. You may have to do a little housekeeping before moving your load. After you have checked out the load and route you're going to travel, the following steps should be taken for your safety in lifting:
>
> 1. Get a good footing close to the load.
> 2. Place your feet 8 to 12 inches apart.
> 3. Bend your knees to grasp the load.
> 4. Bend your knees outward, straddling the load.
> 5. Get a firm grip.
> 6. Keep the load close to your body.
> 7. Lift gradually.
>
> Once you've lifted the load, you'll eventually have to set it down — so bend your legs again — and follow the lifting procedures in reverse. Make sure that your fingers clear the pinch points. And, finally, it's a good idea to set one corner down first.

After Bill's speech ended, the employees immediately returned to work. By the end of the day, however, everyone in the plant had heard about the training fiasco, and all, except the president, were laughing about it.

Questions

1. Evaluate the company's on-the-job training program. Should it be changed?
2. Should the company install an employee orientation program for new factory workers, or isn't one necessary?
3. What changes should be made in the company's safety training program?

EXERCISE:
DESIGN AND EVALUATION
OF TRAINING PROGRAMS

I. *Objectives:*
   1. To help you determine which training methods are most appropriate for achieving particular objectives.
   2. To show you the linkages between training objectives, training methods, and training evaluation.
   3. To help you learn how to identify and write training objectives.
   4. To build skill in the evaluation of training programs.
II. *Out-of-Class Preparation Time:* 1 hour
III. *In-Class Time Suggested:* 45 minutes
IV. *Procedures:* Prior to the class meeting in which this exercise will be discussed, read the entire exercise and complete Forms 1 and 2 in pencil or on a separate sheet of paper. At the beginning of the class period, the instructor should divide the class into discussion groups of three to five students.

Each group should begin by completing Form 1. If you are unfamiliar with any of the training methods listed, consult your text or ask your instructor.

Look at each training objective/outcome and then determine which training methods would be *most* appropriate for achieving each of the six training objectives. Since each group member comes into the class period with his or her own ideas on which training method is most appropriate for achieving which objectives, there may be a need for some discussion and negotiation before a group consensus can emerge.

Put an "x" beside the method that seems *most* appropriate for achieving each objective or outcome. For example, if you believe that a lecture with questions would be a good method of facilitating knowledge acquisition on the part of a training program participant, put an "x" in that space. Then put an "x" wherever the particular training method seems appropriate for achieving particular training objectives or outcomes. For each of the six objectives or outcomes, you should have at least three, but no more than eight, training methods which are identified as most appropriate.

Now look at the data in Exhibit 6.1. These data are taken from a training needs analysis of Corporation X. The percent opposite each occupational group indicates the percentage of members in that group citing *any* training need at all. The numbers under that, opposite each of the two training needs identified for each group, indicate the percentage of that group requesting training in those subject areas.

This company has had no previous formal training programs for its employees and the newly hired Director of Training has asked your group to answer the following questions:

1. Which two occupational groups should I provide training programs for during my first year? Why?
2. What training objectives should I set for each occupational group and training need?
3. What training methods should I use to meet these objectives?
4. What training evaluation method should I use to evaluate each training method or program?

Before completing Form 2, review the information in Form 1 and Exhibit 6.1. Select the two occupational groups which you feel should be the new Director of Training's top training priority for the coming year. Then select only one training need for each occupational group. For example, if you feel training programs for executives are a priority, choose *either* strategic planning *or* marketing. Write the two occupational groups you choose and one training need for each on Form 2.

Now develop specific objectives for each of the two training programs you are recommending be offered. If your group selected strategic planning for executives as one of the two programs, then possible objectives might be increased knowledge about the process of strategic planning or successful development of a strategic plan for the corporation or the executive's department. Likewise, an objective for a performance appraisal program for middle managers might be the design of an appropriate performance appraisal form and process for the individual middle manager's particular situation.

Once the objectives are determined, they usually fit under one of the six major objectives or outcomes listed on Form 1. Based upon your previous analysis in Form 1, select up to three training methods for achieving these objectives with the particular occupational group. For example, achieving the objective of helping executives improve their strategic planning skills might involve on-the-job coaching by consultants or other executives skilled in this process, business games, lectures, or cases.

The final step is to determine the most appropriate method of evaluating the particular training program or programs. The four major methods of evaluation in order of their degree of complexity and difficulty are as follows:

1. Participant reaction—usually determined by a questionnaire immediately at the conclusion of the training program.
2. Learning—assessment of knowledge about or attitudes toward a particular subject, both before and after a training experience.
3. Behavioral change—changes in on-the-job behavior or performance as measured by performance appraisals, subordinates, perceptions, supervisor's perceptions, and/or individual productivity data.
4. Organizational effectiveness—decreases in departmental or organizational costs, turnover, absenteeism, and grievances, and increases in departmental or organizational sales, income, or productivity as compared to a control group of those not attending training.

Complete Form 2 by selecting up to four training evaluation methods for the training methods you have selected. If you selected three training methods, then use all three columns and fill in as many evaluation methods as you feel are appropriate.

Now look at the questions on Form 3 and answer them in your group. Once all the questions are answered, raise your hands and let the instructor know your group has finished the exercise. Appoint a spokesperson to discuss your group's recommendations. When all groups have finished, compare results in each of the groups and discuss possible reasons for differences between the groups.

Exhibit 6.1 Results of a Training Needs Assessment Survey by Occupational Group

Top Two Areas of Training Need by Occupational Group	Percentage Citing Need
1. Executives	67
Strategic planning	38
Marketing	27
2. Middle managers	84
Performance appraisal techniques	44
Employee motivation	32
3. Professionals	27
Effective communication skills	16
Principles of supervision	14
4. Salespeople	28
How to close a sale	22
Effective communication skills	12
5. First-line supervisors	47
Employee motivation	31
Principles of supervision	21
6. Production workers	22
Discipline	16
Production scheduling	10
7. Office/clerical staff	38
Time management	25
Assertiveness training	20

Form 1 The Effectiveness of Alternative Training Methods for Achieving Various Training Objectives/Outcomes

Training Method	Knowledge Acquisition	Attitude Change	Problem-Solving Skills	Interpersonal Skills	Participant Acceptance	Knowledge Retention
Information Processing:						
Lecture (with questions)	✓					
Conference (discussion)	✓					
T-Group		✓		✓		
Laboratory training		✓	✓	✓	✓	
Observation	✓					
Closed-circuit TV	✓					
Programmed instruction	✓					✓
Correspondence courses	✓					
Movies	✓					
Reading lists	✓					

Simulation:					
Cases					
Incidents					
Role playing					
Business games					
In-Basket					
On-the-Job:					
Job rotation					
Committee assignments					
On-the-job coaching					
Feedback from performance appraisal					
Apprenticeships					

Form 2 The Relationship Between Training Objectives, Methods, and Evaluation Methods

Occupational Group:

Training Need:

Training Objectives	Training Methods	Training Evaluation Methods		
		Training Method 1	Training Method 2	Training Method 3
1.	1.	1.	1.	
2.	2.	2.	2.	
3.	3.	3.	3.	
		4.	4.	

Occupational Group:

Training Need:

Training Objectives	Training Methods	Training Evaluation Methods		
		Training Method 1	Training Method 2	Training Method 3
1.	1.	1.	1.	
2.	2.	2.	2.	
3.	3.	3.	3.	
		4.	4.	

Form 3 Questions

1. Why did you select the particular two occupations for the highest priority in training?

2. Once you had determined the occupational group, training need, and training objectives, how did you determine which training method would be most appropriate?

3. What problems might you encounter if you attempted to implement evaluation processes based on improvements in individual participant behavior or organizational effectiveness? Why?

4. What are the most effective training or educational methods to facilitate your own learning? Why?

5. Consider the most complex job you have ever had. What would have been the most effective method of training for that job? Why? What method (if any) was actually used?

EXERCISE:
ON-THE-JOB TRAINING

I. *Objectives:*
  1. To make you aware of the problems a supervisor may encounter when training employees.
  2. To provide you with practice in conducting on-the-job training.
  3. To teach you how to prepare training aids.
  4. To teach you how to evaluate on-the-job training.
  5. To familiarize you with the major on-the-job training steps.
II. *Out-of-Class Preparation Time:* 1 - 2 hours

III. *In-Class Time Suggested:* 45 minutes

IV. *Procedures*:   An important task for most supervisors is to instruct new employees on the methods and procedures necessary to perform various operations involved in a job. Initially, the employee may be totally unfamiliar with a particular task. This places an additional burden on the manager to make his or her instructions as clear and precise as possible. In this exercise you will be asked to train one or more other members of the class on how to perform a task. After the training is complete, it will be critiqued.

During the class period prior to the one in which this exercise will be conducted, the instructor will divide the class into groups of three to five members. Each group should then meet outside of class to prepare for the exercise. They should begin by selecting the task they wish to teach one or more class members. For example, they could pick one of the following:

1. How to lift heavy objects safely.
2. How to fold a napkin like they do at fancy restaurants.
3. How to tie a special knot used by tree surgeons, merchant marine personnel, or those in the Navy.
4. How to fix a dripping faucet such as one a plumber might fix.
5. How to use a volt-ohm meter such as an electrician might use.

In selecting a task, pick one which is performed in industry, one which most class members don't already know how to perform, and one sufficiently complicated that trainees can't perform it instantly. Remember, you will have to provide all of the materials necessary to perform the task.

Once the group has selected a task, it should develop, and make copies for each class member, of a training aid such as the ones used by Ramada Inns, Inc. Its aids include:

1. Training objectives.
2. Benefits of performing the task for the employee, the company, and the customers.
3. A list of tools, materials, and equipment necessary to perform the task correctly.
4. A list showing each step in sequence necessary to perform the task, including the necessary illustrations.
5. An evaluation form to evaluate the trainee.

Finally, you must choose the best approach for conducting the training (lecture, demonstrations, etc.) and the steps which will be followed when conducting the training. A spokesperson (the one who will actually conduct the training for the group) should also be selected.

At the start of class, the instructor will select four or more groups to actually conduct on-the-job training. Depending upon the task, the instructor will also select one or more students to serve as trainees. At this point, the spokesperson for each group selected will hand out a copy of the training aid to each class member and, one at a time, conduct training. This will be followed by a critique of each training session and training aid by all class members. Toward the end of class, those groups which did not actually conduct training during class will be asked to distribute a copy of their training aid to all class members.

INCIDENT:
ZAN MARSHALL'S
INTRODUCTION TO GROTTO FISH

Zan Marshall graduated from Bentley College anxious to start her career at Grotto Fish as a financial analyst. She felt it was clear from how the interview process had gone that they genuinely wanted to hire more women eventually, and she thought it would be exciting to be the first female recruit.

It was understandable that no females had worked there in the early days of the company. Working in a smelly factory cleaning and filleting fish wasn't appealing to anyone. But now the company had grown considerably and Zan would be located in the new administrative offices across the street from the factory. She felt that taking the position would pave the way for other women.

Besides, she grew up with four brothers and knew now to function as the "lone female." Since most of her childhood friends were male, she felt confident that she would get along well at Grotto Fish.

Two months into her job she did grow somewhat tired of dealing with the funny looks and teasing comments: "How does it feel to be the only crab in a flounder net?" "What's a nice girl like you doing working in a dirty business like this?"

But she tried not to let it bother her. She shrugged it off thinking they were a fun-loving bunch of guys. Though she did sometimes wonder if they really didn't want her around, she didn't really think they were singling her out to tease.

. . . until one day in late June.

Since her first day on the job people had been promising her a tour of the plant, but had never gotten around to it.

As Zan tells the story:

I didn't even think it was unusual that they would pick the day I wore a white skirt and jacket. I even had on white sandals.

My boss and another analyst took me over and began the tour. They were very proud of the equipment and all the magical things it could do, so I was trying to do a lot of "ooing" and "ahhing" at the right time. As we were

Contributed by Diane McKinney Kellogg of Bentley College.

standing at one machine, I noticed that the two men working on it had walked away just as the machine stopped. So had my tour guides. As I turned around to see what was happening, my boss said, "The machine is beginning its cool down cycle." And just then there was a great big swish of water which surrounded the machine, and me!

They burst out laughing, along with everyone else in the plant. And there I was worrying about whether the water would come any higher than my already-wet hemline.

I was so mortified I didn't know what to do, but I wasn't about to look mortified! So I gathered all the cheerfulness I could as the water subsided, and said: "What's next?"

Questions

1. Should Grotto Fish have prepared other employees for Zan's arrival? If so, how?
2. Do you think the organization should have given Zan a "special" orientation program to better prepare her for the organization culture of Grotto Fish?
3. Should all organizations develop special orientation programs for women? For minorities?

SKILL BUILDER:
IDENTIFYING TRAINING NEEDS THROUGH TASK ANALYSIS

I. *Objectives:*
>   1. To introduce you to the process and purposes of assessing training needs.
>   2. To give you practice in determining training needs for a job.

II. *Time Required to Complete:* 2 - 3 hours

III. *Instructions:* There are generally three analyses used to determine an organization's training needs: organization analysis, task or operations analysis, and person analysis. This assignment allows you to perform a task analysis for a particular job by interviewing and observing a job holder. A task analysis involves systematic collection of data about a specific job. Its purpose is to determine what an employee should be taught to perform the job at the desired level. It generally includes a description of the major tasks of the job, standards of performance, how the tasks are to be performed to meet the standards, and the skills, knowledge, and abilities necessary. You will conduct the task analysis by following the steps:

Step 1: Select a job to analyze. You may choose a job currently held by a relative, friend, fellow student, etc. (If you completed the Job Description Exercise in Part III, you may use that job.) Ask the job holder if you may interview him or her about the position and/or also observe him or her performing the job.

Step 2: Obtain a job description for the job you selected or prepare one by interviewing the job holder. The job description should describe in general terms the worker's major duties and responsibilities. For example, a job description for an accounts receivable clerk might include the following duties and responsibilities:

a. Invoice shipments to customers on a monthly basis.
b. Prepare journal vouchers at the end of the month to record cash receipts and sales by product lines.

When preparing the job description, be sure to include those things that are critical to performing the job satisfactorily, no matter how infrequently or briefly they occur and the knowledge, skills, and abilities needed.

Step 3: This step involves identifying the tasks associated with performing each of the major duties of the job. You are to identify the overt, observable behaviors that are involved in performing the job. Arrange (if possible) to observe the worker performing his or her job and develop a list of the tasks involved. A task listing includes behavioral statements of how the job is to be performed. Using the example presented earlier for the accounts receivable clerk, the tasks associated with invoicing customers might include:

a. Pull and review invoice master
b. Extend and update invoice master
c. Add correct discount and freight charges
d. Make necessary amount of copies on copy machine.

When you complete this step, you should have a report which includes the title of the job, the major duties (responsibilities) of the job, the tasks associated with the each duty/responsibility, and the knowledge and skills required of job incumbents.

Step 4: Once you have completed steps 1 - 3, answer the following questions and include them in your report:

a. What training would benefit a person performing the job? If you had to design a training program for the job, what content areas would be needed based on your analysis?
b. What training method would be best? Why? (On-the-job training, seminars, apprenticeships, vestibule, etc.)

Part 7

Labor Relations

The presence of a labor union in an organization often results in less management autonomy and flexibility in the design and implementation of personnel/human resource management policies. In recent years, there has been a decline in overall union membership and a growing recognition by both management and labor of the need for joint efforts in addressing productivity and efficiency problems in the workplace. This recognition has had a profound effect on the nature of collective bargaining with greater instances of concessionary bargaining and union willingness to exchange wage gains for job security. Both line managers and personnel professionals should be familiar with current trends in the labor movement, the unionization process, the factors that cause employees to join unions, the legal aspects of labor-management relations, the collective bargaining process, and contract administration.

The materials in this section focus on both the traditional aspects of labor relations and the more current issues confronting organizations today. The "Union Organizing at SGA Industries" case involves a union-organizing campaign in an industry threatened by foreign competition. The implementation of a joint labor-management quality-of-work-life program is the focus of the second case in this section. The collective bargaining role play gives you practical experience in negotiating a labor contract under conditions existing in many labor-management negotiations today. The "Labor Arbitration" exercise allows you to examine the different perceptual sets in the arbitration process. The incident, "Who Should Empty the Trash Cans?" focuses on the kinds of issues that arise in the day-to-day administration of a labor contract. The second incident, "The Two-Tier Wage Structure," allows you to examine the use of two-tier wage structures in the airline industry. The skill builder gives you practice in developing an effective company communication during a union campaign.

CASE:
UNION ORGANIZING AT SGA INDUSTRIES

Introduction

President White sat in his office at SGA Industries thinking about the union election taking place down at the plant auditorium. He felt that the company had waged a successful campaign to persuade workers that their best interests would be served only if the company remained union free. As he awaited the election results, his mind began to wander back to the events leading up to today's election.

Background

SGA Industries is best known as the world's largest producer of women's hosiery and employs approximately 6,500 people in ten plants in five communities in Georgia and South Carolina. The company's headquarters is located in Anderson, Georgia. The company's sales subsidiary, SGA Inc., has twelve offices in major market areas throughout the United States and sells its products directly to distributors around the world. The company's strategy of strong identification with the customer has made the SGA name one of the most recognized in the entire hosiery industry.

SGA was founded in 1907 by Sam Gerome Anderson. Anderson built the company and the community was named after him in 1910. Ever since, the fortunes of Anderson residents have been interwoven with those of SGA. Over the years the company supported the community, donating land and money for churches, schools, hospitals and providing jobs for nearly a third of the town's residents. As the years passed, further expansion and product diversification occurred, and the company gained a reputation as an industry leader in the design, production, and marketing of women's and men's hose and undergarments.

After the death of the last family member, Alexandra Anderson, SGA was managed by four chief executive officers in less than a dozen years before the company was purchased for $250 million by Jack Phillips. The new owner was a well-known Atlanta entrepreneur and business leader. Soon after the purchase, Phillips appointed Ted White as President of SGA.

Labor-Management Relations

Over the years SGA enjoyed a reputation as a steady job provider in an unstable industry. The company provided for its workers and treated them like family members. Many believe that the company's generosity to its employees and the

Contributed by Gerald Calvasina of the University of North Carolina at Charlotte.

town of Anderson helped to defeat an earlier union organizing drive by the Textile Workers of America by a vote of 3,937 to 1,782. At the time of the vote, the Chairman called it "an expression of confidence by employees." The SGA vote was viewed as a severe blow to union organizing efforts in the South.

When Phillips purchased SGA, he announced that his major goals would be to improve the community and to improve the quality of life for SGA employees and their families. Phillips invested over $100 million to reach these goals. The total included funds for pay increases, new job benefits, capital improvements, including the use of robots, community improvements and other contributions. These improvements were also accompanied by a shift in management philosophy. The theme of the new management approach was self-sufficiency, and it signaled an end to the benevolent paternalism that had so long characterized employee relations at SGA. Greater emphasis was placed on employee performance and productivity.

During the mid-eighties, the entire hosiery industry experienced major problems. Growing foreign competition and imports had a negative impact on domestic hosiery manufacturers. Many manufacturers attempted to reverse the impact by intensive capital investments in new technology, reorganization and downsizing of plants, and by instituting programs to improve employee productivity and efficiency. SGA was not spared from this competition. Its international sales fell dramatically from $26 million to $10 million. Faced with increasing imports and weak consumer sales, the company was forced to lay off 1,500 employees, reduce pay scales, and to rescind many of the perks that the workers had enjoyed under the Anderson family. Many of these changes drew worker protests and created a good deal of tension between workers and management.

Wages in the industry had been rising steadily but were still lower than wages in the manufacturing sector in general. On a regional basis, the differential was still quite wide, with a study showing that wages ranged from $4.46 per hour in South Carolina to $7.90 in Michigan. In addition, as technology advanced, more skilled operatives were required, thus increasing cost of turnover to companies. Employers in the industry also were becoming increasingly more dependent on women and minorities for employees. At SGA 40 percent of the employees were women and 35 percent of the total work force were minorities. Minorities and women made up less than 2 percent of the management staff.

The Election Campaign

Despite its earlier defeat, the Amalgamated Clothing and Textile Workers Union (ACTWU) was back in Anderson, armed and ready for an organizing effort that would divert the attention of SGA management for several long and tense months.

While many employers learn of union organizing efforts by their employees only after the National Labor Relations Board informs them, the ACTWU's efforts to organize SGA employees were clearly out in the open a full nine months before the election. With a union office in downtown Anderson and a healthy budget, the ACTWU, led by Chris Balog, engaged in one of the most sophisticated union organizing efforts ever seen in the area. Using computerized direct mailing to stay in touch with workers and extensive radio and television advertising, the union effort at SGA attracted wide attention. Many observers felt that the outcome of ACTWU's drive would have significant implications for the ability of labor unions to make inroads into traditionally nonunion regions of the country.

Union's Campaign

The campaign issues developed and communicated to workers were for the most part predictable. Job security was brought to the front early and was easily introduced to the campaign in the wake of over 1,500 layoffs and selective plant closings by SGA management. In addition, in attempting to become more competitive in the face of increasing foreign competition, increased workloads and reduced wage rates were key issues raised by the union. The union repeatedly accused Phillips of engaging in unfair labor practices by threatening to sell or close the company if the union were to win bargaining rights for SGA workers. To a certain extent, the union did expand on the traditional wages, hours, and working conditions issues typically raised in organizing efforts. As the campaign progressed, Phillips became a focal point of union rhetoric, and the union attempted to portray Phillips as a greedy and ruthless city slicker from Atlanta not interested in the long-term survival of SGA and its employees.

Management's Campaign

While Phillips became a focal point of union criticism as the campaign wore on, his role in management's response to the organizing efforts was critical throughout the months preceding the election. With President White leading the anti-union campaign, backed by a sophisticated strategy developed by an Atlanta law firm specializing in anti-union campaigns, SGA was able to quickly respond to every issue raised by the union.

The SGA strategy to defeat the union organizing effort included extensive meetings with community, business, and religious leaders in an attempt to influence workers' views about the union. Extensive use of anti-union films was required viewing for workers on company time. Letters sent to workers' homes by President White and Phillips emphasized the need for team spirit, not only to keep the union out, but to overcome the threat created by hosiery imports. President White put it this way: "We intend to do everything that is proper and legal in this campaign to defeat the union. This is essential if we are to remain competitive in the hosiery business. Every day we are facing more and more foreign competition. Not only do our workers understand this, but I think the public does also. We have been able to communicate with our workers in the past, and we don't need a third party voice. We all must work together as a team. The only way SGA can beat the encroaching foreign competition is to streamline and consolidate our operations."

White and Phillips made repeated visits to plants to shake hands and listen to

workers' concerns. The weekly employee newsletter was filled with anti-union letters written by workers and community members. Late in the campaign a letter
was sent to all employees from Jack Phillips explaining to SGA workers why they
should vote against the union (see Exhibit 7.1). In response to the union claim that
Phillips was attempting to sell the company, Phillips also told the workers that
"SGA is not for sale, but if I determine that the company cannot operate competi-
tively, I can and I will cease to operate SGA. This is entirely up to me and
nobody can stop me — including this union."

Employees' Views

The employees were divided over the union organizing campaign. Several
employees formed an Anti-Union Committee which organized a SGA Loyalty
Day. A statement by Terry Floyd, a shift leader, summed up the view expressed by
some employees: "We, as employees of SGA, do not feel that it is in the best interest of our company and its employees to be represented by ACTWU. Many
generations of the same families have worked at this plant; part of our strength is
family heritage. I'm afraid a union will destroy that strength. We feel that a union
is not needed and that we can work with management as a team." At one rally
sponsored by the Anti-Union Committee, "No Union" badges, "Be Wise — Don't
Unionize" t-shirts, and "Vote No" hats were worn by several hundred employees.

Other workers expressed support for the union. One worker stated, "We need
a union for protection. At least it would give us a voice. Supervisors can be too ar-
bitrary." Others pointed to pay increases and bonuses for top management in the
wake of wage cuts and layoffs for plant workers. Many older employees, who
remembered the generosity of the Anderson family, also expressed bitterness
toward SGA.

Questions

1. What was the impetus for the union organizing effort at SGA Industries?
2. Discuss SGA's strategy in managing the representation campaign.
3. Discuss any potential unfair labor practice charges SGA management might
   face as a result of their campaign strategy.

Exhibit 7.1 Letter to SGA Employees

TO ALL SGA EMPLOYEES:

It is only fair for you to know SGA's policy on unions. Our policy is quite simple. We are absolutely opposed to a union at any of our plants. We intend to use every legal and proper means to stay non-union.

As you know, the hosiery industry has been under great pressure and competition from foreign firms. Sales in the industry have dwindled over the past few years and we are in a poor profit position. Our government has done little to protect your jobs and stop the imports from eroding our sales. Only you and I can save this company and your jobs.

Our whole industry has been forced to modernize our production process to make it more efficient. In fact you know that many firms have merged together to strengthen their market position. Our company, too, will have to explore the possible advantages of pooling resources and products. In the long run such strategy can only benefit employees and management alike. I know bringing in the ACTWU at this time will only drive up our operating expenses and jeopardize our chances of making such arrangements. Only management has the right to decide how to operate this company. If we find we cannot operate this company profitably, we may be forced to consider other options.

We are convinced that unions have the tendency to create an adversarial relationship between employees and management. Cooperation and teamwork cannot exist in such a hostile environment. It is only through cooperation and teamwork that we will get through this crisis.

No SGA employee is ever going to need a union to keep their job. We know that ACTWU cannot help this company or you and will probably cause us to lose even more of our market and threaten your job security. I urge you—do not vote for the union—let's all pull together and remember the goodwill of the Anderson family and how it has stood behind you all of these years.

Sincerely,

Jack Phillips

Jack Phillips
Chief Executive Officer

CASE:
THE FRUSTRATED QUALITY
CIRCLE TEAM

Background

During the 1980s, one of the many U.S. Postmaster Generals initiated an innovation in labor management relations labeled "Employee Involvement — Quality of Work Life" (EI/QWL). The purpose of the innovation was not to supplant collective bargaining but to supplement it with a program of employee participation. Consequently, the mission of the program was to improve working conditions in any areas which did not contradict the collective bargaining agreement negotiated between the U.S. Postal System and the National Association of Letter Carriers.

The structure of the program included a local team, the manager of each facility, and the local Joint Steering Committee for the metropolitan area. The local team always included a member of management, a union representative, and two to five union members (depending on the size of the facility). The team met once a week for one hour during the workday to discuss ways of improving working conditions in their own facility. Only areas where there was total consensus could be written up and submitted for approval to higher levels.

Once a consensus on a proposal was achieved, the team wrote up a document detailing the need or problem, reasons for the problem, the proposed solution, and the benefits to the postal facility. This proposal was then sent to the facility manager (the second level in the structure). The manager had to approve or disapprove the proposal within seven days. If the proposal was rejected, reasons had to be given and the team could appeal to the third level in the structure.

The third level was the Joint Steering Committee, which consisted of higher-level union officials (i.e., the President of the union) and top management officials in the larger geographical area. The role of the Joint Steering Committee included training local team members, facilitating the process, resolving problems, and making final decisions regarding rejected proposals appealed from the local level.

The EI/QWL Program

A particular postal carrier facility in the Southwest began an EI/QWL program two years ago. The team consisted of a supervisor, a union shop steward, and three union members who had volunteered for the program. Among the proposals on which the team achieved consensus and recommended to the facility manager were ceiling fans to improve air circulation, fatigue mats for carriers to stand on while sorting mail, and a photocopy machine for the building to avoid driving to the downtown post office.

All of these proposals were accepted in writing by the facility manager within the required seven-day period. The team leader was told that the work orders for these three items had been issued.

After ten weeks, the team was becoming frustrated because none of the items which were "on order" had arrived. Team members, who had shared their approved recommendations with other carriers, began to hear complaints that the process was a "farce," "nothing is going to change," and "you guys are wasting your time." Again, the team leader checked with the facility manager and was told everything was "on order."

After four more weeks without results the team decided to check with the Joint Steering Committee since copies of all paperwork connected with the EI/QWL system were automatically sent to them. The team was told that, as far as the steering committee knew, none of the items had been ordered. Other than the initial approval by the facility manager, there was no other paperwork. The team then decided to ask the facility manager for copies of the work orders. They were told that none of the work orders had been kept (even though postal system rules require retention of work orders until the item is received).

The Decisions

By then, the team was extremely frustrated. Two team members suggested simply not meeting again until the approved items were received. Several other teams in the metropolitan area had done just that as a result of similar frustrations. However, the team eventually decided to use the system rather than abandon it. This meant they would bring the problem to the attention of the Joint Steering Committee and hope that the committee would put pressure on the facility manager to implement the recommendations.

The team spent two weeks discussing how to go about implementing this approach. All members of the team agreed on a course of action except for the supervisor. The problem was that the supervisor reported directly to the facility manager. The supervisor was concerned about his own promotion prospects and salary increases if he signed the problem statement indicating the facility manager was the problem. Since all proposals had to be a consensus, he reluctantly agreed to sign the document which accused the facility manager of approving all proposals but not implementing any. The team leader then gave the facility manager a copy of this document and sent the original to the Joint Steering Committee.

Questions

1. How would you explain the facility manager's behavior? What is his management style? What were his goals and objectives? Why?
2. Given the total situation, how would you evaluate the actions of the local team? Did they handle the situation properly? Did the supervisor make the right decision? Why or why not?
3. If you were a member of the Joint Steering Committee, what would you do

now? How would you insure that this type of problem did not recur in this or any other postal facility?

4. Are innovations in labor-management relations, such as EI/QWL, a passing fad or a permanent part of the labor-management structure?

EXERCISE:
COLLECTIVE BARGAINING
ROLE PLAY — BUSH CORPORATION

I. *Objectives:*
   1. To allow you to experience the collective bargaining process.
   2. To help you to understand the skills necessary to successfully negotiate a union contract.

II. *Out-of-Class Preparation Time:* 1 hour

III. *In-Class Time:* 45 minutes

IV. *Procedures:*
   1. The instructor will divide the class in half. Each half will be divided into a union team and a management team. There will be two simultaneous bargaining sessions (A and B).
   2. Read the description of the situation at Bush Corporation before class and familiarize yourself with the current contract and bargaining issues. Also read the role sheets for the union and management provided by the instructor.
   3. During class each negotiation team should meet to develop a strategy for achieving a favorable agreement. Each team should consider three items: (a) degree of flexibility on each provision; (b) issues which are most critical; and (c) willingness to take a strike. Preparation of the bargaining strategy should take no more than 10 minutes. Alternatively, teams may meet prior to class to develop their strategy.
   4. Your instructor will designate the amount of time for the actual bargaining session.
   5. Each team should appoint a chief negotiator and a secretary who will complete Form 1 indicating all the issues agreed upon in each of the areas under negotiation.

Negotiating Rules

1. At the beginning of the bargaining session, each team's chief negotiator should present an opening statement (1 minute or less) stating its objectives.
2. Each team is allowed two, three-minute caucuses during the bargaining session.
3. Each team is required to bargain in good faith and make every effort to reach an agreement. Failure to reach an agreement will lead to a strike.
4. Once a settlement is reached on a contract provision, that issue cannot be reopened.

Situation

Bush Corporation is a general aviation and business aircraft firm located in a large western city. The company manufactures aircraft, aircraft parts, avionics and other aircraft accessories in addition to providing aircraft maintenance and overhaul services. The company's major aircraft models—fanjets and propjets—are generally used for business and recreational flying. The company's products have fared well in a highly competitive market. However, in the first half of the last decade there has been a slump in the market for new general aviation aircraft. Industry experts attribute this slump to high aircraft costs and overcapacity in corporate flight departments. Many large corporations are increasingly turning to on-demand charter flights to meet their business flying needs. A combination of weak market demand and high product liability insurance rates have plagued the industry and have forced many to cut back production and lay off workers. Economic forecasts indicate that demand may pick up in the latter half of the decade as international sales increase. Top management at Bush is very concerned about keeping down labor costs in order to remain competitive. Last year the company had to close down one production line and lay off 450 workers for six weeks. The aerospace industry is becoming increasingly automated, and Bush is planning to increase its use of robots in the production process.

A majority of Bush's 2,500 production employees are members of the International Association of Machinists. A relatively good labor-management relationship has become somewhat strained because of the large-scale layoffs last year. While the union is aware of the company's economic situation, it is most concerned with employment security and a better position in terms of benefits. The present three-year contract (see Exhibit 7.2) is set to expire, and contract negotiations are set to begin. Union and company bargaining proposals are shown in Exhibit 7.3.

Exhibit 7.2 Major Provisions of Present Three-Year Contract
Between Bush Corporation and the International Association of Machinists

1.	Wages	Average union hourly wage = $14.48
2.	COLA adjustment	Prepaid increase of 2% and 1 cent for each 0.3 point rise in CPI; adjustments made annually
3.	Shift differential	15 cents/hour for third shift
4.	Overtime	All overtime paid at time and one-half
5.	Layoff notice	Minimum of two weeks notice
6.	Paid sick leave	2 but less than 4 years of service = 1 day 4 but less than 6 years of service = 2 days 6 but less than 8 years of service = 3 days 8 but less than 10 years of service = 4 days 10 but less than 25 years of service = 5 days
7.	Vacations	1 but less than 3 years of service = 1 week 3 but less than 10 years of service = 2 weeks 10 but less than 17 years of service = 3 weeks 17 but less than 25 years of service = 4 weeks 25 or more = 5 weeks
8.	Holidays	7 (Christmas Day, New Year's Day, Good Friday, Fourth of July, Memorial Day, Thanksgiving Day, and Labor Day)
9.	Life insurance	$10,000 group life plan; accidental death and dismemberment (AD & D) $7,500
10.	Health insurance	Major medical: $250,000 lifetime; company pays 75 percent of individual medical insurance
11.	Pensions	$20 per month per year of credited service
12.	Union security	All employed by the company who fall under the jurisdiction of the union shall, as a condition of employment, become members of the union at the expiration of the sixty (60) day probationary period.

Exhibit 7.3 Bargaining Program: Union and Company Proposals

Issue	Union Proposal	Company Proposal	Industry Average
1. Wages	$1.25 general wage increase per hour	75 cents	Average hourly rate $11.94 in aerospace industry (local labor market $11.75 for skilled workers)
2. COLA adjustment	1 cent increase for 0.175% CPI rise; adjustments made quarterly	Keep current provisions	1 cent increase for 0.3% increase in CPI; adjustments made quarterly
3. Shift differential	20 cents/hour second shift; 30 cents/hour third shift	Keep current provisions	40 cents/hour for third shift only
4. Overtime	Double time for all hours worked outside of normal assigned shift; time and one-half for Sunday and holiday work	Keep current provision	All overtime paid at time and one-half
5. Layoff notice	Minimum of four weeks	Keep current provision	Three weeks
6. Paid sick leave	7 days per year after 10 years of service	Keep current provision	5 days per year after 10 years of service
7. Vacations	1 but less than 3 yr = 2 weeks 3 but less than 10 yr = 3 weeks 10 but less than 17 yr = 4 weeks Over 17 years = 5 weeks	1 but less than 3 yr = 1 week 3 but less than 10 yr = 2 weeks 10 but less than 17 yr = 3 weeks Over 17 years = 4 weeks	1 but less than 5 yr = 2 weeks 5 but less than 10 yr = 3 weeks over 10 yr = 4 weeks
8. Holidays	Additional 3: Christmas Eve New Year's Eve Friday after Thanksgiving	Keep current provision	11 holidays

continued

Exhibit 7.3 *continued*

9. Life insurance	$15,000 group life insurance policy; AD&D $10,000	Increase AD&D to $8,500	$15,000 Life Insurance; $8,000 AD&D
10. Health Insurance	$750,000 lifetime major medical; company pays 85% to individual medical insurance	$500,000 lifetime major medical; company pays 75% of individual medical insurance	$500,000 lifetime major medical; company pays 90% of individual medical insurance
11. Pensions	$24 per month per year of credited service; increase retirees' monthly benefits by $.50 for each service year	$20 per year for past service; $22 for future service	$22 per month per year of credited service
12. Union Security	Union membership required after 30 days	Keep current provision	60 day requirement

Other Bargaining Issues Not Covered by Present 3-Year Contract

Management would like to:

A. Include a contract clause to establish a lower-wage structure for new employees beginning in the new contract year. These new employees would have an average hourly rate of $10.50.

B. Establish a joint committee to work toward containment of health care costs.

Union members would like to:

A. Include a contract provision to protect workers affected by new technology. This provision would require Bush to:

1. Notify the union six months in advance of the purchase or projected introduction of any technological change that would affect employees' jobs or job content.
2. Provide the union with full information about this new technology.
3. Handle any reduction in work force through normal attrition and turnover.
4. Not reduce the pay of any employee who is transferred or displaced because of the new technology.
5. Provide workers with cross-training and retraining for jobs created by the new technology.
6. Provide employees who cannot be retained with training for jobs outside of the company and outplacement assistance.

B. Include a contract provision providing for an employee savings plan with a Section 401k feature.

1. Wages

2. COLA adjustment

3. Shift differential

4. Overtime

5. Layoff notice

6. Paid sick leave

5. Vacations

8. Holidays

9. Life insurance

10. Health insurance

11. Pensions

12. Union security

13. Other issues

EXERCISE:
LABOR ARBITRATION

I. *Objectives*
>   **1.** To familiarize you with the arbitration process.
>   **2.** To give you practice in presenting a case before others.
>   **3.** To examine issues relating to horseplay, assault, insubordination, and progressive penalty systems.

II. *Out-of-Class Preparation Time*: 10 minutes to read the exercise

III. *In-Class Time Suggested*: 40 - 50 minutes

IV. *Procedures*: Either at the beginning of or before class each student should read the exercise. To start the exercise, the instructor will divide the class into the following three groups:
>   **1.** Union representatives (approximately five individuals)
>   **2.** Company representatives (approximately five individuals)
>   **3.** Arbitrators (all remaining participants, divided into groups of three to five members)

The union representatives should meet together and carefully examine "The Union Position" and prepare to argue and defend this position. The company representatives should do the same with reference to "The Company Position." Meanwhile the arbitrators should read both the union position and the company position and discuss among themselves the arguments for and against each position.

After both the union and company representatives have prepared their position statements, each should present their case to the arbitrators. Each group will be allowed five minutes for their presentation, then an additional five minutes to counter the other group's position.

After all presentations are complete, each group of arbitrators will be given ten minutes to discuss the case and reach a decision. These decisions should be presented, along with the reasoning behind them, to all participants.

Finally, the instructor may (optionally) present the arbitrator's actual decision in this case.

The Issue

Was the discharge of Stanley Walters on October 24 for just cause under the terms of the agreement between the parties? If not, what shall the remedy be?

Contributed by Max. B. Jones, College of Business and Public Administration, Old Dominion University.

Pertinent Provisions of the Union Agreement

Article V (4). Discharge: In the event an employee is discharged, the Company shall notify the Chairperson of the Shop Committee within one (1) workday as to the reasons for such discharge. If the employee believes that he has been unjustly dealt with, the Chairperson of the Shop Committee will arrange a meeting with the Labor Relations Department within two (2) workdays after the discharge. If not settled by the Shop Committee and the Manager of Labor Relations and/or his or her duly authorized representatives, the discharged employee, the Shop Committee, and representatives of the Labor Relations Department must meet within five (5) workdays after the discharge in an attempt to resolve the dispute. The Company shall render a written decision and forward it to the Chairperson of the Shop Committee within two (2) workdays. If not satisfactorily settled, the Chairperson of the Shop Committee will furnish a written reply to the Company as to the position of the Union within two (2) workdays. In the event, at any step above, it is decided that such discharge was wrongful and without just cause, the Company shall reinstate the employee to his or her former position and shall compensate the employee at his or her straight-time hourly rate for the time he or she would normally have worked, less any penalty agreed upon by the Company and the Union.

Background

The Grievant regularly worked the 11 P.M. to 7 A.M. third shift in the Tube Mill. On October 24, the Grievant entered the plant late for work at 12:40 A.M. He then proceeded to an area of the plant near the furnaces and talked with some of the employees. About fifteen minutes later, the Production Supervisor for the third shift, Ron Marshall, called the Grievant over to him from the shop floor. From his office Mr. Marshall had noticed the Grievant come in late. He completed the paperwork he was doing, then he came out to check on the Grievant.

According to Supervisor Marshall, the Grievant was loud, boisterous, and in an ugly mood when he came to work. On inquiry, he revealed that he was late for work because he had been watching a football game on television and that he had lost money on the game. Mr. Marshall informed the Grievant that his excuse was insufficient, and that he would receive a reprimand, i.e., a written warning. The Supervisor then accompanied the Grievant to another part of the shop where he assigned the Grievant a task of loading pieces of pipe, called "pushers," onto a rack, referred to as a "mini." The Grievant responded by calling the task a "s___ job," refusing to do the job, and declaring that he would go home. The Supervisor then agreed that he should go home and turned to leave.

The Grievant's version of this incident revealed that he had indicated the job was too much for one person, that it would take all night by himself, that he had asked for assistance, and feared that a blister on his thumb from an earlier injury would break open while handling the pipe through the shift.

Supervisor Marshall testified that, to attract attention as he was leaving the scene, the Grievant picked up a metal drum that had been used as a stool and threw it crashing to the floor, thereby making a resounding noise. On turning to face the Grievant, Mr. Marshall was told by the Grievant, "If I ever catch you on the street, I'll whip you good!" and, "We're going to settle this." Then, the Grievant with clenched fist pushed Supervisor Marshall on the shoulder or upper arm, shoving him back a step or two. The Grievant was then ordered to leave; a guard was called and instructed not to let the Grievant back into the plant.

The Company Position

The Company takes the position that the Grievant's insubordinate conduct, culminating in a physical assault on his Supervisor, mandated the penalty of discharge in the interest of maintaining order and discipline in the plant. The Company's rules of conduct addressed to all employees specifically state:

> Some individual infractions of proper conduct may be of such serious nature as to require immediate disciplinary suspension or discharge without the prior application of verbal or written reprimands. These include, but are not limited to acts of misconduct such as activities of a criminal nature, gross insubordination, fighting, theft of Company or employee property, etc.

The Company stressed that the Supervisor's disciplining of the Grievant for his lateness and his reaction to the Grievant's insubordinate conduct when given his work assignment demonstrated remarkable restraint on Mr. Marshall's part. Even if this had not been the case, the Grievant had recourse through a negotiated grievance procedure and had no cause to take matters into his own hands by challenging his Supervisor's actions. Extending such challenge to physical assault on his Supervisor is of such paramount severity as to require immediate discharge. The Company takes particular exception to the Union's effort to mitigate the severity of the Grievant's conduct under the alleged guise of horseplay.

The Company further contends that unless there is compelling evidence to show that the Company had abused its discretion or had acted arbitrarily or capriciously, the Arbitrator is not free to substitute his or her judgment for that of the Company.

The Union Position

The Union takes the position that the Grievant's discharge was not for just cause. The Union asserts that the Grievant did complain about the amount of work and requested help, which his Supervisor denied. This was in light of an injured thumb for which he had secured first-aid treatment earlier. The Union introduced testimony suggesting that Mr. Marshall had falsely accused the Grievant in an earlier "tire incident" and had seized this opportunity to make an example of the Grievant.

The Union protested the Company claim that the Grievant had a violent tendency, was chronically tardy, and tended to flaunt Company rules. This picture simply did not fit the Grievant's record of eight years' seniority with the Company with not a single disciplinary action in his record for the entire period. The Union brought out in testimony that the Grievant had never filed a grievance before the present incident, preferring to resolve any problems informally. This was consistent with the loose atmosphere that permeated the third shift.

Union testimony revealed that on numerous occasions Supervisor Marshall had been party to traditional horseplay activity including getting thrown into the showers or a rinse tank. In turn, the Supervisor had derogated the Grievant with insults. Testimony revealed that on one occasion Supervisor Marshall had engaged in a good-natured sparring match with the Grievant who is quite skilled as a boxer. These incidents revealed an atmosphere on the third shift characterized by rough language, rough activity, and general laxness. Under these circumstances the Union cannot accept that the Grievant's push on the arm of the Supervisor with an open hand constituted physical assault. For these reasons, the Union requests that the discharge be set aside, and the Grievant be reinstated with all rights and full back pay.

INCIDENT:
WHO SHOULD EMPTY
THE TRASH CANS?

This incident involves a local union of a large international labor organization and a company that is located in the United States. The Company provides wastebaskets adjacent to employees' work stations in Department 17. These wastebaskets are for the convenience of the employees when disposing of personal trash during the work shift. On February 6, Inspector-Packers in this department filed Grievances 6 and 7 protesting their supervisor's instruction to empty wastebaskets at the end of the work shift into a larger trash receptacle located in the department. The grievances claimed the supervisor's action amounted to harassment, discipline without cause, unfair treatment, and confusion in that the duty of emptying the smaller cans was properly that of the Utility Janitor position and included in the job description for that position. Emptying wastebaskets is not specified in the job description for Inspector-Packers. The Company denied the grievances, and, failing resolution, these grievances were submitted for arbitration along with several other critical issues.

Contributed by Max. B. Jones, College of Business and Public Administration, Old Dominion University.

The Issue

Did the Company violate its Agreement with the Union by having Inspector-Packers in Department 17 empty wastebaskets at their own work station? If so, what shall the remedy be? (Grievance Nos. 6 and 7)

The Union Position

The Union takes the position that it has always been the duty of the Utility Janitor to empty the trash bags from the smaller cans into the larger trash receptacle. The Union contends this duty is not part of the Inspector-Packers' job classification, and the improper switching of the duty from the Utility Janitor classification violates Article 14 of the Agreement which covers the job evaluation plan in effect.

The Union noted that on the eve of the Hearing in this matter, the Company had the small wastebaskets removed in an effort to undermine the Union's case and to claim that the issue no longer exists. The Union considers the trash baskets just as necessary to the Inspector-Packers as to any other employees.

The Company Position

The Company takes the position that the emptying of the small trash baskets by the Inspector-Packers at the end of each work shift is the most efficient allocation of employees' efforts. The task is adequately covered in the job description of the Inspector-Packer under "performs other related duties as directed by supervisor" (Union Exhibit #7). The Company contends that Inspector-Packers as well as the Utility Janitor have been known to empty the trash cans, and the task requires only a minute's time once a day.

Questions

1. Whose duty is it to empty the trash cans? Justify your answer.
2. Do the supervisor's actions amount to "harassment, discipline without cause, unfair treatment, and confusion" as the union has argued?
3. What does this case suggest about the relationship between the union and the company management?

INCIDENT:
THE TWO-TIER
WAGE STRUCTURE

Able Airlines is the number five carrier in the highly competitive airline industry. Over the past ten years, Able has grown from primarily a regional carrier to the point where it is presently attempting to secure international routes. Able is also currently preparing to negotiate a new collective bargaining agreement with its pilots. In the last contract it negotiated with the pilots, Able was able to secure a two-tier wage system. Under this system, all pilots hired after November 1983 earn half the pay of pilots hired before then. The contract also included a Cost of Living Escalator Agreement where the new pilots' wages would be adjusted twice a year for inflation.

While many of Able's competitors were able to secure similar wage systems, many of Able's larger competitors did not. Since 1983, the labor market for pilots has tightened and the increased demand for pilots has caused some of Able's second-tier pilots to move to airlines that pay full rates. As the current contract nears expiration, the Industrial Relations staff is facing several dilemmas. The two-tier wage system certainly has reduced costs, but at the expense of some good young pilots. In addition, morale among pilots hired after 1983 who have stayed is beginning to deteriorate. The IRS staff is not in complete agreement with respect to the negative aspects of the two-tier wage system. Some members of the staff feel that the new pilots knew what the pay was when they took the jobs and have no right to complain.

The average wage of the second-tier pilots is $75,000 a year while the average wage for all pilots is $95,000. Presently, of the 350 pilots employed at Able, 150 are in the second (lower) tier. The average retirement age for pilots is 58, while the average age of pilots in the first (higher) tier is 48 years of age and 35 in the second tier. The turnover rate among pilots had been averaging 3 percent a year prior to 1983, but has been over 6 percent since the last contract:

Able Airlines Turnover

1978	2.8%
1979	3.2%
1980	3.0%
1981	3.3%
1982	2.7%
1983	3.0%
1984	6.0%
1985	6.6%
1986	7.1%

Contributed by Gerald Calvasina of the University of North Carolina at Charlotte.

The industry turnover average for pilots has also been up, from 3.4 percent in 1978 to 5.2 percent by 1986.

Able's contract with its flight attendants also contains a two-tier system with a similar escalator clause. This contract, which still has another year to run, is receiving a great deal of criticism from the flight attendants. Their union leaders are paying close attention to the pilots and Able management's negotiations.

Questions

1. As the manager responsible for developing Able's bargaining strategy, assess the pros and cons of the two-tier wage system presently in place at Able.
2. What can be done to overcome the negative aspects of the two-tier wage system presently operating at Able?
3. Should Able eliminate the two-tier wage system? Why? Why not?

SKILL BUILDER:
EMPLOYEE COMMUNICATIONS DURING UNION CAMPAIGNS

I. *Objectives:*
   1. To give you practice in preparing an effective company communication during a union campaign.
   2. To help you understand the practical application of the National Labor Relations Act.

II. *Time Required to Complete:* 1 hour

III. *Instructions:* Your company, Fruit Canners, Inc., has recently become aware that the United Food and Commercial Workers Union is attempting to convince employees in your plant to sign authorization cards. Management is somewhat surprised by the campaign because employee relations have generally been good. Prepare a one-page letter to be sent to all plant employees stating the company's position on the union drive and the company's desire to remain nonunion. Be certain that the content of your letter does not violate the provisions of the National Labor Relations Act.

Part 8

Performance Management and Control

Productivity concerns on the part of organizations have increased interest in performance management and evaluation as a mechanism for influencing employee work performance. Performance management is a broad area which focuses on ways of effectively managing employee performance, including performance evaluation and the control of employee behavior through discipline and employee assistance programs. Performance evaluation systems play an important role in decisions about promotions, pay increases, and terminations. A well-designed performance evaluation system can also influence an employee's behavior and future performance.

The key elements and issues of performance management are addressed in materials in this section. The first case, "The Broken Employment Contract?" focuses on the termination-at-will controversy and highlights the impact of recent legislation and court cases on termination procedures. The second case in this section, "Managing Problem Employees—Graham City," concerns employee behavior in response to a major change in job content because of the introduction of new technology. The "Alcohol/Drug Abuse Program" case describes a drug-testing and employee assistance program developed and implemented by Duke Power Company. This is an important case for students of personnel management because drug abuse is one of today's most relevant and controversial issues. "Eval-sim" is an in-basket exercise which provides an opportunity for you to make decisions involved in administering a performance evaluation system. The second exercise, "The Performance Appraisal Interview Role Play," provides you with practice in giving feedback to employees on their performance. The two incidents focus on employee discipline problems and their resolution. The skill builder requires you to develop written disciplinary policies.

CASE:
THE BROKEN
EMPLOYMENT CONTRACT?

Arthur Wayne walked out of Sara Bell's office shocked. It was hard for him to understand what had just transpired. Bell, treasurer of EcoCare, a large health insurance company located in Michigan, had just told Wayne of the decision to terminate his employment and had requested his immediate resignation in return for a severance pay arrangement whereby he would continue to receive his salary for six months or until he found other employment. As he looked at the date on his watch calendar, May 7, Wayne realized that he had been hired exactly five years ago by Bell. Bell had told Wayne that EcoCare was not satisfied with his administration of the company car program and that given the number of complaints about the program from other employees, it was in the best interest of the company to ask for his immediate resignation. Wayne, Assistant to the Treasurer, had been in charge of the program for the past year. During a meeting the day before with both Bell and the Vice President of Operations, George Findlay, he had been unable to explain why there were so many complaints about the program. One such complaint had involved the claim that someone had "set back" the odometers on several company cars while the vehicles were under Wayne's control.

After his termination, Wayne requested that the decision to ask for his resignation be reviewed by the company president and the chairperson of the Board of Trustees of EcoCare. Wayne felt that he had been wrongfully discharged and that he had been under the impression that he had a contract for continued employment as long as his performance was satisfactory. He further maintained that his supervisor had not properly followed the termination policies and procedures of EcoCare.

In preparation for the review, the president asked the Director of Personnel, Chris Miller, to investigate the facts of the situation and the events leading up to Wayne's termination.

Personnel Department's Investigation

In order to prepare its report for the president, the Personnel Department decided not only to review Wayne's personnel file but also to interview Wayne, Bell, and others involved in the case. Two weeks later, Miller prepared the following summary of what had been learned:

After seven years with a local bank in Michigan, Arthur Wayne sought the assistance of an employment agency to obtain a job that would give him more opportunities for advancement. Wayne had graduated with a degree in business administration and had completed fifteen hours toward his M.B.A. degree in Finance. The employment agency referred him to our company. After several pre-employment interviews and a psychological test, Wayne was hired as an assistant to the company treasurer, Sara Bell. His duties consisted primarily in analyzing and preparing certain financial reports under the direction of Bell. Wayne came to us with excellent work experience and admirable references from his previous employers.

According to Wayne, he felt at the time of his employment that he had a "contract" with EcoCare that was partly oral (Bell's statements during the job interview) and partly written. Wayne told us that during his pre-employment interview with Bell, he had specifically asked about job security and was told that "as long as he did his job" he could remain with the company until he reached retirement age. He further indicated that he had been told by Bell that if he came to EcoCare he wouldn't have to look for another job because she knew of no one ever being discharged. Wayne also told us that a copy of the "Supervisory Manual" was handed to him during his interview with Bell. He said he specifically recalled reading through the sections of the manual which pertained to discipline and termination procedures at that time (see Appendix for relevant sections). At the end of that interview Bell made Wayne a job offer which he accepted. As you know, the manual is given to all management employees as an aid in supervising persons in their charge and not as a declarative of the contract terms of an employee's hire. Our personnel policy has always been to discharge for "just cause only" pursuant to the procedures described in the manual. These procedures apply to all EcoCare employees who have completed their probationary period.

During his five years as assistant to the treasurer, Wayne received above-average performance ratings. Last year he was given the responsibility of administering the company car program. In April of this year, other employees began complaining to Bell and Findlay about Wayne's handling of the program. Wayne indicated that he had only a brief conversation with Bell about these complaints before the meeting of May 6.

We also spoke with Bell and Findlay about Wayne's employment and subsequent termination. According to Bell, she did tell Wayne during the interview that he would have a job as long as his performance was satisfactory. Bell told us that she made that statement based on her understanding of our company's policies and did not intend her statement as a promise of a permanent job.

Bell and Findlay report that Wayne was fired because of continued personality conflicts with other employees. They report that he was unable to work with other employees and that this was an important job requirement for anyone managing the company car program. After receiving numerous complaints about Wayne's handling of the program, they finally requested from him various reports and documents concerning the odometer discrepancies. Ultimately, they called a meeting with Wayne in an attempt to resolve the problems. During the May 6 meeting, Wayne was reported to have been defensive and insubordinate and unable to provide any satisfactory answers to their questions. At the conclusion of the meeting, they both felt that it would be in the best interest of the company if Wayne were asked to resign. Bell called Wayne into her office the next day and asked for his resignation.

APPENDIX
EXCERPTS FROM SUPERVISORY MANUAL

Section IV. Disciplinary Procedures

(Note: If the unacceptable behavior is repeated between six months and one year, the last disciplinary action will be applied. If the behavior is repeated after one year, it will be treated as a new occurrence for disciplinary purposes.)

A. All discipline shall be administered in a fair, consistent, and reasonable manner within EcoCare.

B. Whenever the work performance or personal behavior of an employee is below department standards, a series of progressive, corrective steps will be taken. Before any of these steps are undertaken, however, the employee shall be counseled about his or her performance discrepancy, what he or she must do to improve the performance, and the action the supervisor will take if the performance is not corrected.

C. Within our discipline system, discipline will be given only for cause. Furthermore, the disciplinary action should fit the problem it is intended to correct.

D. All disciplinary action should be duly documented and reported by the supervisor in Form 29B. The form also requires the employee's signature.

E. The following series of steps shall be followed in administering discipline within EcoCare:

1. *Oral Warning:* Supervisor should discuss the unacceptable behavior with the employee and document such by completing Section A of Form 29B and obtaining the employee's signature.

2. *Written Warning:* A written warning should be issued if the unacceptable behavior continues. The supervisor completes Section B of Form 29B and gives the employee the blue copy. The Personnel Department receives the canary copy.

3. *Suspension:* If the employee's behavior continues uncorrected, the employee shall be suspended for a given time off without pay. Normally, suspension should not exceed five working days. Supervisors should consult with their immediate supervisor and the Personnel Department before implementing this action. The supervisor shall complete Section C of Form 29B and also include the date the employee should return to work.

4. *Discharge:* If the employee's behavior is not corrected, the employee shall be terminated. Due to the serious nature of termination, it is recommended that the supervisor review the case with both his or her immediate supervisor and the Personnel Department before discharging the employee. Examples of reasons for termination without prior corrective discipline are covered in Section V. Note, however, that in such cases the employee should first be suspended according to the following procedures:

   Suspension Pending Discharge: (This paragraph applies to all proposed discharges except those which are a result of application of the normal disciplinary procedures.)

a. When an employee's misconduct warrants immediate discharge under Section V, the employee should be first suspended without pay.

b. At the time of suspension, the employee should be informed by the supervisor to leave the premises and that he or she will be notified if and when he or she is to return to work.

c. The supervisor should document the suspension by completing an Employee Discipline Report. The supervisor should consult with Personnel to determine the appropriate course of action.

Section V. Termination
(Reasons for Immediate Termination):

1. Misconduct, such as fighting, gambling, or use of profane or abusive language toward others.
2. Furnishing proprietary company information to unauthorized agents or persons.
3. Refusal to obey direct orders from the immediate supervisor (insubordination).
4. Willful damage of company property.
5. Failure to notify supervisor or manager during three successive working days of absence.
6. Engaging in a business likely to conflict with the business of the company without prior permission.
7. Dishonesty, falsification of employee's own or other employee's time cards, company records, employment application, etc.
8. Illegal use or possession of alcohol, drugs, etc.
9. Reporting to work or engaging in company business under the influence of alcohol or drugs.

Questions

1. Did Wayne have an employment contract either oral or written with EcoCare? Why or why not?
2. What problems, if any, do you see with EcoCare's pre-employment process?
3. Can an employer's written personnel policies ever be construed as a contract between an employer and an employee?
4. Was Wayne terminated for "just cause"? Why or why not?
5. How can companies protect themselves against a claim of "wrongful discharge"?

CASE:
MANAGING PROBLEM
EMPLOYEES — GRAHAM CITY

Background

Graham City is a very large housing complex with over 45,000 residents located in a major U.S. city. Due to the concern of residents of the complex that the crime rate in the surrounding area is unacceptably high, the management maintains its own security department in addition to the metropolitan police force. The security department undertakes many of the same activities as the metro police: patrolling the complex grounds and surrounding area, responding to emergencies reported by residents of the community through an emergency telephone number and taking reports of criminal incidents. The department consists of seventy-five security officers, a director, four assistant directors and other administrative and clerical staff. The mission of the security department is to protect the residents of Graham City, to educate the residents to take the precautions necessary to reduce their risk of being victims of crime, to collect data on crime statistics for use in designing more effective patrol strategies, to keep management informed of criminal activity, and to work with the metro police to reduce crime in the area.

Security Administrative Services, headed by the Assistant Director Brenda Markus, is responsible for performing administrative functions associated with the operation of the Security Department. Her staff consists of a secretary, two clerks, an administrative assistant, and a staff assistant. The staff assistant is primarily responsible for Officer Training. The administrative assistant is primarily responsible for maintaining crime reports and preparing special reports for management. Daily summaries of criminal activity are prepared from the crime reports received within a twenty-four-hour period and distributed to management. Between six and twenty incidents are reported in a twenty-four-hour period. Many of these are not actual crimes, but reports of lost items, burglar alarms triggered, and suspicious activity. A very detailed crime report is completed on the scene by the attending officer, from which a short narrative is prepared by the sergeant on duty. At the end of the twenty-four-hour period, these narratives are compiled into the daily summary report (DSR). The report is reviewed by the administrative assistant in conjunction with the crime reports, revised as necessary, and typed by one of the clerks. After final proofreading by the administrative assistant, the DSR is distributed. The administrative assistant also prepares special reports requested by the director and assistant director, as well as several periodic reports based on the crime reports. Since many functions for the complex are centralized, such as payroll and purchasing, the department is responsible for doing a certain portion of those tasks and working with other departments to complete the tasks. The clerks handle most of these administrative tasks, such as pay-

Contributed by Deborah Ramirez Bishop of Saginaw Valley State University.

roll, some accounting, and typing. The secretary performs day-to-day duties assigned to her by Ms. Markus. She seldom works directly with either of the clerks, but all three work together in the same area and so engage in friendly conversation.

The Situation

One summer, the director and assistant directors decided to implement two new computer systems in the Security Department. A microcomputer was purchased for use by the security dispatcher, with exclusive responsibility for software development and training given to the administrative assistant. The second system involved using the complex's mainframe computer to develop a data base of information obtained from the detailed crime reports. This data base would then be used to prepare the DSRs and other reports. A great savings in time in preparing special reports was anticipated by having computer access to the information. The data base could also be used to quickly identify trends in criminal activity, which could lead to increased patrol and greater protection of the members of the community. The administrative assistant was also given primary responsibility for designing this system and training the clerks in data entry and report preparation.

The administrative assistant was not happy with the new responsibilities given to him. Although he had some background in computer programming, he had hoped to use his present position to move into a different field. A few months after the project was initiated, he handed in his resignation to the assistant director. Early in 1980, Marie Sanchez was hired into the vacant position. She had graduated from a local college in 1978, and had been working in another department of the complex since that time. She was enthusiastic about the transfer, since she had been seeking a position in which she could use her computer programming skills. Ms. Markus gave her complete control of the projects and the authority to use the services of the two clerks in the office and one clerk in the director's office when the time came to train them to operate the systems. She, however, maintained the authority to hire, fire, and make salary decisions.

One of the two clerks, Evelyn, had poor typing skills and she was often late for work. She had not gotten along well with the previous administrative assistant. Everyone in the department knew of the friction between the two. The Staff Assistant, Jim Lawrence, had told her on numerous occasions that she needed to change her "bad attitude." Lawrence warned Marie that she might expect some problems from Evelyn, based on past experience. The second clerk had not experienced any problems in the office, but, for reasons unrelated to the job, had left Administrative Services before the arrival of Marie Sanchez. Shortly after Marie arrived, Cheryl was hired by Ms. Markus to fill the second clerical position. According to the job descriptions of the two clerks, they performed the same work for the office. In practice, however, Evelyn did the major portion of the clerical work involving the DSR's and report preparation while the second clerk handled the majority of the duties associated with payroll for the security officers. Payroll computations were often very complex due to the large number of overtime and shift bonus calculations that had to be made. Since Evelyn's numerical abilities were weak, most of those tasks were usually left to the other clerk. Cheryl was very capable in handling computational tasks, and so she handled the major portion of the payroll duties. She also did most of the typing needed by Jim Lawrence, although Evelyn did some typing for him since the payroll duties took up a lot of Cheryl's time.

During the first six months that Marie was on the job, most of her time had been spent on the first project assigned to her: programming the microcomputer for the dispatcher. The clerk in the director's office was being trained in data entry for this project, so neither Evelyn nor Cheryl was involved. During this time, Marie's contact with Evelyn and Cheryl was limited to assigning reports to be typed, as well as engaging in nonwork-related conversation with them and with the secretary who was located in the same office area. Evelyn and Cheryl were about the same age, and only a year younger than Marie. Cheryl was attending a secretarial training school at night, and had high hopes for advancing her career. Evelyn showed little interest in going back to school, although she seemed to admire Cheryl's enthusiasm. Both clerks had been told at the beginning of the project that they would be trained in data entry and report preparation using the computer terminal as soon as it was ready.

The Problem

By October the second system was ready for trial operation. A single terminal, which used hardcopy display, was going to be shared by Marie, Evelyn, and Cheryl. Selected information from each crime report was entered into the data base. DSRs were printed on the terminal, revised, copied, and distributed. During the transition period, a large backlog of DSRs accumulated. Even after Evelyn and Cheryl were trained and operating the system on their own, poor scheduling resulted in occasional backlogs. By the time the system was put into final operation in January, most of the technical problems had been corrected. Evelyn enjoyed working on the computer terminal. Marie asked her for suggestions in improving the method of data entry, and a few modifications were made. Although she made quite a few typographical errors (which were not unexpected based on her typing skills), they were minor and she would make the corrections quickly. Her attitude toward work seemed to improve markedly. She made less negative comments about work and even became more punctual in arriving for work. She seemed to gain a certain amount of satisfaction from producing the final report that resulted from her efforts.

Cheryl, however, felt quite differently about the new duties she was expected to perform. Although she was able to enter data faster than Evelyn and with less errors, she constantly complained about all the time that she had to spend using the computer terminal. When it was her turn to enter data, she would put off the task until as late as possible. When the deadline approached for submitting payroll cards, she would announce to Marie that she couldn't enter data because the payroll deadline was approaching. Marie suggested that she schedule her work around payroll, but every week the same situation occurred. Evelyn began to complain that Cheryl was not doing her share of the work.

Cheryl complained to Ms. Markus that the data entry work was taking too much time away from her payroll duties. Although Markus felt that Cheryl was spending more time on payroll than was necessary, she attempted to resolve the situation by allocating more of Cheryl's payroll duties to Evelyn to give Cheryl more time to perform data entry. (Because of the previous high turnover rate, she did not want to give all the payroll tasks to Cheryl and all the data entry tasks to Evelyn. If one of the clerks left the job, she wanted the other clerk to be able to handle all of the tasks.) When Markus told Cheryl that she would have to give more of her payroll tasks to Evelyn, she said, "Forget it. I can handle everything." After this meeting, her complaints intensified. Although she and Evelyn had worked out a new schedule, Cheryl still delayed in getting to work on the data entry. This caused increasing backlogs of DSR's and limited usefulness of the interactive capability of the system to assist in analyzing crime patterns.

Questions

1. How should Marie and Brenda Markus handle this situation?
2. Why did Evelyn develop a positive attitude toward the new computer system while Cheryl developed a negative attitude?

CASE:
THE ALCOHOL/DRUG ABUSE PROGRAM

Company Profile

Duke Power Company, with headquarters in Charlotte, North Carolina, is the seventh largest investor-owned electric utility in the nation, with a 20,000-square mile service area in North Carolina and South Carolina. Duke's three nuclear stations, eight coal-fired plants and 26 hydroelectric facilities provide electricity to more than 1.4 million customers.

Duke's retail customers are served through 96 district and branch offices. The company also sells electricity at wholesale and contractual rates to bulk users. The company has a reputation for industry leadership and efficient management. Duke has twice received the Edison Award, the electric utility industry's highest honor. In 1985 the award presented by the Edison Electric Institute praised Duke for excellence in the design, construction, and operation of nuclear power plants and for its successful voter awareness program, Power in Citizenship. The company is one of the largest employers in the state with over 20,000 employees.

Fitness for Duty Program

In June of 1986, Duke Power implemented an Alcohol and Drug Abuse Program. This program is really an extension of their Fitness for Duty Program which had been in effect since the summer of 1984. Additionally, the company had a well-respected and popular Employee Assistance Program (EAP) which has been in operation for over ten years. The Fitness for Duty Program arose from a need identified in 1977 to conduct training for supervisors of employees requiring unescorted access to nuclear stations. This "behavior reliability" program was broadened in 1984 to the overall Fitness for Duty (FFD) Program and was extended to encompass all employees. At the time of its implementation, Bill Lee, CEO, told employees, "Your top management team upon examining this particular program decided the information in this training would be of benefit to all employees. Basically, a decision was made that no matter whether you're operating a computer terminal, whether you're forty feet up a pole, or whether you are in a nuclear plant, it didn't matter."

FFD is a broad concept that deals with anything that might affect an employee's ability to perform his or her job in a safe and efficient manner. The backbone of the program is behavior observation with supervisors and employees both being charged with the responsibility for taking appropriate action when unusual behavior is recognized in a subordinate or a fellow employee. Management's overall objective has been to encourage employees who need help to get it. The FFD program focused on personal, sleep-related, physical and psychological/emotional problems but did not put specific significance on the alcohol and drug issue.

Development of the Alcohol/Drug Abuse
Management Procedure

As media attention became increasingly focused on the growing drug abuse problem in the United States, management at Duke Power Company began addressing the possible impact of drug abuse in the workplace. Jim Bavis, Vice President of Human Resources, described that concern as follows: "We did not want to be ostriches about this growing community problem even though we feel so strongly about the ethics of the people we hire and the backgrounds of the people who work for us. Even though we're in the Bible belt and that might make a difference, we didn't want to be misled by all of that. We felt that we were probably a microcosm of what was going on in society to some extent. We are a public organization and are keenly aware that the public eye is focused on us and what we do. In May of 1985, we decided to take more specific action and examine whether or not we should have a formal policy on drug and alcohol abuse."

During the spring of 1985, a twenty-three-member task force, chaired by Bavis, was appointed to study the need for a policy. Every major operating department was represented on the task force. During its early meetings, the task force reached unanimous agreement about the need for a program. Task force members expressed concern not only for the employee who might be a drug user, but also the possible impact on co-workers of the employee. From the outset, the task force agreed that whatever was done had to benefit the health and safety of employees. The philosophy of the program would emphasize: (1) helping people in need of help and not a "gotcha" effort; (2) educating employees about the negative health effects of alcohol and drug abuse; and (3) educating employees about the impact of alcohol/drug abuse on fellow workers.

Once these basic objectives had been decided, two subcommittees were broken out from the task force to work on the details and actual development of the policy. The Visit Subcommittee's major tasks were to research literature on the subject and to collect information on the programs and policies of other companies. The Visit Subcommittee developed a structured questionnaire and gathered information from twenty-one other companies. Most of these companies were also in the utility industry. The other subcommittee, Education, Training and Communication, was charged with overseeing the initial training and education of employees and to follow through on subsequent training and education needs.

The extensive research done by the committees helped to identify several key issues that had to be resolved in developing a policy on alcohol and drug abuse. Among the more difficult issues were: (1) How do we handle employees "on call" who may have used alcohol? (2) If we test someone and that test is positive, what are we going to do about it? (3) How should we handle consumption of alcohol at company-sponsored events? and (4) Who should be tested? In regard to the latter question, it was decided early on that testing of current employees should not be random, but confined to employees in sensitive positions (e.g., nuclear station operators, crane operators, and bus drivers). The task force spent much time on this particular decision. They agreed that sensitive positions would be defined as those jobs requiring employees to take a periodic physical examination. The drug test would become part of the routine physical taken by these employees periodically. Once all of these issues were resolved, the task force drafted a report of its recommendations.

These recommendations were thoroughly reviewed and discussed by Duke's Salary Committee (an operating committee), which consists of senior officers and is chaired by the President. A consultant, Peter Bensinger, former director of the Drug Enforcement Administration, also reviewed the proposed policy and recommended no major changes. The policy was approved by Duke's Executive Committee during the fall of 1985. The new policy became effective June 1, 1986, for current employees, and pre-employment testing began in March, 1986.

To communicate the new policy to employees, several methods were used. The President sent a letter to all employees in January announcing the new policy (see Exhibit 8.1). A training program was designed which emphasized a "We Can, We Care" approach. This approach reflected the company's objective of helping those employees who need help. Training began in January with managers. These managers had the major responsibility of spearheading the training at their respective work sites. The training program included presentations by Peter Bensinger on illegal drugs from a national and international perspective and by the company's medical director on the deleterious effects of drugs and alcohol on the body. At the training sessions, employees were also given an in-depth review of the new procedures and the opportunity to ask questions about the implementation of the new policy. Prior to the training sessions, all employees received a revised Fitness for Duty Booklet containing a detailed description of the new policy (see Exhibit 8.2 for major features of the policy). The training programs were well received throughout the organization. In addition to informing its employees, Duke also notified its usual recruitment sources (including college placement offices) of the new policy so that potential applicants would be aware of the procedures. Local and regional law enforcement agencies were also made aware of the new program.

Aftermath

Management had concerns as to how employees would accept a drug and alcohol abuse program — especially since few employers in the area had such programs. However, employee reactions to the program have been favorable. In fact, after the initial training efforts, several employees expressed an interest in sharing what they had learned with their families. In response, Duke sponsored several "Family Nights" outlining the activities of the Employee Assistance Program and the health effects of alcohol/drug abuse for employee family members.

Duke's innovative and proactive approach to the drug abuse problem in the workplace also attracted the attention of other companies in the region. In fact, the company received so many requests for information about its program that it held a special half-day seminar to accommodate the demand.

To measure the impact of the program, the human resources staff is monitoring attendance data, accident rates (vehicle and personal), the number of corrective actions in departments, number of referrals to the EAP, and the number of positive drug screens. However, as noted by David Abernethy, Director of Human Resources Administration, it may be difficult to directly measure the program's impact. "Perhaps our best measurement may be the attitudes of our employees and the community," he said.

Questions

1. Discuss Duke's reasons for starting the Alcohol/Drug Abuse Program.
2. Evaluate Duke's approach to developing its program.
3. Does the drug testing infringe upon employee rights?
4. What responsibility does the program place on an employee's immediate supervisor?
5. How should Duke go about evaluating the effectiveness of its program?

Exhibit 8.1 Letter from Douglas W. Booth, President
and Chief Operating Officer, to All Employees

January 23, 1986

TO: ALL DUKE, MILL-POWER AND CRESCENT LAND
AND TIMBER EMPLOYEES:

A new drug and alcohol abuse procedure will be implemented company-wide on June 1, 1986. This procedure is an extension of the Fitness for Duty Program that was introduced early last year.

We are adopting this new procedure because we recognize that drug and alcohol abuse is a growing problem in society. We do not believe we have an extensive problem in our company, but any level of drug and alcohol abuse is a cause for concern. Abuse can cause serious health, safety, and emotional effects on users and can bring about financial hardships for the abuser and family. It can likewise affect the health and safety of non-users who may be exposed to unsafe acts of users. We care too much about our employees—both those who abuse drugs and alcohol and those who do not—to stand by and do nothing.

This new procedure is very important. All employees will undergo training before the June 1 implementation date. I urge you to join with all the members of the Duke Family in implementing the procedure to create a healthier, safer, and more productive work environment for us all.

Warmest regards,

Doug Booth

Douglas W. Booth

Exhibit 8.2 Excerpts of the Alcohol/Drug Abuse Procedure

STATEMENT

It is the policy of the Company that employees shall not be involved with the unlawful use, possession, sale, or transfer of drugs or narcotics in any manner which may impair their ability to perform assigned duties or otherwise adversely impact the Company's business. Further, employees shall not possess alcoholic beverages in the workplace or consume alcoholic beverages in associ-

continued

Exhibit 8.2 *continued*

ation with the workplace or during working time. If we are to continue to fulfill our responsibility to provide reliable and safe electric service to our customers and a safe working environment for our employees, employees must be physically and mentally fit to perform their duties in a safe and efficient manner.

IMPLEMENTATION

Off the job illegal drug activity or alcohol abuse which could have an adverse effect on an employee's job performance or which could jeopardize the safety of other employees, the public, Company equipment or the Company's relations with the public will not be tolerated.

The Company considers alcoholism and other drug addictions to be treatable illnesses. Absences directly or indirectly caused by the use of alcohol/drugs, for the specific purpose of Company-approved treatment, will be excused.

Illegal drugs are those drugs defined as illegal under federal, state and local laws which include, but are not limited to:

- marijuana
- heroin
- hashish
- cocaine
- hallucinogens
- depressants and stimulants not prescribed for current personal treatment by an accredited physician.

Training is provided to assist management in recognizing potential symptoms of alcohol/drug abuse that may lead to or be causing a performance problem.

USE OF THE EMPLOYEE ASSISTANCE PROGRAM

Employees experiencing problems with alcohol or other drugs are urged to voluntarily seek assistance through the Employee Assistance Program to resolve such problems *before* they become serious enough to require management referral or disciplinary action.

Participation, in itself, in the Employee Assistance Program for an alcohol/drug problem will in no way jeopardize an employee's job. In fact, successful treatment will be viewed positively. However, participation will not:

1. Prevent normal disciplinary action for a violation(s) which may have already occurred; nor
2. Relieve an employee of the responsibility to perform assigned duties in a safe and efficient manner.

continued

Exhibit 8.2 *continued*

CONSEQUENCES OF ALCOHOL/DRUG ABUSE

Drug Abuse: The use, sale or personal possession (for example, on the person, in a toolbox, desk or vehicle) of illegal drugs while on the job including rest periods and meal periods or on Company property is a dischargeable offense and may result in criminal prosecution. Any illegal drugs found will be turned over to the appropriate law enforcement agency.

Employees taking prescription or non-prescription drugs must report this use to supervision or a member of the Medical Staff when the use of such drugs may affect the employee's ability to perform assigned duties.

Alcohol Abuse: The use or personal possession (for example, on the person, in a desk, toolbox or locker) of alcohol during work time or on Company property is a dischargeable offense.

1. For all employees, alcohol consumption is prohibited during the workday, including rest periods and meal period. Notwithstanding this, there may be occasions, removed from the usual work setting, at which it is permissible to consume alcohol in moderation, with management approval. Employees who consume alcohol under such circumstances shall not report back to work during that workday.

2. The possession of alcohol in a Company or personal vehicle on or off of Company property is not prohibited by this procedure, provided such possession is in compliance with state and local laws.

Any employee, in any job, who is perceived to be under the influence of alcohol will be immediately removed from service and evaluated by medical personnel, if reasonably available. Management will take further appropriate action (i.e., referral to Employee Assistance Program and/or disciplinary action) based on the medical information, past history, and other relevant factors such as performance, record of disciplinary actions, etc.

Off-the-job selling, distributing or manufacturing of illegal drugs by a Duke Power employee is a dischargeable offense. Likewise, illegal selling, distributing or manufacturing of alcohol is a dischargeable offense. Decisions regarding discharge shall be made by management after consultation with the Human Resources Department.

SPECIAL ACTION

The Company will take whatever measures are necessary to find out if alcohol or illegal drugs are located on or being used on Company property. These measures will not be taken unreasonably, but when the Company believes

continued

Exhibit 8.2 *continued*

them to be completely justified and necessary. The measures that may be used will include, but not be limited to the following:

1. Trained dogs may be used to search company property, facilities, or equipment. Dogs will not be used to search people.
2. Federal, state and/or local authorities may be called upon to assist in an investigation.
3. Unannounced drug screens of groups of employees may be conducted where a reason to suspect exists. Refusal to participate in a drug screen will result in immediate removal from service and may result in termination for insubordination.
4. Searches of company property, facilities, or equipment may be conducted by authorized personnel.
5. Searches of people, and of personal property located on Company premises, may be conducted by security officers, if available, or by management if security officers are not readily available.

The decision to use the measures described above, or similar measures, must be approved by a Senior Vice President or above after consultation with the Vice President of Human Resources, except where time is critical to the success of the search.

DRUG TESTING

1. Drug tests will be conducted as a routine part of the pre-employment physical examination for all regular full-time and regular part-time job applicants and co-op students prior to employment. If the drug screen indicates the presence of drugs or controlled substances, the applicant will not be considered further for employment.
2. Drug tests will be conducted as a routine part of promotion or transfer into positions for which a Company-mandated physical is required and/or which may directly affect public safety or employee safety. If the drug screening indicates the presence of drugs, other than prescription drugs, the employee will not be considered further for the position. Positive results on a drug screening for promotion or transfer will be cause for referral to the Employee Assistance Program and/or consideration for disciplinary action.
3. Drug tests will be conducted as a routine part of company-mandated physicals for certain positions considered to be sensitive from a health and safety standpoint. Positive results on a drug screen will be cause for referral to the Employee Assistance Program and/or consideration for disciplinary action.
4. Drug and/or alcohol tests may be conducted at the option of manage-

continued

Exhibit 8.2 *continued*

ment as part of the investigation involving an accident (vehicular or personal) or "near-accident" in which safety precautions were violated and/or unusually careless acts were performed. Also where an employee's work record indicates a history of accidents, and/or "near accidents," or in accidents which are the fault of the employee testing may result.

5. Drug and/or alcohol tests will be conducted when an employee's supervisor has cause to believe that the employee is "unfit for duty."

6. Drug tests will be conducted where there is reason to suspect use or possession of illegal drugs.

7. When there is a change in group behavior, a high rate of accidents or injuries, reliable information about drug involvement and/or reason to suspect the use of illegal drugs within a work group, there may be cause for testing all employees in the work group after approval of a Senior Vice President or above.

CONSEQUENCES OF A POSITIVE DRUG TEST

1. In the case of a first time positive result on a drug screen, but where no evidence exists of use on the job, the following steps will be taken:

   a. The employee will be removed from service.

   b. The employee must visit the Employee Assistance Program staff at least once to learn what drug counseling resources are available. The employee will be required to seek treatment for drug abuse from a recognized professional and/or institution. Refusal to do so will be viewed as insubordination and the employee will be subject to discharge.

   c. The employee must have a negative test result in a screen administered by the Company within a period of six weeks from the date of removal from service. In the event the employee fails to do so within this six-week period, the employee will be discharged. If, after negative results within such six-week period, an employee is unable to return to work for good reason (e.g., participation in a treatment program not yet completed), the time at which such employee shall return to work may be extended beyond the end of the six-week period.

   d. Employees who have been removed from service following a positive drug screen and who have subsequently had a negative test result will be subject to random screening for an indefinite period of time. Supervisors shall have the responsibility, with Employee Assistance Program staff assistance, of determining when and if to require follow-up random screening.

continued

Exhibit 8.2 *continued*

2.   An employee in a job where a physical is not required or public/employee safety is not a factor will be allowed to return to work upon receipt by the Company of a negative test result.

3.   Employees in positions where a physical is required and/or which may affect public safety who have a first time positive drug screen and a negative follow-up screen within six weeks will be allowed to return to their position *only* upon providing to the EAP certified documentation from a recognized professional which would give a reasonable degree of confidence that the individual would be capable of performing his/her assigned duties without impairment.

4.   Employees who have been removed from service for a positive drug screen and allowed to return to work, in accordance with this procedure, will be discharged for a positive test result on a subsequent drug screen.

EXERCISE:
EVALSIM — A PERFORMANCE EVALUATION IN-BASKET

I. *Objectives:*

  1. To familiarize you with some of the problems related to the use of performance appraisals and to provide alternative approaches for solving these problems.

  2. To give you practice in making decisions and writing memos to employees regarding performance appraisal issues.

  3. To familiarize you with the major duties or tasks which personnel specialists must perform with regard to a firm's performance evaluation system.

II. *Out-of-Class Preparation Time:* 20 minutes to read exercise plus 1 - 2 hours to discuss In-Basket items with group members and write memos

III. *In-Class Time Suggested:* 45 minutes to discuss all In-Basket items

IV. *Procedures:* You are to begin by reading all of the material presented in this exercise. Your team is to assume that it is responsible for developing and maintaining the O'Leary Organization's performance appraisal system. You are to assume further that the items that follow were waiting in your in-basket when you arrived at work after a three-week vacation. You are to respond to each item in two different ways. First, write a response to the employee who wrote you the memo. Secondly, explain in writing on a separate sheet of paper what additional actions you would take with reference to each item. For example, if you believe that you should gather additional information before making a final decision on the item, explain what information you want. Or, if you believe that additional memos or discussions with someone in the company are needed, explain this. Your team should bring both the memos and the "Additional Action" sheets to class. Be prepared to present and defend these materials during class discussion.

Situation

The O'Leary Organization is a medium-sized organization whose headquarters is located in the midwestern United States. You may assume that the organization is a manufacturing company, a hospital, an insurance company, a university, or virtually any other medium-sized organization with which you are familiar.

The O'Leary Organization's Personnel Department is organized in the manner shown below:

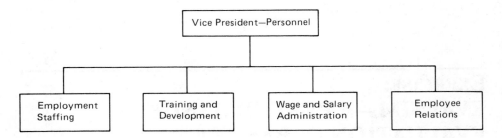

The Training and Development section consists of your team. In addition to conducting training, one of your team's other major duties is that of having full responsibility for the organization's performance evaluation system. Included among your duties are:

1. Determining which employees will be evaluated.
2. Determining how frequently employees will be evaluated.
3. Determining which appraisal format should be used.
4. Determining which job categories will be used to evaluate the employee's job performance.
5. Determining who should evaluate each employee.
6. Insuring that all evaluators know how to complete the organization's performance appraisal form and to conduct evaluation interviews.
7. Establishing the performance appraisal system and insuring that all employees adhere to it.
8. Maintaining all performance appraisal records.

The O'Leary Organization's present performance appraisal system, which you are to assume your team designed, requires that all employees be evaluated by their supervisor on a periodic basis. All employees are evaluated at the end of a ninety-day period (the probationary period) and on a yearly basis thereafter. The performance evaluation form used by the organization is shown in Exhibit 8.3. Supervisors are required to complete this form covering each of their employees at the appropriate time, discuss the evaluation with him or her, ask the employee to sign the form at the end of the evaluation interview, and return the completed form to the Personnel Department.

Exhibit 8.3 The O'Leary Organization Performance Appraisal Form

NAME   SOCIAL SECURITY NO.

TITLE   DEPARTMENT

TODAY'S DATE   APPRAISAL PERIOD   Annual
                                                    FROM _____ TO _____   90 day
                                                                              Special

PART I Performance Rating
(All Employees)

	1	2	3	4	5
Ability					
Attendance					
Attitude					
Appearance					
Conduct					
Initiative					
Work with Group					
Promotability					
Quantity of Work					
Quality of Work					
Overall Level of Performance					

continued

Exhibit 8.3 *continued*

REMARKS

Prepared by _____ Title _____
COMMENTS BY REVIEWED EMPLOYEE:

Employee's Signature _____ Date _____
(Employee signature does not indicate agreement, merely acknowledgement
of this report.)

1 — Unsatisfactory   2 — Below Average   3 — Satisfactory
4 — Good   5 — Excellent

IN-BASKET ITEMS

Item 1

M E M O R A N D U M

TO: Personnel Department
FROM: Tom Morrison, Accounting Department
SUBJECT: 90-Day Employee Evaluation

I just received my 90-day employee evaluation and received mostly "3's" on
it. My boss explained his evaluation to me by saying that I was making good
progress on the job. He added that, if I continue to show improvement, I will
receive "4's" and "5's" like the more experienced employees do. Why am I
being evaluated against older, more experienced workers? That doesn't seem
right. I believe that considering my limited experience I deserve "excellent"
evaluations.

Item 2

M E M O R A N D U M

TO: Personnel Department
FROM: Paul Lands, Computer Center
SUBJECT: Performance Evaluation

    Joe Meena and I both started together at the O'Leary Organization two years ago. We are both in the Computer Center doing the same job, only he works one shift, and I work another. Two weeks ago when we compared our performance evaluations, I discovered that he received all "5's" whereas I received mostly "4's." The thing that irks me is that he and I both know we are doing an equally good job. His boss is just more lenient in his evaluation than is my boss. I don't think this whole system is fair, particularly since he may get promoted (based on his performance evaluation) before I do. Can't something be done about this?

Item 3

M E M O R A N D U M

TO: Personnel Department
FROM: Jill Best, Manager
SUBJECT: Lost Performance Appraisal Form

    Six weeks ago when our offices were being remodeled, one of the janitors accidentally threw away a small stack of papers. Included in the stack was a performance appraisal form which I had just completed on one of my subordinates, Karen Whitmore. I know you need this form, but it is gone. What should I do?

Item 4

M E M O R A N D U M

TO: Personnel Department
FROM: Sue Peters, Supervisor
SUBJECT: Administering Employee Evaluations

    I have recently received from your office a request to conduct evaluations this month on three of my employees. As you probably know, I was promoted to this supervisory position just one week ago as a result of the former supervisor's termination. I don't feel that I can presently conduct a fair evaluation of these employees. Do you want me to do them anyway?

Item 5

MEMORANDUM

TO: Personnel Department
FROM: Sandra Kelly, Supervisor
SUBJECT: Evaluation of Karen Bicknell

Yesterday afternoon I conducted an evaluation interview with Karen Bicknell, and when I told her I gave her a "3" on "Work with Group" she got quite upset and defensive. She said the evaluation should have been at least a "4" and probably a "5." I attempted to explain my evaluation to her, but she wouldn't listen. Instead, she continued to argue with me. Karen received a "4" evaluation last year on "Work with Group" and a 3.5 overall evaluation this year. What should I do if this happens again?

Item 6

MEMORANDUM

TO: Personnel Department
FROM: Howard Adams, Supervisor
SUBJECT: Necessity of Signing Evaluation Forms

Recently I conducted a performance evaluation interview with Harold Wallace. At the end of the interview, when I asked him to sign the appraisal form at the bottom, he refused. I asked him if the evaluation was accurate, and he said yes. I also explained to him that signing the form only represented an acknowledgment that he had been evaluated. He replied that he had nothing to gain from signing the form, and, therefore, why sign it? I don't know what I should do. Harold is somewhat of a problem and is often quite stubborn.

Item 7

MEMORANDUM

TO: Personnel Department
FROM: Margaret Windell, Purchasing
SUBJECT: Annual Performance Review

I have a rather troublesome question to ask you. I would ask it of my boss, but she is currently in the hospital. For the last 23 years I have received an overall performance review, and my evaluations have all shown that I am an excellent employee. I am six years from retirement and, frankly, I have reached the point where performance evaluations aren't of any consequence to me. I know I am doing a good job. I know I won't get promoted or transferred, and I am at the top of my pay grade. So why should I continue to be evaluated formally?

Item 8

MEMORANDUM

TO: Personnel Department
FROM: Sarah Wade, Maintenance Engineer
SUBJECT: Employee Appraisal Form

When I was over in the Personnel Department yesterday looking at my personnel file, I saw the appraisal form which was completed on me one month ago. I was shocked to see the following statement written on it under "Remarks": "Sarah has a very poor work attitude and doesn't appear willing to change it." My boss, Marilyn Turner, had also changed my evaluation on "attitude" from a "4" to a "2." I am positive the negative statement was not on the evaluation form when I signed it. Needless to say, I want you to do something about this!

Item 9

MEMORANDUM

TO: Personnel Department
FROM: Chris Green, Supervisor
SUBJECT: Performance Evaluation of Bill Young

Next week I must conduct a performance evaluation interview with Bill Young who works by himself in the evenings. While I was completing the evaluation form on him, I realized that it was impossible for me to evaluate him on one of the evaluation categories, "Work with Group." What should I do? I am afraid if I leave it blank it will affect his "Overall Level of Performance" score and hence his chances of promotion.

Item 10

MEMORANDUM

TO: Personnel Department
FROM: Jeff Skala, Finance Department
SUBJECT: Confidentiality of Performance Evaluation

As you know, I have been experiencing a series of personal problems during the past year all of which have adversely affected my job performance. These problems reflected themselves on my recent performance evaluation as my "marks" slipped from mostly "4's" to most "2's." I can't disagree with my evaluation, but I don't think it was right for my boss, Helen Jackson, to tell two of my co-workers that she had given me a "1" on "Quality of Work." It seems to me that this type of information should be none of their business.

EXERCISE:
PERFORMANCE APPRAISAL INTERVIEW ROLE PLAY

I. *Objectives:*
1. To allow you practice in conducting a performance appraisal interview.
2. To compare and contrast different approaches to the performance appraisal interview.
3. To help you develop sensitivity toward communication problems in performance appraisal interviews.

II. *Out-of-Class Preparation Time:* 20 - 30 minutes
III. *In-Class Time Suggested:* 45 minutes
IV. *Procedures:*
1. Read the exercise before coming to class.
2. Four students should be selected to participate in two different performance appraisal interviews (A and B). Two of you will play the role of the employee and two will play the role of the supervisor. Role assignments should be made in the prior class period or before class begins. The instructor will provide role sheets.
3. The persons playing the role of the employee should read "Employee's Role."
4. The person playing the role of supervisor A should read the "Supervisor Role A" and the person playing the role of supervisor B should read the "Supervisor Role B."
5. During the class period where the role plays will occur, all role play participants should be taken outside of the classroom and given time to prepare their respective roles. All other members of the class are to observe the two different sets of interviews and record their observations on separate sheets of paper.
6. Supervisor A conducts a 10-15 minute appraisal interview with one of the employees in the front of the class. The other role play pair remains in the hall outside the classroom until their turn.
7. After the first role play is completed, the second role play pair enters the classroom and conducts its appraisal interview. The first role play team joins the rest of the class to observe the interview.
8. The entire class discusses both interviews.

SITUATION

Tri-City Health Services is a large non-profit center providing basic out-patient health services and health education programs to low-income families in the Southwest. The center employs over 40 physicians and nurses and over 200 other workers in various staff positions. Pat Smith has been working as a junior assistant in the Fund Raising and Grants Department for the past two years and has worked on the children's health care program. Pat has done well in performing the job — all performance objectives have been met or surpassed for the year. However, this year Pat has been consistently late for work on many occasions. Each year on the anniversary date of the employee's hire, his or her supervisor must conduct a performance appraisal interview. Chris Jackson, the supervisor, has completed the performance evaluation form shown in Exhibit 8.4 and is ready to discuss the evaluation with Pat.

INSTRUCTIONS FOR OBSERVERS

Your task is to evaluate two different sets of performance interviews. As you observe the interviews, consider the following:
1. How did the supervisor begin the interview? Was the purpose of the interview clearly stated?
2. What type of interview approach did the supervisor use? Who did most of the talking?
3. Did the supervisor learn how the employee feels about the job? About his or her performance?
4. Did both parties gain a clear understanding of the problem and its solution?
5. Were any specific action plans made to resolve the problem(s)?
6. Are there any ways in which the supervisor could improve the interview? How?
7. Which interview was most effective? Why?

Exhibit 8.4 Performance Evaluation Form

I. RATING CATEGORIES

Performance Dimensions	Performance Level	Points (Maximum = 5)
Quality of Work (The degree to which the employee's work is free of flaws)	*Excellent*	5

continued

Exhibit 8.4 *continued*

Quantity of Work (The total amount of acceptable work completed within time and resources available)	*Excellent*	5
Attendance (Includes absences and tardiness)	*Poor*	1
Cooperation (The degree to which the employee cooperates with and is respected by co-workers	*Average*	3
Initiative and Self-Reliance (The degree to which the employee is independent and self-directed)	*Excellent*	5
Work Timeliness (The degree to which the employee exhibits skill in planning and scheduling activities)	*Average*	3
Responsibility (The degree to which the employee is willing to accept responsibility for details in work)	*Above Average*	4
Total Points		*26*

II. OBJECTIVES AND GOALS

A. Did the employee set any specific work-related goals this performance period?   Yes (X)   No ( )

B. If yes, what were they?
To complete and implement a fund-raising program by April 1.
To obtain a 15 percent increase in federal grants by April 1.

C. To what extent were they met?
Employee met or exceeded both objectives. The fund-raising effort was very successful (over $25,000 was raised) and federal grants have been increased by 18 percent this year.

Overall evaluation of goal achievement? *Excellent*

continued

Exhibit 8.4 *continued*

III. OVERALL EVALUATION OF EMPLOYEE PERFORMANCE
(Support evaluation with comments.)

The employee has done a fine job on performance objectives but continues to have a problem with tardiness. Based on this, the overall rating for the year is average (26 out of 35 points). I do not recommend the employee for a promotion at this time.

Supervisor Signature	Date	Employee Signature	Date

INCIDENT:
ROLLER DERBY
WITH THE FORKLIFT TRUCK

The warehouse of a large plant in St. Paul was divided into several sections with a different supervisor heading each section. Joe Lewis was the supervisor in charge of the dismantling department. Joe believed in a free reign style of management. His employees were given considerable freedom over their activities.

Joe's employees had continually higher job performance than those in the other warehouse sections. They thought very highly of Joe; in fact, they considered him one of the gang.

One night, while on overtime, Joe's section started to goof around as they always had in the past. This time, however, it got out of hand. Before the night was over, one of Joe's workers had driven a forklift truck through one of the plywood partitions of the warehouse. It wasn't long before Joe noticed the gaping hole in the wall. He immediately confronted the employees in his section saying, "O.K., who's been playing roller derby with the forklift?" Everyone stared at one another, but nobody answered.

Contributed by Arno F. Knapper, School of Business, University of Kansas.

Questions

1. What course of action should Joe follow now? Why?
2. Should Joe discipline all of the employees if he can't determine who is guilty?
3. If someone confesses to the "crime," what action should Joe take?
4. Evaluate Joe's apparent leadership style. Should it change?

INCIDENT:
SPIKED MILK

A reputable northeastern construction company employs six experienced construction supervisors for its various construction jobs. These supervisors have the overall responsibility of hiring and firing and seeing that the construction proceeds as close to time and cost schedules as possible. They also have the responsibility of overall quality control of the construction.

Larry Werst, age 55, has been a supervisor for this company for many years. He is never absent and has established a reputation for getting the job done close to schedule and doing it right. He has supervised the construction of several prominent buildings and is now supervising the construction of a college fraternity house. Larry's approach to handling his employees is firm and sometimes harsh. He doesn't take any back talk, and everyone who works for him usually earns his or her pay or isn't on the job for very long.

The owner and manager of the company had become concerned about Larry because rumors implied that he was an alcoholic and that he drank on the job. The owner knew that Larry drank a lot and had a stormy, cavalier home life, but he didn't know whether he was drinking on the job.

One day, the manager was talking with Larry and noticed a definite bad-breath odor smelling quite alcoholic. This happened on several occasions, and office and storeroom employees noticed the odor when they talked to him. Also, the storeroom clerk noticed that almost every day he would come in and buy two cokes at a time and then take off in his company truck, presumably back to his job site.

The manager decided to talk to Larry about this subject. When he confronted Larry with the rumors, the bad breath, and two cokes at a time, Larry denied that he was drinking. He said that the rumors were just that and that the two cokes were for himself and his carpenter supervisor. The manager told him that he would have to let him go if he were ever caught drinking on the job. He reminded Larry that the firm's progressive discipline system included a rule that states, "No

Contributed by Arno F. Knapper, School of Business, University of Kansas employee is permitted to go on duty or remain on duty if he or she possesses, is under the influence of, or is consuming an alcoholic beverage. Violation of this policy will result in dismissal."

About a year later, when the construction season was again in full swing, stories began floating around about Larry's drinking. The employees on his job talked about the quart of milk he drank every day. They wondered why he had started drinking so much of it lately and wondered if he "spiked" it and used it to combat his odorous breath. Sometimes his speech seemed definitely slurred, but Larry was gravel-voiced and had sloppy speech habits anyway. The workers also got a lot of amusement from the stories he'd tell about things that had happened to him. They were just stories, of course, but lately they were getting pathetically far-fetched and made no sense at all.

The manager couldn't help finding out about some of the things that were said about Larry, and he wondered what he should do. Larry had never actually been caught drinking. His construction job was going up satisfactorily, but it was a little behind schedule due to the inability to get good carpenters and laborers at the beginning of the construction season. Worker turnover was perhaps a little higher on this job than the average.

Questions

1. What course of action should the manager follow? Why?
2. To what extent should the manager go to try to catch Larry drinking on the job?
3. What action, if any, should the manager take if Larry confesses to being an alcoholic?
4. Does the manager presently have sufficient proof that Larry is working under the influence of alcohol?
5. Critique the firm's alcoholism rule.

SKILL BUILDER:
WRITING/DEVELOPING EMPLOYEE
DISCIPLINE POLICIES

I. *Objectives:*

    1. To familiarize you with how organizations resolve employee discipline problems.

    2. To allow you practice in writing a model discipline policy statement.

II. *Time Required to Complete:* 2 - 3 hours

III. *Instructions:* Go to the library and read four articles which deal directly with one of the topics below and write a brief summary of them. Look for articles which explain how companies handle or should handle these employee problems. (Make sure you include a full bibliography.) Once your research is completed, develop a written "model" policy statement for a medium-sized manufacturing company for the topic you selected. Be sure that your statement specifies the rules and disciplinary procedures that apply.

Topics

1. Stealing/Theft/Dishonesty
2. Absenteeism
3. Insubordination
4. Tardiness
5. Alcohol/Drug Abuse
6. Safety Rule Violation
7. Sexual Harassment

Part 9

GROUP PROJECTS/TERM ASSIGNMENTS

PERSONNEL SYSTEM EVALUATION

I. *Objective:*   To help you to critically analyze a personnel system, identify problems, and recommend constructive improvements.

II. *Out-of-Class Preparation Time*: 30 - 40 hours per group (10 - 15 hours per individual student)

III. *In-Class Time Suggested:*   None, unless an oral report is required by the instructor

IV. *Procedures:* You should identify a real organization, form groups of two to three people, and receive permission to study the organization from either the CEO or the personnel director.   Once permission is received, your group should arrange to interview as many of the following as possible: the personnel director, other personnel department employees, employees performing different functions at different levels in the organization, and labor union officials (if any).

V. *General Purpose:*   The study will focus upon the selected organization's personnel and employee relations objectives, structures, policies, practices, and selected administrative problems. It will give you the opportunity to learn firsthand about the management of personnel systems in actual organizations. It will also provide you with the opportunity to develop field research methodologies and evaluation skills that should prove beneficial in future academic and professional assignments. Finally, for the organization cooperating with each of the student projects, the results of these studies should be helpful in future efforts to improve the efficiency and effectiveness of their personnel systems.

The final product of this study will be a comprehensive written report to be submitted no later than two weeks before the end of the term. Each of you should assume the stance of an outside consultant who has been called in to evaluate the personnel system of the particular organization. At a *minimum*, the paper should reflect the items contained in the Evaluation Guide that is found below. Alternatively, your instructor may permit each group to focus on a few selected parts of the organization's personnel system.

EVALUATION GUIDE

I. *The Organization and Its Mission*

    A. When and why was this organization established?

        1. Under what statutory or legal authority was it created?

        2. What are the principal needs and objectives that the organization is designed to fulfill?

    B. What are the structural components of the organization?

        1. How is the organization organized to carry out its objectives?

        2. Where is the focus of decision-making authority for carrying out these objectives?

    a. How centralized or decentralized is the decision-making process with respect to

        i. organizational planning?

        ii. operational management?

    b. What is the relationship between the leadership of this organization and

        i. elected public officials?

        ii. other public officials?

        iii. leaders in the private sector?

        iv. representatives of employee organizations or associations if any?

        v. professional and technical staffs?

3. What budgetary constraints confront the organization?

    a. What are the sources of revenue for this agency?

        i. for capital expenditures?

        ii. for operating expenditures?

    b. What changes have occurred in the organization's budget in recent years?

        i. Have there been any noticeable increases or decreases in budget allocations?

        ii. Have there been any new sources of funding?

        iii. Have any old sources of funding been reduced or eliminated?

        iv. How have these trends affected management of the organization?

4. What is the total employment complement of the organization?

    a. How are these employees distributed throughout the organization?

        i. by department or operational function?

        ii. by skill, e.g., managerial, professional, technical, clerical, skilled craftsman, semi-skilled operatives, unskilled laborers, etc.?

    b. What have been some of the noticeable employment trends in recent years?

    c. What are the major problems and opportunities confronting this organization? Up to this point, how well has the organization responded to these challenges? What are your recommendations? Why?

II. *The Role of the Personnel Function*

    A. Does this organization have a formal and identifiable personnel function (department)?

        1. When was this department or function formally established and why?

    2. How is the personnel function or department organized to carry out the objectives of the organization?

    3. How many individuals are directly associated with the personnel function or department?

    4. What are the academic and employment backgrounds of those involved in the organization's personnel function?

B. What is the focus of decision-making authority on personnel matters within the agency?

    1. Who establishes the objectives and policies related to personnel matters?

    2. What is the relationship between the personnel functions and other operations of the organization in the administration of personnel policies and practices?

C. What is the perceived importance of the personnel function or department relative to other functional operations of the organization?

D. What recommendations do you have (if any) for reorganizing the personnel function? Why?

III. *Employment Decisions*

A. Who is responsible for human resource planning and forecasting for the organization?

    1. What methods are used to determine staffing needs?

    2. Does the organization focus primarily upon short-run or long-run human resource needs, or both?

    3. Are job analyses and job descriptions made for each position in the organization?

    4. What specific problems have been encountered in the human resource planning process?

        a. To what can they be attributed?

        b. What are the major alternatives for resolving these problems?

        c. Which solutions are most feasible, and why?

    5. If no human resource planning is done:

        a. Why not?

        b. Has the lack of human resource planning had any negative impact? Why?

    6. Does the organization provide career planning and career counseling for employees? Why?

B. Once staffing needs are established, what procedures are utilized for filling job vacancies?

    1. Who is responsible for staffing the organization, the personnel department, or the respective functional departments?

    2. What methods are used to recruit new employees?

    3. What methods and criteria are used for evaluating and selecting job applicants? Have these methods been validated? How?

    4. To what extent are new employee recruitment, evaluation, and

selection procedures aided or restricted by:
- **a.** established policies or practices of the organization?
- **b.** provisions contained in employment laws?
- **c.** factors associated with local labor markets?
5. Does the organization seek to fill existing job vacancies from among present employees or by recruiting new employees, and why?
6. What specific problems have been encountered in the employment staffing process?
- **a.** To what can these be attributed?
- **b.** What are the major alternatives for resolving these problems?
- **c.** Which solutions are most feasible, and why?

IV. *Determination of Working Conditions and Rewards*

A. Is an occupational classification system utilized by the organization?
1. Who is responsible for determining the classification system?
2. What are the basic features of this system?
- **a.** Does the classification system appropriately reflect variations in job skills?
- **b.** Is it used effectively as a mechanism for identifying career paths? Explain.
- **c.** Have there been any recent reviews and evaluations of the performance of the classification system in relation to organizational and personnel goals?

B. How are wage and salary levels and annual improvements determined?
1. Does the organization conduct periodic internal and external wage surveys?
2. Are salary levels adequate to enable the organization to attract and maintain an effective work force? Why or why not?
3. Do differentials in salary grades appropriately reflect differentials in skills and responsibilities?
4. Are large proportions of employees grouped into particular salary grade levels?
5. How do salary levels compare with those of other comparable organizations for the same or similar occupational and experience groupings?
6. What trends have taken place in salary levels over the past few years?

C. What methods are used for evaluating employees for the purpose of determining their effectiveness and any merited salary increases?
1. Do employee performance appraisal systems actually reflect job performance? Why or why not?
2. How adequate or inadequate are the performance appraisal methods currently being used? Why?

D. How adequate are non-wage fringe benefits?

      1. How are they determined?

      2. How do they compare with those of other organizations?

E. Has the organization introduced any special programs or activities to improve safety and health conditions on the job?

F. What efforts, if any, are utilized to maintain employee morale and job satisfaction?

G. What improvements in compensation and employee motivation should be made? Why?

V. *Employee Training and Development*

A. Has the organization supported programs for employee training and development? Why or why not?

      1. What kinds or programs have been established? Have they been oriented toward:

         a. job skills?

         b. supervisory and leadership skills?

         c. basic educational skills?

      2. Does the organization maintain its own training staff or are outside organizations used for training purposes?

      3. What proportion of employees have participated in training and development programs supported by the organization?

B. To what extent has the organization's programs of employee training and development been used in making decisions related to promotions and transfers within the organization?

      1. Are promotion decisions based primarily upon the measured and observed abilities of employees or upon their seniority in the job?

C. What problems, if any, have been encountered in the administration of employee training and development programs within the organization? What suggestions for improvement can you make? Why?

VI. *Employee Frictions*

A. What methods and procedures are available for resolving employee complaints and grievances?

      1. Have there been large numbers of such grievances? Why?

      2. Has the volume of grievances been growing or declining? Why?

      3. What are the major problems eliciting the majority of employee grievances?

B. Have there been many problems of employee discipline?

      1. Are there clearly spelled out formal procedures within the organization for handling discipline cases? What are they?

      2. How often are employees disciplined or discharged?

         a. What are the major causes of such problems?

         b. How have these been dealt with by the organization?

C. To what extent have employee lateness, absenteeism, and turnover been problems?

1. Have these problems be studied to determine their most likely causes? What are they?
2. What steps have been taken to resolve these problems, if they exist? What steps should been taken? Why?

D. Have any of the employees sought to join labor organizations for the purpose of engaging in collective bargaining over wages, hours, and working conditions? Explain.

1. Why have, or have not, such organizing activities taken place?
2. What is the official position of the organization toward acceptance or rejection of unionism for its employees?
3. If a labor union exists in this organization, what effect has the union had upon:
   a. overall decision-making within the organization?
   b. the efficiency and productivity of the organization?
   c. the administration of the personnel function?
   d. the relations between the managers of the organization and its non-managerial personnel?
   e. the interpersonal relationships among non-supervisory employees?

E. What has been the relationship between management and union leaders? (e.g., cooperative; neutral; cold; hostile?)

1. Have there been any noticeable changes in the nature of this relationship in the recent past? Why or why not?
2. Have there been any work stoppages among employees of the agency in order to pressure management into agreeing to union demands?
   a. What were the issue(s)?
   b. Why did the dispute occur?
   c. How was it resolved?
   d. What has been its subsequent impact upon:
     i. the operation of the agency?
     ii. employee performance?
     iii. the work environment?
     iv. the decision-making process involved in personnel matters?

F. What suggestions would you make for minimizing employee grievances and improving the labor relations climate (if applicable)? Why?

VII. *Summary and Evaluation*

A. How effectively is the personnel function of this organization contributing to the fulfillment of its mission and objectives?
B. What are some of the problems of personnel administration that have been adequately solved or are now in the process of being solved by the organization?

C. What are some of the major personnel problems that remain to be confronted and solved?

D. What would appear to be among the most desirable solutions to these problems? Provide specific detail and justification for your recommendations.

PERSONNEL MANAGER INTERVIEW

I. *Objectives:*

    1. To analyze the role of personnel/human resource managers in organizations.

    2. To allow you to gain a better understanding of the nature of a personnel manager's job.

    3. To help you understand the interface between personnel and line managers.

II. *Out-of-Class Preparation Time:* 8 - 10 hours

III. *In-Class Time Suggested:* None unless instructor wants an oral report.

IV. *Procedures:*

    1. This assignment is to be done individually by each student.

    2. Locate a personnel manager to interview. You may select a personnel generalist or a personnel specialist. After the manager understands the research project and agrees to cooperate, conduct the interview. The interview should take about 45 minutes to one hour.

    3. Also interview a line manager in the same organization to gain his or her views of personnel.

    4. A suggested interview outline is given (in Exhibit 9.1) for the questions to be asked. You are expected to prepare additional questions. The final interview questions and the name of the organization and manager you will interview should be turned into your instructor for approval prior to conducting the actual interview. Additionally, you should gather research information on the company before the interview if possible.

    5. Prepare a report (8-10 pages) of the results of the interviews which covers: (a) a description of the overall operations and role of the personnel department; (b) a description of the personnel function they explored in-depth; (c) the type of interaction between personnel and line managers; and (d) the extent to which the organization's personnel practices conform to theoretical prescriptions. If differences are found, discuss why they exist.

Exhibit 9.1 Interview Outline

Part I: Organization Information

   a. Type of business/industry/organization
   b. General description of company's products/service/operations
   c. Brief company history
   d. Number of employees: managerial, clerical, operative, etc.
   e. Organization structure
   f. Size and structure of the personnel/human resource department

Part II: Background of the Personnel/Human Resource Manager

   a. Title
   b. Academic preparation (highest degree earned and field of study)
   c. Years with organization
   d. Years of personnel experience
   e. Other work experience
   f. Professional associations/organizations

Part III: Personnel/Human Resource Management Functions

Ask the personnel manager to check off and rate the personnel activities listed in Form 1.

Part IV: Role of Personnel/Human Resource Department

Ask the personnel manager the following general questions:

   a. What is the role of personnel in your organization?
   b. To what extent is the personnel staff/department involved in strategic business planning? Explain.
   c. In your opinion, what are some of the most pressing human resource issues faced by organizations today? Why?
   d. What was the most difficult organizational problem faced by the personnel department in the last five years? How was it resolved? Why?

Part V: In-depth Review of P/HRM Function

Explore in depth one of the personnel functions with the personnel manager (for example: recruiting, selection/staffing, compensation, training and development, performance evaluation, etc.). You should first review the material in the text on the personnel function you choose and then prepare a set of questions for the manager relating to how that function is carried out in the organization. During the interview be sure to get enough information so you can describe their function in detail. Ask the executive to comment on the effectiveness of the function and his or her interaction with line managers in carrying out the activity. Try to obtain examples of forms and/or materials used.

Part VI: Interface with Line Managers

Once you have interviewed the P/HRM manager, also interview one of the line managers in the organization. The purpose of this interview is to understand the way in which personnel "interfaces" with other managers in the organizations.

Ask the manager:
- **a.** To rate the activities listed in Form 2.
- **b.** What kinds of things are done by personnel that support you in your position?
- **c.** What do you "ideally" expect from personnel in performing your job?

Form 1 Form for Ranking of Personnel Activities by Personnel Manager

Instructions: Place a check next to the personnel activities under your responsibility and indicate the importance of these responsibilities using a scale of 1 (very important) to 5 (not very important).

	Personnel Activities	Importance
1.	Ensure fair and consistent implementation of personnel policies and procedures.	_____
2.	Advise and counsel management on employee problems.	_____
3.	Design appropriate staffing and recruiting policies and programs.	
4.	Assist department managers in interviewing, selecting and hiring of employees.	_____
5.	Design and implement performance evaluation system(s).	_____
6.	Administer direct and indirect compensation programs.	_____
7.	Ensure compliance with federal and state fair employment laws and other legal restrictions in all employment practices.	_____
8.	Counsel employees on job-related and/or personal problems.	_____
9.	Develop and maintain employee personnel records.	_____
10.	Develop EEO policy and communicate EEO policy to all managers.	_____
11.	Ensure compliance with safety and health standards.	_____
12.	Oversee fair application of employee grievance procedures.	_____
13.	Provide state-of-the-art solutions to employee relations problems.	_____
14.	Plan for future human resource needs.	_____
15.	Work with top management on human resource implications of business plans and strategies.	_____

continued

Form 1 *continued*

____16. Design and implement employee training and career _____
         development programs.
____17. Negotiate the collective bargaining agreement. _____
____18. Administer and enforce provisions of the collective _____
         bargaining agreement.
____19. Other(s) write in. _____

_____

_____

_____

Form 2   Form for Ranking of Personnel Activities by Line Manager

Instructions: Here is a list of typical activities performed by personnel departments in organizations. Please indicate the importance of the activities performed by the personnel department in your organization using a scale of 1 (very important) to 5 (not very important).

Personnel Activities	Importance
1. Ensure fair and consistent implementation of personnel policies and procedures.	_____
2. Advise and counsel management on employee problems.	_____
3. Design appropriate staffing and recruiting policies and programs.	_____
4. Assist department managers in interviewing, selecting and hiring of employees.	_____
5. Design and implement performance evaluation system(s).	_____
6. Administer direct and indirect compensation programs.	_____
7. Ensure compliance with federal and state fair employment laws and other legal restrictions in all employment practices.	_____
8. Counsel employees on job-related and/or personal problems.	_____
9. Develop and maintain employee personnel records.	_____
10. Develop EEO policy and communicate EEO policy to all managers.	_____
11. Ensure compliance with safety and health standards.	_____
12. Oversee fair application of employee grievance procedures	_____
13. Provide state-of-the-art solutions to employee relations problems.	_____
14. Plan for future human resource needs.	_____

continued

Form 2 *continued*

15. Work with top management on human resource implications of business plans and strategies. ____
16. Design and implement employee training and career development programs. ____
17. Negotiate the collective bargaining agreement. ____
18. Administer and enforce provisions of the collective bargaining agreement. ____
19. Other(s) write in.

_____

_____

_____

GROUP DEBATE PROJECT: CONTROVERSIAL P/HRM ISSUES

I. *Objectives:*
1. To help you understand both sides of controversial personnel/human resource management issues.
2. To allow you to apply personnel/human resource management concepts in understanding the policy implications of the issues.

II. *Out-of-Class Preparation Time:* Equivalent to time required for students to complete a major term paper assignment

III. *In-Class Time Suggested:* 45 minutes

IV. *Procedures:*
1. Each debate will consist of two teams: an affirmative team which upholds the proposition and a negative team which opposes it. Debates can be scheduled throughout the semester to coincide with course content. For example, the comparable worth debate should be held after compensation is covered in the course. Alternatievly, all debates could be held at the end of the term.
2. Students should be divided into groups of three or four depending on the number of debate topics to be covered during the semester. The number of debators on each side should be equal and the time allowed for each side is the same.

3. Each group should be assigned to either the affirmative or negative side of a topic.
4. Each team conducts research on its topic. Because of the current nature of the debate topics, you are encouraged to consult current periodicals (e.g., use the *Business Index, Business Periodicals Index*, etc.) in addition to academic journals and books. You may want to review the list of journals in the skill builder in Part 1.
5. Each team prepares a written paper (8 - 10 pages) analyzing both sides of the topic in addition to presenting its arguments. The paper should be divided into three major parts: Introduction, Discussion, and Conclusion. (See additional instructions that follow.)
6. The debate is held in class and the two sides alternate in presenting their arguments with the affirmative side opening and closing the debate.
7. A chairperson presides over the debate and keeps time.
8. The debating teams' presentations are evaluated by the rest of the class and the instructor (see Form 1).

ADDITIONAL INSTRUCTIONS FOR DEBATE TEAMS

Structure of Classroom Debates

First Affirmative		6 minutes
First Negative		6 minutes
Second Affirmative		6 minutes
Second Negative		6 minutes
Rebuttals:	Negative	5 minutes
	Affirmative	5 minutes
Audience Cross-Examination		10 minutes

Tips on Oral Presentation

1. All of the speeches in the debate, *except* the first affirmative speech, should be given extemporaneously by the debators. They should not be read. Essentially, the debators' comments must reflect what was presented in the previous speech.
2. The first affirmative speech should be used to build the affirmative case. It is a good idea to give an overview of the major arguments you will use to uphold the proposition.
3. The first negative speech must be presented with the content of the first affirmative speech in mind. The aim of the negative speech is to cast doubt on the affirmative's arguments. The second speeches on both sides attempt to reconstruct and rebuild arguments as needed.
4. The rebuttal should directly address the arguments made by the other side.
5. Two excellent sources on debating are: Arthur N. Kruger, *Modern Debate:*

Its Logic and Strategy. New York: McGraw-Hill, 1960 and Thomas K. Hanley, *An Introduction to Debate.* Boston: Ginn & Company, 1965.

Suggested Debate Propositions

1. Resolved: That drug testing in the workplace makes good business sense and does not infringe upon employee rights.
2. Resolved: That affirmative action is a fair method of achieving equal opportunity for minority groups and women.
3. Resolved: That smoking restrictions are needed to assure a safe working environment for nonsmokers.
4. Resolved: That employment-at-will or termination-at-will should remain the basic doctrine governing employee dismissal and should not be subject to legislative restrictions.
5. Resolved: That comparable worth should become an accepted means of addressing sex-based wage gaps.
6. Resolved: That labor unions in the United States have been a positive force for both employees and the economy.
7. Resolved: That paper and pencil honesty tests are a good method for screening out dishonest employees and preventing employee theft.
8. Resolved: That employers should be legally required to give employees prenotification of plant closings or relocations.
9. Resolved: That federal laws regulating safety in the workplace have done more harm than good.

Suggested Paper Format

Your written paper will follow a form known as a "full brief"—a comprehensive analysis of both sides of a given proposition, outlined logically from which the debator can develop his or her case. Each team should have a minimum of ten references (in most cases you will have many more). The paper will consist of three parts: Introduction, Discussion, and Conclusion:

Introduction:
   a. Statement of the proposition and your group's position.
   b. Why is the issue important?
   c. Origin and history of the issue—keep brief.
   d. Outline the conflicting arguments—why is there a controversy?

Discussion: (This is the major section of your analysis.)
   a. Present your arguments to support your position.
   b. Be sure to use sound reasoning and evidence.

Conclusion:
   a. Summarize the main points of the discussion—recapitulate your major points.
   b. End with an affirmation or denial of the proposition (depending on whether you have the affirmative or negative position).

Form 1   Debate Evaluation Form

DEBATE:

Use the following Scale to write in a rating on each item below for each team.

1	2	3	4
POOR	FAIR	GOOD	SUPERIOR
		Affirmative Team	Negative Team

I. Analysis
(Was the analysis reasonable, complete, and clear?)

II. Reasoning and evidence
(Were the arguments structured soundly based on research facts and examples? Were arguments logical?)

III. Organization
(Was each speech clearly organized and cogently organized so that you could follow the structure of the debate?)

IV. Rebuttal
(Were unsupported points and assertions challenged by the opposing team?)

V. Delivery
(Was each speech effectively presented? Consider voice inflection, eye contact and tone.)

VI. Questions
(Did the team adequately answer audience questions?)

VII. Overall team rating
In my opinion, the better debating was done by the _____
      (Affirmative or Negative)
Comments for Affirmative Team:

Comments for Negative Team: